The Triumph of Instrument Flight

Aviation's instrument flying challenge was conquered in less than five years. Not bad for a goal that was never defined and had no heroes to accept medals at festive banquets. Salesmen just wanted to go from Chicago to Kansas City, on schedule. Like the train, only faster.

Other books by Franklyn E. Dailey, Jr.

Joining the War at Sea 1939-1945
0966625102

My Times with the Sisters and Other Events
0966625110

The Triumph of Instrument Flight

A Retrospective in the Century of U.S. Aviation

by **Franklyn E. Dailey, Jr.**

Dailey International Publishers
19 Brookside Circle
Wilbraham, MA 01095
www.daileyint.com

First Edition, 2004

Printed in the United States of America

Cover design and front cover montage by Paula Nestor.

On the front cover, the pilot with autograph is Boston & Maine Airways pilot, Hazen Bean. The original photograph, with Stinson *Trimotor*, was provided by airline Captain, Robert Mudge. The low frequency radio range illustration concept is by the author, executed by graphic artist Claire Keefe. The gyro horizon indicator came from Navaer publication 00-80W-7, 1945. The back cover photo of the DC-3 taxiing was provided by Captain Mudge. The tower in the background was a familiar scene for pilots and passengers at Logan Airport, Boston, Massachusetts.

Illustrations edited by Leo Pilares.

ISBN: 0966625137

I thank the following persons who have read parts of this story at various stages of its creation. They have made suggestions, caught errors in fact and in grammar, given more than hints as to where the story went off the track, and still have offered encouragement.

Franklyn E. Dailey III
Philip T. Dailey
Frank Davis
Genevieve Kvam
Eric Mills
Robert Mitchell
Robert M. Mudge
Morris Rosenthal
Mike Schrupp
W.B. "Billy" Wood

I would also like to thank Sally Dailey, who introduced me to a copy of *Adventures Of A Yellowbird* by Robert M. Mudge, and Paul Larcom of the Beverly (MA) Historical Society, who helped me select photos for illustrations and provided the text of his original article on Operation *Bolero*.

In the Appendix the reader will find citations of sources.

Franklyn E. Dailey, Jr.

Table of Contents

List of Illustrations

Less Known "Firsts" in Aviation

A number of aviation firsts will be encountered in this book. Many were claimed as record-making flights. Most of the records are forgotten, like a non-stop flight in a single engine plane from Tokyo to Wenatchee, Washington.

A few of those events are unforgettable. Citizens around the world, including young people just learning to read and write, joined in the triumph of Charles Lindbergh's 1927 solo non-stop flight from New York to Paris. That flight spanned two calendar days, leaving Roosevelt Field on Long Island in the early daylight of May 20, 1927 and landing in the early evening at Le Bourget Field, Paris on May 21, 1927.

In differing sectors of the aviator spectrum in the 1920s were barnstormers, mail pilots, military pilots and very late in that decade, a few airline pilots. The diversity in human interests is reflected in the fact that pilots in these very different flying professions had almost all come to aviation as the result of the impetus given to aviation by World War I.

Two flights, known now to almost no living persons, come frequently to the author's mind. One was recorded in two small-town newspapers. The other was recorded only in human memory. These occurred within two months, and within two years, respectively, after Lindbergh and his *Spirit of St. Louis* made it to Paris.

In July 1927, a barnstormer came to my town, Brockport, New York, in his biplane. He landed on Gifford Morgan's farm, just east of the town. Morgan was a leading citizen in Brockport. After pilot Ray Hylan made his peace with owner Morgan for temporary landing rights, he solicited "ride" business from the "locals."

The Peters family lived just down and across the street from our home on South Avenue. Their eighteen-year old son, Stephen, had graduated from high school and was working in Ed Simmons' drug store for the summer. Steve was greatly admired by the small fry on our street. In July of 1927, Stephen and his parents had just returned from a trip to New York City where Stephen had taken two local flights over the harbor in a seaplane. Upon his return home, Steve was quite excited to discover a Curtiss biplane, a *Jenny*, in a field right next to his hometown. The *Jenny*, with pilot Ray Hylan, was ready to take up passengers.

Steve took two flights in the afternoon of July 19, 1927, in the front passenger seat of the *Jenny*, with Hylan, the pilot, at the controls in the rear seat. Then, after attending a twilight baseball game, Steve drove back to the "airfield" and made a deal with Hylan to go up once more. It was now dusk. News reports from the July 21, 1927 editions of the Brockport *Republic Democrat* and nearby Holley, New York's *Holley Standard* provide details on what happened next.

From the lead lines in the *Republic Democrat:* "A very sad accident occurred at 10 minutes after nine Tuesday evening when Stephen Peters Jr., 18-year old son of Mr. and Mrs. Stephen Peters of South Avenue, was instantly killed when the plane in which he was riding crashed into the roof of Dr. Morris Mann's house on State Street. Steve, as he is better known to his many friends, had two previous rides in the plane and was very much enthused about flying."

The *Holley Standard* began its story with these lines.

"In order to gratify a desire for 'some extra thrills' expressed by Stephen Peters of Brockport at the beginning of a flight Tuesday night, the pilot of the plane, Roy Hylan of Rochester, attempted a tail spin which ended in a crash in which Peters lost his life and Hylan was severely injured. After leaving his landing field a half-mile east of Brockport, Hylan took his plane up gradually until he was six hundred feet above Main Street where he decided to satisfy Peters' flare for thrills by going into a tail spin."

Steve Peters was dead at the scene while Hylan was taken to the Brockport Sanitarium. When Hylan regained consciousness, he stated, according to the *Holley Stamdard*, that he "made a tailspin which he could not control."

The Brockport paper closed its coverage with these lines.

"Many people have remarked about the plane flying very low and the pilot was questioned about it the afternoon of the accident. Mr. Hylan claimed he always flew 500 feet or more above the ground and that that height was considered safe."

Both news sources referred to the pilot as Roy Hylan, but he later became well known in aviation circles as Ray Hylan. He operated the Hylan Flying School in Rochester for many years. In 1959, he was in the news for the donation of his Boeing F4B-4 Navy fighter to the Smithsonian Institution. Hylan died in 1983. When the *Jenny* crashed in Brockport, Ray Hylan was just three years older than his eighteen-year old passenger. The Brockport paper had noted, "He (Hylan) has piloted aeroplanes for the past year and was considered one of the best drivers in this section."

That accident was not an isolated experience in U.S. aviation in the 1920s. For this writer, then six years old, it was a first connection with aviation and a first connection with death.

Illustration 1 shows a Curtiss *Jenny*. It is one of the carefully restored vintage airplanes at the Curtiss Museum in Hammondsport, New York, located in the southern part of the state at the foot of Keuka Lake. This type of aircraft saw considerable service as a training plane for U.S. World War I pilots. The plane was used to carry mail in the early U.S. airmail service, and was a favorite of barnstorming pilots in the 1920s. The *Jenny* at the Curtiss Museum is equipped with a Curtiss ninety-horsepower OX-5 liquid cooled aircraft engine.

Illustration 1 - A *Jenny* at Glenn H. Curtiss Museum

Barnstorming is a segment of flying that has no counterpart today. Russia's space program sold seat space to Dennis Tito for $20,000,000 for his rocket flight to the space station. That might herald the birth of a new era of barnstorming. With the moon and Mars on the U.S. space agenda, more self-financed astronauts may get in line.

Pilots, especially, hearken back to their own first flight. The author's occurred, as a passenger, at Leroy, New York in the summer of 1929. The airport, way ahead of its time and a prototype for airport design, was the Donald Woodward Airport. It was named after a local aviation enthusiast who put up the money to complete an air facility in 1928, with four paved runways, hangar with corner tower, passenger ramp and space for parked aircraft.

The Leroy airport was an early general aviation airport that few small cities, let alone small towns, would ever match. Before the airport took shape, the western New York village of Leroy was known mostly for being the home of the Jell-O manufacturing plant. The airport added to the town's prominence. Leroy was also the site of one of those early light beacon links in the visual flight navigation path spanning the United States.

My hometown, Brockport, New York, was not far from Leroy. Young boys had no difficulty claiming some of the prominence of a nearby town. This occurred most frequently when the nearby town generated some excitement. Aviation was excitement.

At the Leroy Airport, a World War I aviator, Lieutenant Commander Russell Holderman, USNR, piloted a Stinson *Detroiter* aircraft on a summer Sunday in 1929 in which my father, mother, sister and I were the passengers. Pilots like Holderman were the civil aviation instructors of the era, the pilots of Sunday rubberneck flights, and the contract pilots flying the U.S. mail.

Illlustration 2 is a reproduction of a photo that includes the *Detroiter*. It is the little single engine high wing monoplane in the mid-background of the photo. The plane in the foreground is a Boston & Maine Airways' Lockheed 10A *Electra*, whose instrument panel this story will come to later.

These aircraft are on the ramp of the Boston airport, the "home port" of Boston & Maine Airways. That airline became Northeast Airlines. It expanded from its original New England region to become the last trunk airline formed in the United States. Portions of its story will be found in Chapter 5.

Illustration 2 - Stinson *Detroiter* in near background

The photo has been cropped to feature the Stinson. The original photo is in the Walker Transportation Collection of the Beverly, Massachusetts Historical Society.

Eddie Stinson, and the Stinson family, located in Detroit, Michigan, designed and produced a number of fine aircraft. The *Detroiter* was one of them.

I did not know it at the time but Russell Holderman was also the Donald Woodward Airport's Manager and had a hand in the airport's design.

The Stinson at Leroy in 1929 had a glass panel in the bottom of its small cabin through which the three passengers in the rear could look straight down. This was an opportunity they exercised just once during that flight, pleading later that they did not like the feeling it gave them.

The right front seat of the Stinson was mine for this, my first, flight. It did not permit the downward vertical look. Through the window on the right side forward, one could see Niagara Falls. As flights go, it was just a 20-minute tour of western New York State. My father paid 30 dollars to a ticket agent near the plane. My younger sister and I went for $5 each and the adults had to pay $10 each.

I do not believe Dad ever flew again. Near Huntsville, Ontario, we vacationed for short periods in two summers at a resort named Limberlost. The resort was on one of those countless, see-to-the-bottom, lakes of Canada. Mother took many rear cockpit flights there in a single engine biplane, pontoon equipped. The aircraft was a DH (de Havilland) *Moth,* and it was piloted by a Major Wrathall.

Russell Holderman later became the Gannett Newspapers' chief pilot, in command of a coveted Lockheed *Lodestar.* About 30 years after that 1929 flight, I had left active duty as a Navy pilot and transferred to the Naval Air Reserve. My father invited me for lunch at the Rochester Club on East Avenue in Rochester, New York. Dad was a stockbroker and occasionally took clients to the Club. This day, my Dad had an ulterior motive. He introduced me to Lieutenant Commander Holderman, who, I learned, was a regular at the Club, with his own accustomed luncheon table.

It takes no stretch of reason to figure out that the Gannett Newspapers' *Lodestar,* with its experienced, instrument qualified pilot, was a major help in newspaper owner Frank Gannett's effort to build a national newspaper empire from a two-newspaper base in Rochester, New York. The flagship publication of that news organization is *USA Today.*

At Leroy on that summer Sunday in 1929, there were other aircraft parked at the airport. Most were the single engine biplanes of early aviation. A few of the aircraft parked at Leroy that summer were single engine, high wing monoplanes. All were painted orange. I was told that the plane type was a Curtiss *Robin.*

Pilots and mechanics based at Leroy were themselves recognized, by better known aviation peers, as key contributors in aviation's early years. For that reason, when Donald Woodward's airport at Leroy held fly-in events, it attracted many well-known national and international figures, all pioneers in early aviation.

With the entrepreneurial investment of Woodward, and the pioneering pilots that his foresight attracted, the town of Leroy was early on aviation's map. In just a few years after 1929, larger U.S. cities became the essential airline embarking and debarking points for the growing number of paying passengers. As the pilot proficiency base grew and radio aids were installed across the United States, the introduction of radio receiving instruments became a requirement for commercial aircraft. The tools for instrument flying were falling into place. Scheduled flights with paying passengers multiplied. Towns like Leroy drifted into history. California, Texas and Illinois became leaders in the number of aviation early adopters. Distance was a spur to flying.

Many pilots, like Russell Holderman, moved on to salary-producing aviation careers. The barn-storming pilots elected to make their living in more of a free form that perhaps identified them more as lovers of flight for the sake of flight and not as just an alternate means of transportation. Even the famed Charles Lindbergh did time as a barnstormer.

An imaginary arrow, with a U.S. mail pilot in a Jenny at its feathered end, and a pilot like Holderman in a Stinson up toward its flint arrowhead, would be pointed along the path toward instrument flying. Holderman in his *Lodestar* had arrived.

Every time an airplane went overhead in the early years of flight, persons of all ages turned their eyes skyward. Most vivid is my memory of the giant Navy dirigible, the USS *Akron*, passing over my home in western New York in 1931 on November 11, Armistice Day. She was creeping along under a very low overcast in restricted visibility, trying to stay in visual contact with ground reference points on the south side of Lake Ontario as she made her way back from a western trip to her home port of Lakehurst, New Jersey.

That dim gray wraith that took up so much space in the moisture laden sky was a discussion topic for folks in our town for months afterward. I can make a pretty good conjecture now that the

Akron's Commanding Officer that day did not feel that his dirigible, his flight instrumentation, and he, were capable of simply plunging into the clouds and heading directly for Lakehurst. Visible checkpoints like nearby Rochester on the south shore of Lake Ontario were the navigation aids he trusted.

A man-made connection existed between two U.S. dirigibles and heavier than air flight. The *Akron* and her sister ship, the USS *Macon*, were both rigged with a hangar and suspension for a small aircraft. A number of aircraft flights from the two dirigibles and airborne recoveries to them were made successfully. Both dirigibles met their ends in separate crashes that involved fatalities. These crashes had nothing to do with their embarked aircraft.

Today, I see giant C-5 jet transport planes taking off from or approaching Westover Air Reserve Base (ARB) in Chicopee, Massachusetts. I hear sleek Boeing and Douglas jet transports shushing overhead toward Bradley International Airport at Hartford, Connecticut, as they pass down the instrument runway approach path directly over my home. When I am out in my neighborhood, I always turn my head skyward on the chance that the approaching aircraft will "break contact" as it emerges from clouds.

Franklyn E. Dailey, Jr. June 3, 2004

Aviation Humor

The first 32 pages of the December 2003 issue of the National Geographic magazine represent a major commitment to the story of aviation. On page 13, the issue quotes Arlen Rens, a Lockheed Martin test pilot:

"Airplanes are now built to carry a pilot and a dog in the cockpit. The pilot's job is to feed the dog, and the dog's job is to bite the pilot if he touches anything."

Aviation Becomes a Subject

T his story of instrument flying is told in the context of progress in United States aviation. The period of closest examination for the transition from flight strictly by visual flight rules to instrument flying will be 1929-49.

An instrument flying capability emerged in all industrialized nations in about the same time frame. It was well implemented by the time that war clouds approached in 1939.

In the early years of flying in the United States, most pilots did not fly when the weather was threatening. The more experienced pilots who were flying to accomplish some mission beyond sight of their home airfield learned to avoid weather.

Flying attracted great public interest in the first three decades of the 20th century. The Wright brothers were first in powered heavier-than-air flight in their December 1903 flights at Kitty Hawk, North Carolina. Their achievement was an historic first in aviation's many firsts. The brothers were slow to publicize their accomplishment.

Flying emerged as a major news item in Europe before the Wright brothers flight became broadly known in the United States.

Many early aviators, first among them the Wright brothers, brought innovative ideas and practical engineering skills to their objectives. There was not much in the literature available in 1900 about what it would take to fly. The Wright brothers' combination of theory, practical development, testing and risk-taking brought success. A number of aviation pioneers soon followed the Wrights. World War I added great stimulus, not just in airframe and engine development, but in interest on the part of a much wider spectrum of young men who wanted to fly and also wanted to assist their country.

Many would agree that the Wright brothers' breath-taking accomplishment in 1903 was fittingly capped by Lindbergh's historic flight in 1927. By then, the major players were onstage. These were the airframe with its wings, the flight controls, the reliable power plant (engine) and the pilots. Lindbergh was the pilot's pilot - a man who was willing to take a risk but who then did everything possible to improve the odds in his favor. The Wright brothers took risks, but as inventor pilots.

In 1927, a critical element needed to advance aviation, the gyro horizon, was waiting to come onstage to make instrument flying practicable. The change from piston engine to jet engine was further in the future and blind landings would require almost the full century.

By the late 1920s, accumulation of flight experience and achievement of self-defined milestones in speed and endurance by more aviators gave aviation expanded space in newspapers and magazines. The press itself became a sponsor of aviation achievement. Flying the U.S. mail was another daring venture that helped keep aviation in the news in the 1920s and early 1930s. An episode in the history of airmail, along with the formation of airlines, brought attention to the imperatives that would lead to instrument flying.

Aviation Becomes a Subject

A few aviators had begun to chafe at the constraints that weather imposed on flight options. Weather was a factor cited by some aviators in their flight attempts to set new point-to-point speed records. On February 5, 1929, Captain Frank Hawks of the Army Air Corps flew a Lockheed Vega monoplane called the *Air Express* from Mines Field, Los Angeles, to Roosevelt Field on Long Island. His elapsed time was eighteen hours and twenty-two minutes. He told newsmen that he could have made the trip in three hours less except for the storms he encountered. (Standard Quarterly Review, Vol. II, No.1. April 1929 page A-4)

Without any master plan, airframe and engine designers, influenced by pilots, began to add instruments and other aids that responded to a need to know more about their aircraft's performance, helping to improve the pilot's preflight and in-flight decision making.

For farming and other pursuits not directly applicable to aviation, the United States Weather Bureau was regularly upgrading its forecast and reporting capability. One of the outcomes of a radio broadcast capability in the relatively new AM (amplitude modulation) radio frequency band was the addition of weather forecasts. As radio receiver design improved, weather information became accessible to a greater audience. Aviators who followed this progress spread the news of greater flight information availability in aviation discussion groups.

Pilots began to carefully assess newly available flying aids with the realization that knowledge of weather formation and weather movement was important to their flying pursuits. Aviation information relevant to safe flight was being accumulated. In the very early days of heavier-than-air flight, those pilots with more experience would pass along their knowledge to those with less experience. From such sharers of information came a new breed, flight instructors. Eventually, flight school by flight school or flying club by flying club, the pilot cadre and its knowledge-base increased.

The cost of operating an aircraft, even in aviation's earliest days, represented a considerable expense relative to the cost of other extracurricular activities a young man or woman might choose to engage in during aviation's formative years. The pilot-aspirant would often hang around airports, and some would do the dirty jobs that no one else wanted to do. Cleaning up spilled oil was one example. Even if they did not directly get paid for such work, those yearning to fly would hope thereby to get flight time with an instructor at the lowest going price.

Flying clubs helped to drive down the cost of both flying instruction and fees for the use of aircraft. An instructor, often the owner-operator of an aircraft, was a businessman. If a flying club presented him or her with a number of students, and these could be structured into lists and schedules, the instructor would be making best use of time and would price services accordingly. Flying clubs were also an effective means of exchanging information. What one heard or read could be exchanged with others. Early flying clubs represented ground school and flight school bundled together.

J. Frank Durham is a senior practicing attorney in Indiana. In 1924, he spotted his first real airplane on the ground in a field north of Highway 40 between Greencastle and Indianapolis. He places the location west of Plainfield, Indiana. The aircraft was a World War I *Jenny*. Growing up, Frank built and flew control-line model planes. (With wireless radio control now available, the control line that mechanically transmitted flight control commands to the model flying plane has made its own passage into history.) By 1935, Durham was completely hooked on aviation and with his buddy, Loren McDonald, helped found the DePauw (Indiana) Flying Club. Monthly meetings of the ten members were held at the Delta Tau Delta Fraternity House at DePauw University. Indianapolis Airport was a favorite venue for hangar talk. Listening, and closely examining parked airplanes, substituted for formal ground school. Loren McDonald persuaded a Flight Instructor at the Bloomfield Airport to fly the latter's Taylor *Cub* over to Greencastle so club members could take turns getting flying instruction. The club student pilots paid $2.50 for a half-hour of in-flight instruction. Frank Durham soloed after four hours of flight instruction.

Aviation Becomes a Subject

The law was to become Frank's career, not aviation. Private pilots were going to share the airspace with career aviators, charter pilots, airline pilots and military pilots. By graduation from the University in 1937, Frank had accumulated the grand total of seven hours of pilot flying time. After picking up flight time over a number of years, often in rented aircraft, he received two days of formal instruction at the Acme Flight School in Texas to take and pass the written exam for a Private Pilot's license. A lady pilot checked him out for the flight portion of the requirement. Durham recalls that the flight check occurred in the Cessna 170B he had purchased in 1954, and in which he and his instructor, Chet Hill of Crawfordsville, Indiana, and another attorney-pilot had flown from Greencastle to Texas. Both Frank and the other attorney took their exams and flight tests and earned their Private Pilot certificates on that occasion. Chet returned independently to Indiana and the two newly certificated pilots flew the 170B, legally, back home.

The circumstances of the purchase of the 170B at Indianapolis Airport involved well-known names in early 20th century flying. Chet Hill went with Frank to Indianapolis to assist him on the prospective purchase. The deal was made and ownership was transferred from Mildred Hurt, the owner, to Frank Durham. Mildred had been an early pilot. Her eyes had failed so she resolved to sell her plane. Her husband was in business with renowned aviator Roscoe Turner. Mildred parted from her Cessna with a flourish. Shortly after the acquisition, Frank Durham received a membership in the Aircraft Owner's and Pilot's Association (AOPA). He discovered that it was a gift from Mildred Hurt.

Although J. Frank Durham owns his own plane now and flies from his own airstrip, he recalls many early flights in rented aircraft. There would usually be a number of aircraft available for rent on a given airfield. Depending on an applicant's experience and flight plan, Frank Durham relates that instruction to fly a given plane would be provided by the Fixed Base Operator (FBO) of an airfield. Sometimes a look in the pilot's logbook would be needed and other times conversation alone would suffice. The person responsible for renting the plane to another person would evaluate the applicant's background and make a judgment call on whether oral instruction on the proposed rental aircraft would be sufficient. Pilots were still enough of a novelty so that a person in one airport community already knew something about a person in a nearby community.

Flight powered by an internal combustion engine, with an embarked human operating flight controls, marked the dramatic beginning of piloted flight of heavier than air machines. In the process, the biplane was born. For propulsion, the Wright brothers had provided two propellers for their Wright *Flyer*, driven through sprocket and chain from one 12 horsepower gas engine. The pilot was conveniently positioned, prone, forward of and between the two propellers. No instrument panel.

The Wrights did not just stumble onto flying with some dumb luck. They were skilled mechanics. They studied the available literature. What had failed to work in the past was evaluated by them and replaced by their contributions to aerodynamics. They did not invent the internal combustion engine but adapted it skillfully to their use, with economy of weight clearly in their mind. They took risk and succeeded. Many who followed were to make enormous contributions, but the Wrights had removed one major obstacle. That obstacle was doubt.

By 1908, just five years after Kitty Hawk, Glenn H. Curtiss was at work advancing the art in first generation aircraft. Military student pilots began training in the United States by 1916 for air combat in the war that the United States would enter in 1917. In addition to their air-to-air combat experience, these men were de facto test pilots in proving a new generation of heavier than air flying machines.

Glenn Curtiss, like the Wrights, began with engineering skill, plus the priceless knowledge from the Wrights' success that flight was possible. Curtiss began with a biplane like the Wright brothers. Though his first craft was still without instrument panel, it had a more coherent look to it. The pilot had a place to sit.

Curtiss began his remarkable career in bicycle repair, then moved on to motorcycles, and then to the design of motorcycle

16

engines. He realized that available engines were not very good. Using an engine of his own design, he set a motorcycle speed record in excess of 130 mph, and for some years was known as the fastest human. Asked to design an engine to move a blimp through the air, he concentrated his engine design efforts on obtaining the highest horsepower per unit weight. This brought him to heavier-than-air craft, and he entered the field of airframe design with the dual motivation to also design appropriate engines to drive propellers for his new aircraft structures.

Glenn Curtiss later launched successfully from the deck of a ship after obtaining some financial support from the U.S. Navy.

Curtiss sat in front of his internal combustion gas engine that turned a propeller which "pushed" the aircraft into the air and sustained it there. His hand wheel, mounted at the top of a "stick," turned the rudder. Back and forth movement of the stick moved the elevator, and Curtiss leaned his body to the left or to the right to add tension to cables which moved his ailerons. Curtiss is credited at the Curtiss Air Museum with the invention of the aileron as a control surface. That control completed the essential air control surfaces in use right down to this day. These control surfaces are the elevator, the rudder, and the aileron.

In the January 1930 issue of the Standard Quarterly Review on page A-32, Dr. William Whitney Christmas is credited as "the inventor of the aileron balancing system which is now used on all planes." Invention claims have been the subject of controversy throughout the history of the U.S. Patent Office. Aviation provided its share of disputed claims. The Wright brothers and Glenn Curtiss were involved in lawsuits initiated by the Wrights.

From France came the third flight surface control modification, putting the aileron under the control of the hand wheel or "yoke," adding rudder pedals to control the rudder, and maintaining the stick for control of the elevators. This configuration settled the control method for aircraft lasting to this day. Without that fairly rapid progression to successful flight controls, flying would have been much slower to advance, holding back successful instrument flying as a subsequent result.

In the next illustration, Curtiss' ailerons can barely be seen as triangles at the tips of the wings. The pilot is forward with the elevators in the far front; a fixed stabilizer is at the rear with a rudder at its center.

This model, atop a pole, greets a visitor at the front of the Curtiss Museum at Hammondsport, New York.

Illustration 3 - Curtiss *June Bug*: Glenn H. Curtiss Museum

It did not take long for Curtiss to reengineer his craft and put the elevators back with the rudder assembly. Some felt that he was a bit reluctant to put the engine in front of the pilot; his later designs had the engine forward.

In both powerplants and airframes, Glenn Hammond Curtiss was successful, becoming a principal U.S. inventor, of aircraft, and of internal combustion engines to power them. And he was a good pilot as well. He was confident enough to be the first to make the first flight in his own designs and then to pilot them to record after record.

Even without the aileron, the number of Curtiss firsts is incredible: the tricycle landing gear; the seaplane; the amphibian aircraft. He made records for sustained flight, one after another; he was winner of the prize to fly non-stop from Albany to New York. Curtiss was first to fly off a ship and the first to fly off a warship. The latter craft's design, and then its execution as an aircraft of interest to the U.S. Navy, earned him the sobriquet, "father of naval aviation."

For high-speed performance, the inline liquid-cooled engine, a legacy of the automobile, propelled many military fighter aircraft right up to and including World War II.

Glenn Curtiss' experience with engine building for his motorcycles led him to the design of a liquid cooled engine series for aircraft. The first one was known as the Model O. Successively he designed and built models in the OX series, the culmination of which was the OX-5, rated at 90 horsepower. This engine was put into what was then regarded as mass production. This engine powered many different aircraft in the early years. An OX-5 Aviation Pioneers club had active chapters in 2003.

Glenn H. Curtiss eventually put all of his patented designs into the public domain.

The next illustration is the cover page of a patent issued in 1927. Inventor Newton F. Foner depicts the cylinder/crankshaft view (not shown here) of his internal combustion engine on "sheet 1" of his three sheet patent application of 1925. Issued as U.S. patent 1626457, the engine is shown *with an aircraft propeller*. Like most patent seekers whose objective is to make their novel idea as generally applicable as possible, Foner's patent adds the words, "may be for any purpose for which it is adapted."

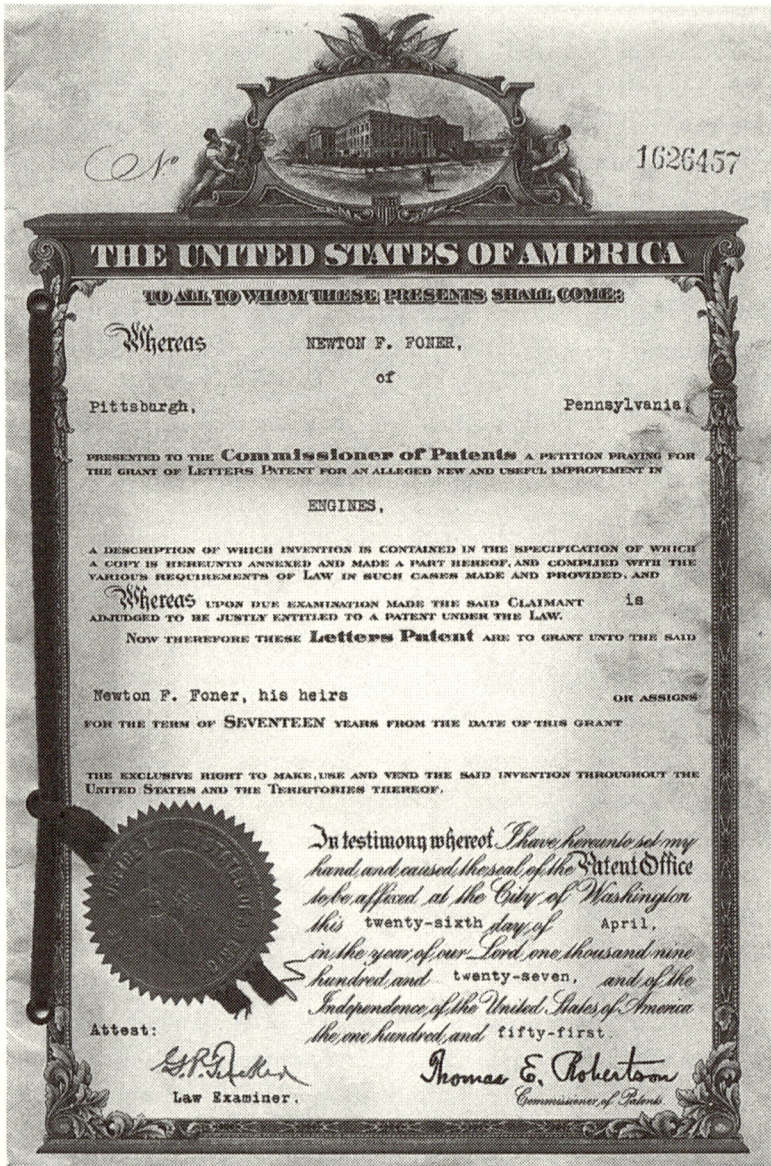

Illustration 4 - Foner's Airplane Engine Patent

Foner's engine was a two-cycle internal combustion engine that the inventor claimed could be operated with several fuels, was liquid cooled, had paired compression and combustion cylinders that the text states had unique cooling advantages, and operated without cam shafts.

The more interesting aspect was the overall layout of the Foner engine. Curtiss' OX-5 and competing engines were inline liquid cooled engines. The eventual winners by 1929 for all but the fastest racing and military fighter aircraft, were the air-cooled radial engines. Foner's engine was liquid cooled but was configured more like the later radial engines.

The only inline vestiges in the Foner engine were the compression-combustion pairs, one behind the other. These were disposed as pairs, but in two geometric planes, radially from the crankshaft. The air-cooled radial engines that powered all successful airline transport planes up to the advent of turbine engines had their cylinder-pairs in the same radial plane. But by then, an in-line look had crept into all radial engines.

As the cylinder count increased, the cylinders could not all be crammed into one radial plan; the solution was that banks of them would be disposed one behind the other. The Pratt & Whitney 4360 that made its appearance at the end of World War II was the last of these, four banks with seven cylinders in each bank, for a total of 28 cylinders. Some called it the "corn cob."

As with other 20th century wars, the end of World War I found war industries at peak production. The excess production of the OX-5 engines at the end of World War I, and their resultant inexpensive availability, found them extensively used in postwar aircraft. A 400-hp Liberty engine was a top horsepower-performing engine that came along at the end of World War I. That engine did not achieve extensive production. Its power was persuasive, but by comparison it was expensive. Cost did not favor its early adoption by aircraft manufacturers.

It took a bit longer for any airframe to achieve mass-production status. One of the first airframe designs to achieve manufacturing scale was the Curtiss *Robin*. St. Louis-based Curtiss-Robertson built 750 of the single engine *Robins* before shutting down in 1930, partially a consequence of the Depression.

Three-engine aircraft made a strong, albeit brief, appearance on the aircraft scene. Passengers, paying passengers, occupied the minds of some aircraft designers and manufacturers. For just a few years, three-engine aircraft appealed to some aircraft manufacturers to be a competitive design that would interest those who might be going into the air transport business.

In the first three decades of aviation, aircraft design was partly a 'cut and try' effort. It was based on disciplined inspiration. Success improved in steps by learning from what did not work after conducting tests and evaluation of airframes. The wind tunnel became a powerful tool. Aircraft engine design efforts included test-stand testing, and continued to take advantage of knowledge gained in the design of automobile engines.

Putting 'best of breed' elements together to create an aircraft system was part of the story of progress. The era in which an aircraft designer was able to design and specify the whole machine, then take delivery of proven results from competing contractors, did not come until much later.

Pilot technique progressed with each generation of aircraft. New aircraft offerings had design failures and pilots who were lost flying them; some pilots lost their lives for the sole reason that they were willing to take a chance on a new craft. Failures as well as successes were teaching experiences. Engines became more reliable, airframes stronger and more aerodynamically efficient. Successful pilots learned the first three essential rules of flying, "keep airspeed, keep airspeed, keep airspeed!"

Technology played a key part in transitioning aviation from the thrill stage to the record-setting stage to routinely successful flight. Training and pilot experience played vital parts. But progress was gained a step at a time with no visionary to claim that he or she saw the ultimate objective and put together the first flow chart to accomplish it.

Aviation Becomes a Subject

With the benefit of experience, we can now say that for instrument flying to succeed, advances in aircraft instrumentation were going to be required. Ground radio facilities and weather reporting schedules would be needed. Airframes and engines had to demonstrate reliability. Speed records, distance records, and endurance records would confirm not only the technical advances, but also reliability. Finally, aviation needed aviators whose motivations were akin to explorers bent on conquest.

There is caution. And there is fear. Pilots have fear. Sometimes fear overcomes all the ambitions of a student pilot, and he or she decides not to pursue the pilot objective. After flight with visual earth reference, the next step in flying for many pilots is flight through instruments. Some find that too steep a challenge and drop that ambition. AVWeb is an aviation website. Reporting through the Newhouse News Service in 2001, writer Dru Sefton reported on a question that AVWeb asked one thousand pilots. "Have you ever had to control your own fear serving as a pilot?" 74% admitted that they had. The biggest fears reported by the survey: "weather," followed by, "making a critical error."

This story is developed from a pilot perspective. The infrastructure composite of airport, airways, air traffic control systems and ground instrumentation, weather forecasting and reporting, and communications, will enter these pages mostly from a pilot's perspective. The evolution, from a series of light beacons in the 1920s for night flying, to our present airways route structure, is an essential part of the story of instrument flight.

The early chapters emphasize civil aviation. Many of the basic challenges were confronted and solved in scheduled airline operations. Civil aviation gradually established the statistical basis for safe instrument flight. It accomplished that objective by piling up flight hours accompanied by the steady improvement (lowering the number of accidents and fatalities per passenger mile flown) in accident statistics. The United States government made its mark by insisting that records be kept and then analyzed.

The Triumph of Instrument Flight

Pilots work hard to make sure that no accident or incident mars their flight records. Unlike the speed, endurance and distance record makers and record breakers to be encountered in Chapter 2, no pilot or group of pilots actually set out with the objective to accumulate a prescribed number of flying hours that supported a claim that instrument flying could at that point be declared safe.

Strict interpreters would argue that "safe" means "freedom from risk" and that flying would never meet that criterion anyway. Many parties with varied backgrounds, academic research, engineering, ground support and of course the pilots themselves, were part of an effort, not always strictly defined, to make flying as safe as it was humanly possible to make it, and to make instrument flying safe in that same context. It was an aggregate of human experience that brought the state of the art from step number one to step number two, the evolution from safe flying to safe instrument flying.

Declarations of safety that cited statistics came after the fact. Government, executive, legislative and judiciary all contributed. An aviation support establishment grew. U.S. pilots and their government participated in an extended shake-down cruise for rules, procedures and equipment that would best insure safe conduct of flight.

The military services made important contributions. They furnished an initial cadre of pilots that had been trained for World War I. In World War II, military pilots, many representing between-the-wars civil aviation, helped extend instrument flying around the globe. Military experiences in instrument flight will be introduced later in the story.

In addition to a pilot bias found here, the reader will also find a geographic bias, the Northern Hemisphere.

A look at polar projection maps of the Northern and Southern Hemispheres is quite revealing. There is very little land-mass between the 50th and 70th southern parallels. There is considerable landmass between the 50th and 70th northern parallels, and parts of it are heavily populated. The northern rims of both the eastern and western hemispheres were a challenge to the early venturing peoples.

Man's curiosity, and the linking ingredients, land and water, were passed on to the air faring descendants of the original seafarers to continue the pursuit of passage through these spaces.

Mankind's deadliest wars have occurred in the northern hemispheres. Most of World War II, and the Cold War nuclear standoff that followed, were waged in the Northern Hemisphere.

Travel distance between major population centers is minimized by use of great circle routes. North of the Equator, these routes arch toward the North Pole. In 1940, progress in exploiting strategic aviation advantages of the north Pacific rim lagged behind experience in the North Atlantic.

There have been orderly steps in pilot licensing, as solo pilots, as private pilots, as instrument pilots, multi-engine pilots, commercial pilots and air transport rated pilots. An instructive journey would take one to technology, to safety efforts that would include such steps as seat belts, then shoulder harnesses, on to weather forecasting and reporting, to radio aids and air traffic control, and the composite would be supported with data. None of those approaches, useful and valuable as they might be, would come across a magic day on which it can be categorically stated that the day for instrument flying had arrived.

Many important events in U.S. aviation's formative years have receded into history. Charles Lindbergh's flight from Roosevelt Field, near New York City, to Le Bourget Airdrome, Paris, in 1927 remains an exception. It was then, and is now, recognized as a defining event. Crossing the North Atlantic, *The Spirit of St. Louis* surmounted or avoided most of the challenges of instrument flight.

Illustration 5 - Lindy and his autograph

Some pilots began to embark on flight plans involving forecasts of weather system movements that were conditioned by uncertainty. These pilots understood that they might encounter weather if a weather system moved faster or slower than forecast. Having an alternate airport in mind before taking off became a good prudential rule. Sometimes, despite all precautions, a flight would become immersed in a weather challenge. Pilots who kept their heads and lived to tell the tale brought back information that helped other pilots.

The reader will discover that each form of water, solid, liquid and vapor, has provided its own unique challenge to safe flight. The solid forms would be snow or ice. The vapor could be invisible water vapor, or vapor that had condensed into tiny liquid droplets as fog.

Aviation Humor

The parachutist training story.

The man was being instructed. "Count to 10 and pull this upper ring. If nothing happens, count 10 again and pull this lower ring on your emergency chute. A motorcycle with a sidecar will be around to pick you up where you land."

He jumped.

He counted 10. He pulled the upper ring. Nothing happened.

He counted 10 again and pulled the lower ring.

Nothing happened.

He looked down, saying to himself,

"Now, I'll bet that motorcycle won't show up either."

Chapter 1 - Speed and Endurance
Records, 1929-31

Note: Unless noted otherwise, the specific details of record-making flights in this chapter were compiled from the quarterly issues, beginning April 1929 and ending January 1932, of World Progress, The Standard Quarterly Review published by The Standard Education Society, Inc. of Chicago, U.S.A.

We have noted that Lindbergh's crossing of the Atlantic in 1927 could be viewed as the climax of aviation's first era. Some might conclude that he was just very lucky. The word lucky was actually used occasionally when Lindy was mentioned.

The events of 1929-1931 in aviation removed all doubts that the operative term, performance, had become relevant to aviation. It was an exciting period during which the progress of aviation's first years would be transformed into performance numbers. There was no calculated plan to do this and no pre-defined agreement that this or that measured characteristic was essential. But it turned out to be a period of taking stock of the subject of aviation.

The year 1929 began and ended with auguries for aviation's future in transport. Pilots of an aircraft named the *Question Mark* took off at the Los Angeles Metropolitan airport on an endurance flight on the first day of January and landed there on January 7, 1929. The craft stayed aloft over six full days, having been refueled in flight by another aircraft which flew overhead and gravity fed the endurance plane through a fifty foot hose. Thus had a heavier-than-air machine beaten a flight endurance record previously held by a lighter-than-air machine, a dirigible named the *Graf Zeppelin*.

As noted previously, on February 5, 1929, Captain Frank Hawks, in a Lockheed Vega monoplane named the *Air Express*, landed at Roosevelt Field, Long Island, just eighteen hours and twenty one minutes after leaving Mines Field, Los Angeles. That is elapsed time from takeoff to final landing. He refueled along the way. February 1929 also found Orville Wright accepting Distinguished Flying Crosses on behalf of himself and his brother Wilbur for the historic flight they had made December 17, 1903, at Kitty Hawk, North Carolina.

Plans were drafted in 1929 to put a floating airport, 1,200 feet long and 200 feet wide, midway between New York and Bermuda. If getting to Bermuda rapidly was the passion for the east-coast jet set of the 1920s, an air transport operator was going to take them there even if it meant a stop along the way.

On March 11, 1929, Major H.O.D. Segrave of England set a new automobile speed record of 231 miles per hour on the beach at Daytona Beach, Florida. The interplay between flight speed records and land speed records continued in the news for several years with the aircraft gradually pulling ahead. Investors in land racing vehicles and their record-smashing drivers finally yielded the headlines to aviation progress.

The American Air Transport Association published data showing that scheduled airlines were flying 42 daily trips, involving 102 cities and over 33,000 route miles by early 1929. Two years earlier there had been no scheduled daily passenger flight trips in the United States.

In May of 1929, Reginald Robbins and copilot James Kelly landed the monoplane *Fort Worth* at Fort Worth, Texas after an endurance flight of 172 hours, thirty one minutes, beating the record of the Army-sponsored *Question Mark*, with its three engines, by nearly a day. On July 6, 1929, Roy Mitchell and Byron K. Newcomb landed their single engine monoplane, *The City of Cleveland*, at the Cleveland Airport, having been aloft an hour and a half longer than the *Fort Worth*. In that same month, pilots L.W. Mendell and R.B. Reinhart closed out a 246 hour, 43 minute flight, at Culver City, California, in their aircraft, the *Angeleno*.

A Curtiss *Robin* aircraft piloted by Dale Jackson and Forest O'Brine, stayed aloft in the St. Louis area, accumulating 420 hours and twenty-one minutes, July 13-30, 1929. Manufactured by the Curtiss Robertson Aeroplane and Motor Company of St. Louis, Missouri, the *Robins* had wooden wings and a steel tube fuselage, all covered with fabric. Configured at first with OX-5 engines from World War I, as aircraft production ramped up, the *Robins* were later fitted with Wright radial air-cooled engines. "Wrong way" Douglas Corrigan's 1938 solo flight across the Atlantic was made in a radial equipped *Robin*.

It took nothing away from the earlier endurance flights that the Key Brothers, Fred and Algene, flew a Curtiss *Robin* J1 Deluxe for 27 days at Meridian, Mississippi from June 4, 1935 to a landing on July 1, 1935.

What these flights had done, beyond confirming pilot stamina and the skill and novel ideas of the in-flight fueling teams, was to attest to the airworthiness of monoplanes like the *Robin*. Just as important was the confirmation beyond all doubt of the reliability of radial, air-cooled, engines. The three flights, in May, June, and July 1929, that set a succession endurance records for refueled flight, were all accomplished in single engine airplanes! *The St. Louis Robin* was powered by a Wright Challenger, 165 horsepower (hp) engine.

The *Angeleno* and the *Robin* J1 Deluxe were each powered by Wright Whirlwind 220 hp engines. Wright engines were setting a standard.

While engine test stands were used to prove that engines could perform reliably over long periods, these flights attested to engine reliability when aloft. The pilots could only do minimal support such as adding gas and oil. The pilots, the airframes and the engines were all being tested. Pilots earned recognition for endurance records. Aviation benefited far beyond any one record flight.

With new levels of performance established, the airplane improved rapidly in both endurance and speed. Aircraft flown by all the world's air carriers from the late 1930s, right up until the conversion to turbine power, were designed using flight performance data derived from these earlier record-breaking flights. Each endurance record and each speed record also added to the store of confidence that both investors and the flying public needed before transport aviation could "go commercial."

For direct bearing on the subject of instrument flying, the most far-reaching event of 1929 in aviation did not capture wide public attention. Major James H. "Jimmy" Doolittle of Cleveland, Ohio, cooperating with the Guggenheim Flight Laboratory, demonstrated on September 24, 1929, a complete sequence involving blind flight from takeoff to landing at Mitchell Field on Long Island. The gyro was certainly involved, but no other details are given in the references available. The lack of corroborating data on the flight does not detract from the central fact that in cooperation with a recognized flight research laboratory, an experimental flight was conducted by a prominent pilot that supported the premise that blind flying was an operational possibility.

The promise of the gyro in aviation had actually been introduced to the public in 1914 when Lawrence Sperry won a prize for the design of an aircraft fitted with gyroscopic control. The printed commentary under the caption, "Gyroscopic Robot" of a photo in the Standard Quarterly Review of January 1930 emphasized control of an airplane under "all conditions of weather and darkness."

"Blind flight" was the popular term of the times to express what was later called instrument flight. Specific numerical values would eventually define the ceiling and visibility conditions that would apply to flight phases. A pilot would be given ceiling and visibility numbers that represented the local takeoff condition, expected cruise flight conditions, and a forecast of the destination-field conditions.

In the 1920s, pilots were contracted by the U.S. Post Office Department to fly the U.S. mail. Eventually, these flights operated both day and night. The pilots encountered weather and figured out how to get around it in order that the mail might go through. Occasionally they had to land at one of the emergency fields along the way cleared for the purpose, while they waited for the weather to pass. While airborne at night, they used the nation's new lighted beacon system.

In one disastrous period for early aviation in the United States, a dispute arose between pilots flying the U.S. mail on contract with the federal government. Active duty Army pilots were assigned the additional duty of airmail service flying. The 1934 replacement was abrupt, and the military pilots had no time to gain proficiency for this service. Many perished.

The Post Office Department of the United States had become serious about transporting mail by air in 1918. The federal government, between 1926 when the Department of Commerce took over responsibility, and 1930, installed nearly 14,000 miles of lighted pathways in the sky. Night or day, from elevated platforms, a 24 inch searchlight rotating at 6 rpm, containing a 1000 watt lamp, swept the sky. This system cast a one million candlepower flash every 10 seconds, lasting one tenth of a second. One of these beacons was installed every 10 miles. If there was no commercial airfield at a defined interval along the path, a bare bones intermediate landing field was prepared to make sure that a safe landing option occurred within 30 miles of the previous landing opportunity. These basic fields each had their own airfield beacon, boundary lights, approach lights and obstruction lights. At some there was a lighted wind cone to tell the pilot the local wind direction. During night hours, there would often be caretakers to assist a pilot with communication, transportation, meals, fuel and repairs. The details for the light beacons referred to in this and the next paragraph were found on a website. The full text, copyrighted by Charles Wood, was found at www.navfltsm.addr.com.

The 10-mile interval airways light beacons produced a pencil of light in a beam about 5 degrees wide and could be seen about 30 miles in average visibility. Underneath the main searchlight beacon were two 500-watt flashing course lights-one pointing forward along the airway and one pointing 180 degrees opposite. Every third beacon had a green course light indicating presence of a landing field. The intermediate two beacons had red lights. These course lights flashed Morse-coded numbers from zero to nine. The code for five (five dots, no dashes) indicated the plane was on the fifth beacon in a 100-mile stretch of the air highway. The pilot had to keep track of the onset of each 100-mile set because the system simply repeated itself. These airways had principal terminal cities, and those cities' name abbreviations became airway names. Chicago-Omaha was CO, and San Francisco-Los Angeles was SF-LA.

The light beacons were the beginning of defined airways. According to the "The History of U.S. Flight Inspection" quoted from AvStop Magazine Online in the next paragraph, airways began as a concept, with no actual routes specified for flying the mail and no continual means for the pilot to determine his navigation position. It was up to the pilot for a given trip on a given day to get the airmail through.

"There were no aeronautical charts, no radio capability for weather, communication or navigation, much less anything resembling air traffic control. There was no civil aviation authority at either the federal or state level. There were no flight rules, nor, at that point, a real need for them. ...With the lack of effective aeronautical navigation, operations were limited to daytime flights in good weather, obviating most of the advantages held by the airplane as a transportation medium. The mid-1920s saw the beginning of federal navigation aids as efforts were made to provide lighted airway beacons along the airways to allow safe nighttime navigational assistance."

Light beacons quickly became obsolete as newer resources heralding the instrument flight age came into being in the 1930s. Just as the last of the light beacon installations were being put in service, the introduction of the first low frequency (low hundreds of kilocycles) radio range stations began. These radio aids became the navigation resource for en-route airways flying in clear and in clouded weather. These new radio facilities were also used for aircraft letdown and runway approach patterns in limited ceiling and visibility conditions. Fixed emplacement of low frequency, non-directional radio beacons also came into use as distance checkpoints along airways and along airport approach patterns. Leroy, New York's rotating light beacon along with the nation's entire network of light beacons quickly faded into aviation history. The light beacons left an important legacy. They had established the concept of airways in the sky.

Many, but not all, of the low frequency radio aids of the 1930s were in turn superseded after World War II by higher frequency installations. The new spectrum allotments were in hundreds of megacycles instead of hundreds of kilocycles. Radio-wave emitting installations known as "omni-range" (the OR in VOR, where V was used for anything involving aviation) and "localizer" facilities came into being. Another important aid was DME for Distance Measuring Equipment. Electromagnetic wave emitters from the aircraft would trigger the receiver-transmitter (transponder) equipment on the ground. The pilot of the aircraft was able to be constantly informed of the distance to the position of the ground equipment.

The changeover for aircraft and ground installations dedicated to communications and navigation, from hundreds of kilocycles to higher frequencies, in the hundreds of megacycles, that occurred during the years of interest here, constituted an advance in degree but not in kind. The earlier advance from light beacons to radio beams was the real steppingstone to uninterrupted position determination while flying on instruments.

Airport control towers continued to use light signals to communicate with local flight traffic well into the 1940s, especially at military primary training bases. With the onset of an air transport industry, voice radio communication between pilots and tower operators or ground controllers or air traffic control personnel became a necessity. More and more aircraft came equipped with appropriate voice radio receivers and transmitters.

In 1929, even with light beacons, it had not yet become accustomed practice to fly passengers at night. Aircraft system developers and ground equipment developers were still making darkness their priority objective, as the solvable impediment to scheduled flight. All-weather flight had not yet become the priority on the agenda of requirements for revenue passenger flight. Although "all conditions of weather" remained a goal, flight in darkness was the immediate objective for the air passenger transport companies that were formed in the late 1920s. The onset of darkness caused the aircraft operators of a number of rail/plane transportation partnerships to land their aircraft and transfer their passengers to the passenger train.

The year 1929 brought a rush to commercialize in aviation. New air carriers entering service that year were:

- National Air Transport, New York-Chicago, using the airmail route via Cleveland and Toledo
- Boeing Air Transport, Chicago-San Francisco, following the air mail route west of Chicago
- Transcontinental Air Transport (TAT), New York to Los Angeles and San Francisco via St. Louis, Dodge City and Las Vegas; this began as an air-rail setup using TAT in the air by day and the Pennsylvania and Santa Fe Railroads at night
- Colonial Air Transport, on New York-Montreal and New York-Boston routes, carrying passengers and air mail

Others that joined or announced plans to join this air passenger business race were Pitcairn Aviation, flying between Atlanta and Greensboro, and Western Air Express operating from Los Angeles to the Missouri River and Denver to Los Angeles.

The year 1929 found Europe's Imperial Airways announcing London-Bombay service which was to originate in London with an 18-passenger plane called *The Great Argosy,* flying by day to Switzerland, where its passengers transferred to rail at night which took them to Italy. *The Great Calcutta,* a giant seaplane, took over at Genoa, flying south to Rome, where it was to "stop an entire day to enable the passengers to rest." Frequent changes of vehicles became the highlight of that lengthy route plan.

As the United States' border neighbor to the north, Canada's efforts in aviation were of direct interest to U.S. citizens. In July 1929, Canadian Airways entered into a contract with their government to connect Montreal and Detroit, initially for airmail only. One flight left Montreal and one left Detroit each morning, arriving at the other country's city each afternoon by four o'clock. Cities served along the route were Toronto, Hamilton, London and Windsor. Canada, with a population of 9.5 million, had 262 registered aircraft in 1929 and forty-three airports. Canada's aeronautics authority recorded a roster of 191 private pilots, 241 commercial pilots and 234 air engineers in 1929. For 1928, the U.S. Department of Commerce reported that 4,346 aircraft had been manufactured in the U.S. These included land, sea, and amphibians.

Lieutenant Herbert Fahy established a new solo endurance record in May of 1929. At Los Angeles, he made a non-refueled, solo flight of thirty-six hours and fifty-six minutes.

In the midst of a summer of endurance records, on June 13-14, three Frenchmen flew from Old Orchard, Maine to a landing on the beach at Comillas, a fishing town near Santander, Spain. This flight was the sixth straight Atlantic crossing if we begin the count with Lindbergh's historic solo flight in 1927. The French crew's destination had been Paris, but a stowaway from Portland, Maine, may have caused slightly increased gas consumption, forcing a premature landing. Their plane bore the name, *Yellow Bird.* This *Yellow Bird* took a route slightly to the south of east, making landfall in the Azores before turning northward toward Paris, and falling just short of that city by 500 statute miles. This flight is notable because by means of regular radio contacts with landmarks and ships along the way, the flight crew adjusted its course based on its fuel remaining, the weather ahead, and alternate airport options. With air-to-ground or air-to-sea communication, flight course could be adjusted along the route. Weather could be avoided.

The series of flights over the Atlantic between the U.S. and Europe, along with the domestic U.S. endurance flights, demonstrated to the potential passenger that flight reliability had been attained. Not just engines, but other aircraft systems were advancing in performance. Over water flights for land-based aircraft demonstrated that short intervals between intermediate airports for possible emergency landings might not be a requirement for safe flight.

U.S. Navy Lieutenant Apollo Soucek broke the flight altitude record in May of 1929 with a flight to nearly 39,000 feet, and just two weeks later, German aviator Willi Neunhofen broke that record by reaching nearly 42,000 feet. While flight at high altitudes was undertaken first by military pilots testing new frontiers in military aviation, in the longer view it meant that high altitude commercial air traffic could fly clear of the low altitude clutter of planes in the air, with the added benefit of lower fuel consumption for point to point flights.

The third anniversary of the aeronautics branch of the U.S. Department of Commerce was celebrated on July 1, 1929. Commerce had taken over aviation rules making and facilities provisioning from the Post Office Department. Thirty thousand air route miles were now being flown domestically, with ten thousand of those miles served by light beacons. First half 1929 totals of passengers and of mail in pounds equaled the totals of all of 1928. 5,830 aircraft were registered in the U.S. in mid-1929. California was way ahead with nearly a thousand, and Alaska had nine. Airline operators, that time 45 in number, had 400 aircraft in their operating inventories.

Charles Lindbergh and President Juan Trippe of Pan-American Airways opened a new passenger route from Miami, over the West Indies and Central America in September of 1929. Havana, and Parambiro, Dutch Guiana, were outbound stops, with Central American stops on the return to Miami completing the route structure. Mrs. Lindbergh and Mrs. Trippe accompanied their husbands on the maiden flights.

In September of 1929, nineteen women participated in the Women's Air Derby from Santa Monica, California, to Cleveland, Ohio. Thirteen completed the flight and Marvel Crosson suffered a fatal crash the second day out.

At Hasbrouck Heights, New Jersey, on September 13, 1929, the first of a planned manufacturing run of twelve Fokker F-32 aircraft made a flight demonstration. Designed for 32 daytime passengers or 16 at night, this plane cruised at 150 mph and was poised to begin service in the transcontinental plane-train system of the New York Central Railroad and Universal Air Lines. There were four engines in two nacelles of the F-32, with the rear engine in each nacelle configured as a pusher engine. In the flight demonstration, first the two rear engines were idled with no loss of altitude, and then the forward engines were idled, with the plane again maintaining stable flight. Passengers sat four abreast, with an aisle between. Tall passengers did not have to stoop down. Two washrooms and one kitchen were installed.

By 1930, the U.S. Department of Commerce was reporting 10, 215 registered pilots nationwide with California leading with 2,076 and New York second with 1,007. In California's total pilot count, there was a subclass of 903 who were designated as transport pilots. Alaska had seven pilots, five in the transport classification.

An airline flying to South America bankrolled a conversion of the Navy's PY-1, a seaplane, for passenger use with space for 20 passengers. Igor Sikorsky was at work in Connecticut on the world's largest seaplane intended for commercial passenger flight with an announced customer, Pan American Airways. Boeing Aircraft pioneered the famed and successful four-engine seaplanes that became known as Boeing *Clippers*.

The U.S. cross-country speed records for single pilot and dual pilot, refueled (stopping at an airport, en route) and non-refueled flight, were changing hands every month in 1930. Lt. Apollo Soucek regained the world's altitude record at 43,166 feet. Amy Johnson flew solo from Croyden, England to Australia. A monoplane, the Bellanca *Columbia,* round-tripped nonstop, New York-Bermuda, putting the floating island airport further into memory's recesses. Lt. Col. Roscoe Turner set a new east to west record, for flight with a single stop, using less than 19 hours in the air.

With two French pilots, the aircraft *Question Mark* made another record. They flew from Le Bourget Field in Paris to Curtiss Field on Long Island. The aircraft landed with 100 gallons of fuel remaining and the motor "needing only a new rocker arm and grease and oil." A French woman taking off from Le Bourget just hours after the *Question Mark* departed set a new woman's record of 37 hours for solo, non-refueled, flight. Captain Hawks set a new Los Angeles to Curtiss Field on Long Island speed record of just under 12 ½ hours. This was accomplished in a *Travelair* low wing monoplane with a Wright Whirlwind engine, averaging over 200 miles per hour for the 2,510 mile route. Dale Jackson and Forest O'Brine regained the endurance record with a 647 hour flight in their original *Robin* now emblazoned with the name, *Greater St. Louis.* Only a crack in the crankcase brought them down. O'Brine determined that this was the difficulty by crawling out on a catwalk during the flight.

While engines with liquid cooling were the engines of choice for the automobile industry, it became evident that the air-cooled radial engine was winning the contest for reliability in the air. With Burbank, California as the objective, departing from her native New York City, Ruth Nichols set a new (actual flight time) cross country east-to-west U.S. record late in 1930 in a Crosley-Lockheed-Vega monoplane. That plane was powered by a new 450 horsepower radial engine.

The 10th west to east flight over the North Atlantic was completed on October 10, 1930. Ex-military pilots Boyd of Canada and Connor of the U.S. flew old reliable *Columbia* from Newfoundland to a beach landing on one of the Scilly Isles off the southwestern tip of England. They had gas left but their gas line became fouled, forcing a premature landing.

The non-refueled flight of a Bellanca powered by a Packard diesel engine broke the endurance record for non-refueled flight by staying aloft for nearly 85 hours. Though the period of use of the diesel engine in flying was short, it exceeded that of the nuclear powered plane later in the 20th century which never quite made it past the drawing board.

Germany's Do-X, a twelve-engine flying boat, made several successful flights in 1931, one to South America. This was a huge aircraft, with only the Howard Hughes seaplane after World War II rivaling it in size. The twelve engines of the Do-X were in six nacelles above the high wing of this huge monoplane, six pulling and six pushing. The "Do" derived from Claude Dornier who designed many successful warplanes for Germany's Luftwaffe in World War II.

A public demonstration was made at Houston's Municipal Airport on May 31, 1931 of one plane whose flight was automatically controlled by a pilot in another plane. A transport pilot was aloft in the plane to be controlled because of a government regulation that there be a licensed pilot aboard any experimental plane flying over an "incorporated city." Control was surrendered for about fifteen minutes to the pilot with the "master key" in the control aircraft.

The National Air Races at Cleveland, Ohio, opened on August 28, 1931. Never before (and never since) had such a large group of the world's leading names in aviation gathered together. Russell Boardman and John Polando had just flown nonstop from New York to Istanbul, Turkey to set a new world distance record for non-refueled flight. They came to Cleveland along with Lt. Al Williams, holder of the U.S. landplane speed record. Also there was Major

Ernst Udet, the German war ace of World War I credited with 62 kills.

The major event of the National Air Races was the race for the Thompson Trophy. It was won in 1931 by Lowell R. Bayles of Springfield, Massachusetts in the Granville Brothers' *Gee Bee*, which set a new record for a closed course race of 236.2 mph. Their chief rival, Major Jimmy Doolittle, was forced out in the seventh lap by an overheated engine.

There was money to be won at the National Air Races in 1931. Major Doolittle was the top money winner with $10,000. Bayles was next with $9,300. These prize winnings were followed by other aviators and aviatrixes who rounded out the top ten money winners:

Mae Haizlip of St. Louis with $7,750;
W.J. Wedell of Patterson, LA with $5,800;
Phoebe Omline of Memphis with $4,250 plus an auto she won, worth $2,500;
John Livingston of Aurora, IL with $6,280;
Florence Klingensmith of Minneapolis with $4,300;
Maud Tait of Springfield, MA with $4,250;
Robert Hall of Springfield, MA with $3,150.

On September 29, 1931, Britain's G.H. Stainforth set a new speed record of 408.8 mph. The engine was a Rolls Royce liquid cooled inline engine that used a refined gasoline containing additives of ethyl and wood alcohol. The engine generated 300 more horsepower than had ever previously been demonstrated, though in its early years this engine had a short maintenance cycle. These inline engines powered most of the land based Allied fighters used in the early years of the battle for Europe in World War II. Though their cooling systems were vulnerable to enemy fire, the Allied fighter and fighter-bomber aircraft could match the flight performance of the counterpart German planes. The U.S. Navy and the Japanese Navy stuck with radial air-cooled engines for their carrier-based fighter planes in World War II.

A flight made in 1931 by Wiley Post and Harold Gatty in their aircraft *Winnie Mae* had long-term implications for both commercial passenger flight and for military flight. Powered by a Pratt & Whitney Wasp engine developing 525 horsepower at 2200 rpm and taking eight days and sixteen hours, the aircraft flown by these two men left New York on June 23. They piloted and navigated their plane around the world in its northern latitudes. Here is a list of the places they put down for fuel. Some of the place names may send the reader to an atlas.

Harbor Grace, Newfoundland;

Chester, England (near Liverpool);

Berlin, then Moscow, then on to

four landings in Siberia at cities just above or below the

50th parallel, at Novosibursk, then Irkutsk, Blagovyeshchensk and Khabarovsk;

then, flying north of east to Fairbanks, Alaska;

next, flying south of east to Edmonton, Alberta;

thence, to Cleveland, Ohio;

arriving back at their original takeoff point in New York City on July 1, 1931.

There was not a great deal of night flying on this route. These two men flew their route in northern latitudes just after the summer solstice for their "round the world flight." The North Atlantic crossing was 2,195 miles and the North Pacific crossing was 2,500 miles. Edmonton to Cleveland was about 1,600 miles and Moscow to Novosibirsk was about 1,100 miles. The rest of the flight segments in Siberia were relatively short, though a forced landing in the mountainous area between any of those stops would have been a concern.

At the end of July of 1931, Hugh Herndon and Clyde Pangborn piloted a flight intended to track the Post/Gatty round-the-world route and break the *Winnie Mae's* record. One of their flight segments led to a situation of political import. Their Bellanca plane named *Miss Veedol* proved too slow and they could not make up sufficient time by shortening the rest and refueling stops. In mid-Siberia, recognizing that the *Winnie Mae's* record was beyond their grasp, they changed flight plans and landed, without permission, in Japan. They were interned, and released only after paying a fine of $1,025 each. When the Japanese newspaper *Asahi* offered a prize of $25,000, the two opportunists then made preparations for a Japan to United States nonstop flight. Over Dutch Harbor, Alaska, their plane was nearly forced down by the accumulation of ice on its wings. The plane was slowed considerably but did not stall, and the two men landed *Miss Veedol* at Wenatchee, Washington on October 5, 1931 after a 41 hour trip from Samushiro, Japan. This time they had a record. No one had flown that 4,458 mile route before. Their Japan to Wenatchee, Washington record may still stand.

An *Asahi* press representative was on hand at Wenatchee to present them with their check. One feature of their Bellanca helped the flight through its icing problem in the Aleutians. They dropped their landing gear when they got out to sea shortly after leaving Japan. *Miss Veedol* had been equipped with reinforced-steel flooring so that it could make a landing without wheels. The jettisoning of over 300 pounds put them in position to make it to U.S. soil and undoubtedly helped keep the aircraft above its stall speed with its ice accumulation near Dutch Harbor, Alaska. The flight is a reminder of the mixture of opportunism and meticulous planning that made aviation's early record-breaking flights possible. After landing, the pilots confided to newsmen that their arrest and internment had been for taking pictures of Japanese fortifications from the air on their way to their landing in Japan, and they speculated that the influence of the newspaper must have helped get them a permit to leave Japan. Their commentary during the interview after their feat does not include any admission (or denial) that they had actually taken those pictures.

Charles Lindbergh made the national news again in 1931. He and Anne Morrow Lindbergh, daughter of the U.S. Ambassador to Mexico, whom Lindbergh had married in 1929, left North Haven, Maine, on July 30. Their aircraft was the 600 horsepower *Sirius*, a low wing, two cockpit, two-pontoon seaplane. Their destination was the

Orient. Anne Lindbergh, a gifted writer, chronicled their flight in her short, excellent, book, titled, "North to the Orient." Their route was north and west over Canada and the Northwest Territories, to Pt. Barrow and Nome, Alaska, then south and west to Kamchatka, the Chishima island group, to Hokkaido and Tokyo, Japan and finally into China. On this flight, Anne was radioman and co-navigator. Always cognizant of the weather, Lindbergh elected not to overfly the option to use visual flight rules for landings in lakes or bays. In one exception that occurred along the Chishima group, an offshore low cloudbank moved in over the shoreline underneath them while higher clouds ahead foreclosed staying on top of the weather. According to Anne Lindbergh's book, they turned back, and her pilot husband made repeated, steeply banked, attempts to slide the aircraft down the side of the mountainous coastline trying to find clear water for landing underneath, finally making it on a third try. (See particularly pages 85-88 of the Harcourt Brace & Company's Harvest Book imprint, first Edition 1967, of "North to the Orient.")

There were no local radio aids where the foregoing event took place. The *Sirius* was equipped with only the most rudimentary direction finder, and Lindbergh did not have the aircraft instrumentation that was needed to make a controlled wings-level letdown to see if he could find a clear space with a sea horizon under the clouds. He had to hang on to that land, because he needed to know *where it met the sea.* An open sea landing out to sea was not an option for *Sirius* even if his aircraft had had the necessary instrumentation.

This chapter has brought to the reader just a few of the highlights of the completion of aviation's preparation age in the years 1929-1931. What those pilots and designers accomplished in first-ever flights set the stage for aviation's air transport era. Many of the names that made the news were dashing young men or women standing next to or sitting in the cockpits of their astonishing aircraft.

There was glamour. But, steadily improving engine and aircraft reliability were the enduring accomplishments.

45

Aviation Humor

·

There is an oft-told story about the SNJ (AT-6) aircraft. When the air speed fell below a pre-set number, for example when the plane was coming in for a landing, a loud horn would sound if the landing gear were still up. This was to warn the pilots to get the wheels down. At the preliminary hearing which followed one SNJ wheels up landing, the tower operator made it clear that he had yelled at the pilot continuously while the plane was on final approach, telling him to get his landing gear down.

The pilot's response at the formal proceeding was, "I knew you were yelling at me but I couldn't hear what you were saying because that horn was making so much noise."

Chapter 2 - A Preface to Instrument Flying

A pilot who takes an aircraft aloft has to pay attention to instruments and has to know what they tell him or her. The instrument communicates with the pilot through an indicator. Throughout the flight, the pilot pays attention to an indicator that tells how much fuel remains. Another indicator informs whether the oil pressure is in a range pre-determined to be safe. Still another tells the pilot the cylinder head temperature on an aircraft powered by a radial, air-cooled engine. If flying a legacy aircraft, coolant temperature would be important for the liquid cooled engines used on many aircraft up to and including World War II. Fuel pressure gauges and fuel flow meters were prominent on the instrument panels of many of the aircraft I flew. The foregoing instruments relate to the engine. They are very important, but they are not the instruments of primary interest in our examination of instrument flying.

Moving from tools derived from automobile experience that were found in early aircraft, a basic airplane instrument panel for all but the earliest aircraft has an indicator that informs the pilot whether the airspeed is in a safe range. The airspeed is a critical piece of flight knowledge. The airspeed indicator is relevant to all flying, including but not limited to instrument flying.

Altitude is another item of numeric data in flying that is monitored regularly. Knowing the height of an airfield above sea level, the pilot can quickly determine the aircraft's height above an airfield when the altimeter is set to the local altimeter setting for that airfield in inches of Mercury. The airspeed and the altimeter are just two of the basic flight situation indicators requiring pilot attention in the conduct of any flight.

Instrument flying, flying on instruments, or flying in instrument conditions are common and equivalent expressions relevant to this story.

Airspeed and altitude can be read from instrument indicators that are found in heavier-than-air flying machines like gliders and aircraft. For "steady" readings of these two essential pieces of information, the pilot is informed of the aircraft velocity in a geometric plane parallel to a plane tangent to the earth at a point directly under the aircraft, and distant from that point by the altitude of the aircraft. This is necessary information but is not sufficient for safe flight under instrument conditions. It works for an aircraft with a visual horizon.

To airspeed and altitude, let us add "rate of climb or descent" information available from one indicator on just about all instrument panels. For the steady condition in the previous paragraph, this needle would be horizontal, indicating no ascent or descent. With those three indicators available for scanning by the pilot on a regular basis, we are nearing preparation for a discussion of the instruments that enabled the transition to instrument flying.

A Preface to Instrument Flying

Wings level, nose on horizon, nose down or up, left wing down, right wing down, rate of turn and rate of climb or descent describe the "attitude" of an aircraft. Making an assumption from the steady airspeed and the steady altitude that the aircraft attitude is wings level, and adding the assumption that its heading is also as steady as its magnetic compass direction of flight can confirm, it should be possible to double check by determining if the "position" of the aircraft is changing in a predictable way.

Borrowing from the language of geometry, 18,000 feet above the earth is a "z" position coordinate, corresponding to altitude. The other two position coordinates, geometrically, are the "x-y" position of the aircraft, its geographic position in earth coordinates. Various measurement pairs confirm an x-y position on or above the earth's surface. "One hundred miles due east of Norfolk, Virginia," is one pair. Latitude and Longitude are another. Control of the aircraft's heading and speed can be confirmed if the expected position is compatible with the current measurement of position. If we flew from Norfolk on an easterly heading at 100 miles per hour for one hour and found our new position after one hour to be one hundred miles east of Norfolk, we have confirmed the basic dynamics of the flight control problem.

Climbing, gliding, and turning with one or the other wing down are some of the dynamic terms that further- define an aircraft in motion. These attitude descriptors are easily inferred by a pilot who has good earth reference. These can be visualized by a pilot through instruments we have yet to describe whether or not he or she has visual earth reference.

A pilot proceeding with reference to an uninterrupted visual earth horizon may not be and may not need to be "on instruments" in the context of our attention here. An aircraft proceeding between layers of clouds with a defined cloud horizon is on an instrument flight even though the pilot can generally infer the aircraft's earth orientation without constant attention to any instruments aboard for that purpose. Clouds that are found in layers have helpfully disposed themselves roughly parallel to the earth's surface. The gyro horizon (known also as the artificial horizon - gyro horizon will be the preferred term in this story) is an instrument that helps the pilot construct a mental picture of earth reference when the ground below cannot actually be seen. This instrument will be accorded its essential space in later pages.

Finally, ground haze that permits visual identification of earth features when viewed straight down, but provides almost no forward visibility, is an instrument condition. Pilots may fly using Visual Flight Rules in those conditions, but it is not advisable. Carrying passengers under those conditions should always demand an instrument flight plan clearance.

In recognition of changing weather conditions, leading to possible information overload for a pilot or hazard overload for the aircraft, there is the judgment call as to whether a flight should be attempted at all. Choosing not to fly under threatening weather conditions, especially when changes are occurring with uncertain predictions, marks a pilot who is attentive to the practice of instrument flight rules.

Successful instrument flight was achieved as the result of a mix of three widely disparate motivations. Tragedy, entrepreneurial ambition, and job opportunity all played roles.

Tragedy occurred when military pilots lost their lives in 1934's misbegotten replacement of airmail pilots. The airmail pilots had been flying the U.S. airmail and had learned to respect, avoid or outfox the weather in the accomplishment of their task. The military pilots ordered to take their place did not have relevant experience, and no training period was provided to them before taking over the responsibility. The airmail story actually began many years earlier.

The military pilot in war had an objective to get the better of an enemy aviator. This came in to play for the United States during its 1917-1918 participation in World War I. In those years, the United States Post Office Department defined air mail as a new domestic mail service that would support a premium price. The military pilot training needs and the entrepreneurial motivations of the postal service seemed briefly to vie with each other for the limited resources of aircraft and pilots, especially in 1918, the last year of World War I. The word "limited" is used in the context of the military who always want all they can get.

In 1918, the U.S. Post Office Department was actually using Army pilots and planes for flying the mail; the Post Office and the War Department were both then full departments of the federal government and were cooperating in a simpler age.

Two contrasting preferences were expressed by mail pilots of the 1918-era for flight under conditions involving clouds or fog. Some mail pilots favored staying under the clouds, even hugging the ground when necessary, as a cloud avoidance method. Others wanted to fly above the clouds, in clear weather, and descend through breaks in the clouds when necessary to land.

The latter group even laid out a number of requirements. Historian Edward Pearson Warner, in the first of his five lectures at Norwich University on November 21, 1937, entitled "Early History of Air Transportation," reported that he found a list of requirements in government conference notes of 1918. In summary, the first four requirements on the 'wish-list' were: meteorological stations to record high altitude weather data, twin engine aircraft, auxiliary fields near destination fields, and radio direction finders. The fifth item on the list was lights to guide aircraft flying at night.

The significant fact is that a list existed. As Dr. Warner noted, lacking any foreseeable implementation of their requirements, the group who wished to fly above the clouds were forced to join the ground huggers in the early years in order to deliver the air mail. But, the flying aids that the "fly above the clouds" group listed showed vision. These proved to be important support elements in the solution arrived at in the 1930s when instrument flight became a reality.

Entrepreneurial ambition was ready to play a major part in aviation. There were investors who bet that the airplane could compete with the train in passenger service. That willingness to make investment capital led to the very first airlines. At first, airline pilots flew by Contact Flight Rules (CFR).

The Triumph of Instrument Flight

Owners and pilots soon figured out that if schedules were to mean anything, their aircraft needed to fly in weather. In early general aviation and in the peacetime military, flights could wait on weather. It was in the airline business that the effort to conquer instrument flight, not as an occasional demonstration of skill, but in every day operations, was waged. By 1933, the basic tools were in place.

A regular job in a period of job scarcity was welcomed by those who aspired to be pilots with steady jobs. Judging by results, there was enough experience and foresight in those first steady job pilots to determine that most foresaw that instrument flying would become a goal. In addition to the two engine requirement on that perceptive list from the Army mail pilot group in 1918, another item featuring the number "two" had come into the 1930s aircraft picture. Two pilots!

In the evolution of the airline business, pilot self-confidence and the airline owner's need to stay solvent and to return something to investors became the nexus of the endeavor. A test of priorities took place. Day by day decisions on what flight should go and what flight should not go, slowly developed into standard criteria at each airline. The line of debate was original within each airline, but it became influenced at all airlines by the gradual arrival of regulation by the U.S. government. These varied protocols converged into procedures that were designed to keep accidents low and yet provide passenger-acceptable on-time flight schedule results across the industry.

The process took several years and the issue that came up most often was confrontation with weather. Issues of maintenance and servicing were also worked out. But the weather challenge and the solution of successful instrument flight in weather evolved into procedures followed by all airlines. These were pilot driven at first and not always written down. Despite competition, and the differing business and geographic origins of the airlines, aircraft operations management processes eventually became standardized.

Sooner or later, irrespective of their status in aviation, most who piloted airplanes acknowledged the need to adjust to the impediments that weather held for safe flight. This prudence was healthy even as the pilots became better equipped through training, experience and aircraft equipment to deal with the challenges.

Safe flight in clouds, and flight which could ascend successfully into overcasts and descend through undercasts became a part of aviation in the years1933, 1934 and 1935. This is the transition period in which airline operations gained their critically important initiative. That was the basis for the ability to maintain schedule for a high percentage of flights.

The capability has received almost no public recognition. Tools had been provided. Implementation had occurred. Airline pilots who were on board for the transition and those who followed them recognized it. Military aviators in World War II recognized it. So, what needed to be said?

Instrument flying rapidly became indispensable to industrialized nations and emerging nations. Though the event required several flight segments, President Roosevelt's early 1943 trip to the Casablanca Conference to meet with Winston Churchill was by air. World leaders and business leaders now proceed by air to both scheduled and emergency meetings.

Public consciousness of flight under instrument conditions has only occurred on the rare occasions when there appeared to have been a failure of man and his flying machine to surmount an impediment in which instrument flight conditions played a part.

While my own pilot experiences will enter later pages, the reader will find that general aviation, airline and other military pilot voices will be heard as well.

A leap forward that one technology development brought directly to a pilot's ability to fly using instruments proved so important, that one exception is made to a general guideline not to dwell on technology in this story. That exception is the gyroscope, shortened by most to "gyro."

Aviation Humor

"If it ain't Boeing,
I ain't going."

Chapter 3 - The Gyroscopic Stabilizer: A New Horizon

T he whole is greater than the sum of its parts. So states an axiom. In order to push aside the barriers to instrument flying in 1930 it became a challenge to discover that the parts were more than the whole.

Pilots face an array of indicators on the panel of any aircraft new to them. Keeping the aircraft in the air on a good day requires attention to the panel indicators. For instrument flying, attention to the panel is essential. It is a more intense indicator-human-action-sequence than simply noting whether the fuel gauge needle has gone down into the warning zone.

A competent instrument pilot is a pilot capable of handling all-weather flight on instruments for long periods in which visual horizons do not exist. In the process of becoming proficient for flight in demanding weather conditions, a pilot learns to trust what the instruments are telling him or her.

The Triumph of Instrument Flight

The subject of flight without visual horizon had no relevance until man first figured out how to fly. Then, the airframe, controls, engine and basic pilot proficiency had to evolve so that flying was reasonably safe and just keeping the aircraft in the air did not make moment to moment demands on the pilot. Anyone engaged in a wrestling match with a machine is hardly in a good position to extend attention to instrument flying.

As flight by visual flight rules in decent weather became almost routinely successful, a flight challenge for transport aviation was to see if schedules could be met along a route on a given day when flight using a visual earth horizon was not possible.

The translation of gyroscope technology, as earlier demonstrated in Sperry's gyrostabilizer, to pilot use involves a challenge in describing how it took place. The whole had arrived before its parts. Discussions that took place in preparation for this story revealed that many pilots, even experienced ones, have but a hazy knowledge of how the gyro arrived to make their wonderful careers possible.

Today's pilots know that the gyro is the basis for their autopilot. Flight training programs are expensive. Skilled instruction costs money. Understandably, most pilot instruction programs provided little understanding of the pivotal role that the gyro plays. Instruction follows innovation in performance; it does not lead. Pilots came before instructor-pilots. Instrument flying was practiced before instrument flight instruction was available. If the first pilot to use gyro-based instruments for successful instrument flight did not write down what his experience was, a gap occurred. Literature searches have provided few sources, but one proved exceptionally helpful..

T.J.C. Martin wrote about aviation matters in the New York Times. In a 1929 article in the Times, he wrote extensively on his interpretation of the implications of the gyro for aviation. It is clear that he understood better than most, and better for sure than the aviation industry, the fundamental importance of the gyro. Some of that article was quoted in the January 1930 issue of the Standard Quarterly Review, page [39], under the heading, "Gyroscopic

The Gyroscopic Stabilizer: A New Horizon

Control of an Airplane." In the article Martin cites a two-axis gyro, one wheel spinning in the horizontal and the other in the vertical. Two of Martin's paragraphs and then a final sentence are quoted:

"The gyroscopic stabilizer, as the latest aero-gyroscope is called, has brought automatic control to the threshold of practicability - a threshold, be it said, that bids fair to make it an indispensable unit of equipment in all long distance passenger transport planes...The method by which it masters the plane's controls is an important forward step."

"A gyroscopically controlled plane is armed against fog, gusts of wind, mist, snow, sleet, and all the rest of the many factors that plague an aviator. It is also independent of the sun, moon, stars, earth, etc. Once the plane has been set on a course and the gyroscopic stabilizer has been set to guide it on that course, not all the elements nor all the errors of men can combine to persuade it off that course, provided that the instrument is let alone."

And here, in that Standard Quarterly Review of 1930, Martin's concluding sentence is quoted:

"Perhaps the day will dawn when this stabilizer will be attached to a gyroscopic compass."

That day did come. It had, technically, already come. The pilot was to become enrolled in aircraft flight control with, not one, but two very important new panel indicators.

Author Martin's view of the gryo device that the Sperry family reduced so successfully to practice was a step or two ahead of aviation's ability to take immediate advantage of what that gyro could provide. Aviation had to negotiate the steps in between, and eventually came to understand that *essential pilot information* was bundled *inside* the new gyroscopic stabilizer.

In the post-World War I decades leading up to World War II, the name Sperry gradually emerged in connection with the gyroscope. Lawrence Sperry became famous before his inventor father became well known. Lawrence was an aviator who earned many first-time flight distinctions in his brief life, which ended in his death in 1923 at age 31 in a flight over the English Channel.

Lawrence, whose nickname became "gyro," was the first to demonstrate that he could drop the landing gear of a plane to save flying weight and then land the plane on skids. His father, who went by his middle name, Elmer, launched his company into the manufacture of gyro devices engineered and mass-produced for a variety of purposes. Sperry gyroscopes helped win World War II. Elmer Sperry outlived his son by seven years and died in 1930. The company he founded expanded dramatically in World War II. One Sperry war production plant on Long Island had parking space for 20,000 cars.

The promise of the Sperry gyroscopic stabilizer device was that a pilot could take a plane off in clear local conditions, get to assigned altitude, set in a prescribed course and altitude, and turn the aircraft's flight control over to the automatic device. Serious thinkers about aviation's future recognized the gyroscopic stabilizer's fundamental advantages. But, the local weather was not always clear. The starting position was the runway of an airport. Weather conditions for takeoff might be a 300-foot ceiling and one half-mile visibility. To get to the point where he could turn the aircraft over to this new device that aviation would come to call the "autopilot," the pilot still had the challenge of taking off and then getting the plane settled down at assigned altitude on the assigned course. He or she would then be able to release hands-on control of the flight control surfaces to the autopilot.

The gyro stabilizer device incorporated functions that would maintain level flight, and maintain the direction of flight. That result would be achieved through the actions of the elevator control surfaces to maintain the nose on the horizon so that the aircraft did not climb or glide, and would hold the course steady through actions of the aileron and rudder surfaces, once the aircraft was turned over to its control.

While the function of horizon definition and control had been built into the gyroscopic stabilizer of 1929, the pilot involved in flight controlled by the gyroscopic stabilizer was not privy to, meaning he could not *see*, the horizon, as the device defined it.

The Gyroscopic Stabilizer: A New Horizon

It became necessary for a gyroscopic horizon function to be *brought out* of the autopilot system in the form of a new display indicator in front of the pilot so that he or she could be in the horizon knowledge loop. This meant that the gyro's sense of the attitude of the aircraft could be given to the pilot, visually. The faith of the pilot in the attitude of his aircraft could be vested in an indicator on his panel. That would correspond to the faith that an actual altitude was coming from the altimeter indicator.

As for controlled flight in darkness, it could and had been accomplished without the gyroscopic horizon, though that device certainly made it easier. For the rest of this story, I will shorten the gyroscopic stabilizer and the gyroscopic horizon to gyro stabilizer and gyro horizon respectively.

The first in importance of the two panel-indicating instruments that evolved from the gyro stabilizer was the *gyro horizon*. Some refer to it as the artificial horizon, and that is the role that it played. The second panel indicator that came from function solutions within the original stabilizer was the *gyrocompass* envisioned specifically by author T.J.C. Martin. Here it will be called the "directional gyro."

Another important panel indicator had arrived before either of them, and used a property of the gyro that is most often associated with error. That was the *turn indicator*. It showed up on instrument panels, packaged with a ball in an arc in the lower portion of the indicator. The turn needle in the upper periphery of the indicator was moved off center by a force, inherent in gyro technology, called *precession*. That device did not evolve from Sperry's gyro stabilizer. The instrument has been variously known as the turn and ball, turn and bank, and needle-ball. Aviation people generally understand that all refer to the same instrument.

Here, in illustration form, are the three instruments that gyro technology brought to aviation as it leapt across the barrier of blind flying to routine flight on instruments.

In the gyro trio of instruments, the instrument whose panel indicator is pictured in Illustration 6 came to instrument panels first.

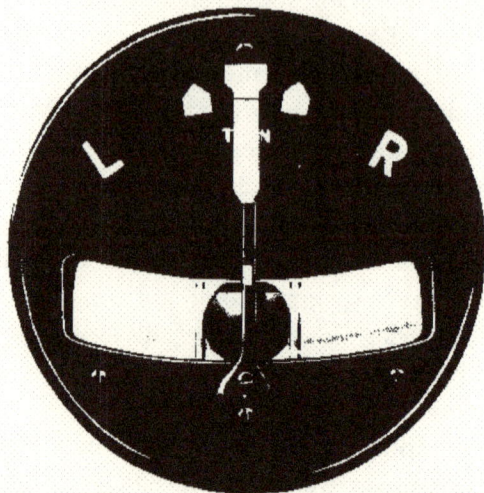

Illustration 6 - The Turn Indicator

The turn indicator that arrived on aircraft instrument panels did not come from the unbundling of the Sperry gyroscopic stabilizer. It was at best a partial answer to the pilot's need when entering clouds.

The next two instruments pictured came to pilot's instrument panels in the same time frame and owe their origin, conceptually, to Sperry's gyro stabilizer. The first to be pictured in Illustration 7 is the directional gyro.

As originally introduced, the directional gyro incorporated no magnetic force input. It did only what its master, the pilot, told it to do. The directional gyro had to be set by the pilot to an initial heading. Then, if the aircraft turned to a new heading, the instrument's indicator would settle on a new indicated heading. The new indicated heading was an accurate indication of the number of degrees the heading had changed from the heading originally set. One technique to manually introduce earth coordinate intelligence was to set the gyrocompass to the true heading of the takeoff runway. In flight, the pilot would later refer to his magnetic compass for magnetic heading from time to time. After calculations that incorporated "variation" and "deviation" corrections to the magnetic heading to arrive at true heading, the pilot would recheck and correct the directional gyro's heading which might have drifted a bit due to precession. Later, an extension of the directional gyro instrument arrived that incorporated earth's magnetic force intelligence directly into the instrument.

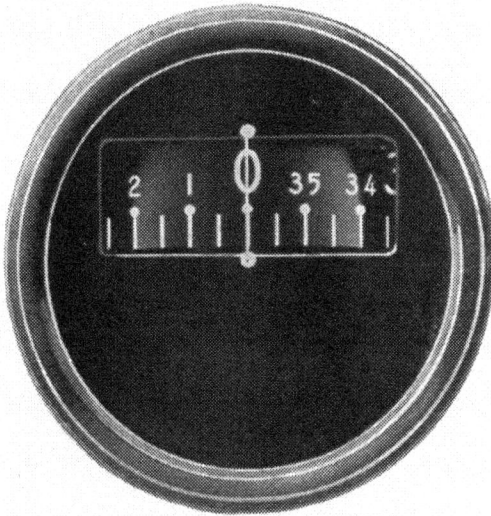

Illustration 7 - The Directional Gyro

The breakthrough instrument in this group of three is the gyro horizon whose indicator is seen in Illustration 8.

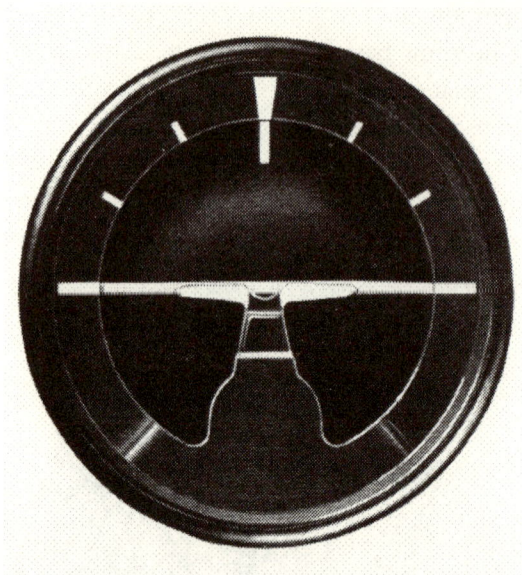

Illustration 8 - The Gyro Horizon

Gyroscopic action derives from the gyro property of *stability*, that is, a spinning rotor resists change. A spinning top is an example.

For both the directional gyro and the gyro horizon, the other gyro property mentioned earlier, *precession*, is treated as an unintended, meaning unwanted, consequence. Precession, in those instruments, meant "error."

In contrast, the turn indicator's *intended action* depended on the gyro property of precession.

The directional gyro was a decided improvement in course control, but an improvement *in degree*. It was not as absolutely crucial as the gyro horizon. The latter, as an improvement *in kind*, was transformational and essential for instrument flying.

The gyros that powered the indicators in Illustrations 7 and 8 were treated with respect by pilots. After landing, they would be "caged." On the Pre-Taxi check-off list for the P2V-5F Lockheed

Neptune aircraft, item 15 was "Gyros...Set & Uncaged." If a pilot, whose aircraft had these gyros aboard, intended to do acrobatics, he or she would be advised to "cage" the gyros for the acrobatics exercise or they would "tumble."

For flight in far northern latitudes, when the magnetic compass' variation was so large that it could no longer help the pilot determine true course with respect to true North, the gyrocompass became essential, even with its precession. For those interested in the subject of precession related to motion, an entrée clue is "Coriolis force."

The spinning rotors at the heart of the three instruments are so vital that engineers for most aircraft designs went to the vacuum pump, direct driven by the aircraft's power plant. The pump furnished suction to drive the gyro rotors. A suction pump indicator on a pilot's instrument panel is the link to the proper action of the vacuum pump in use. Two engines, with a pump on each, provide redundancy. A third source would be "ram" air from the motion of the aircraft.

The autopilot would eventually be accepted, even welcomed, by pilots whose aircraft had arrived at a prescribed altitude in controlled flight. It was a little ahead of its time in 1929. Full gyro control was more than aviation was prepared to accept then. The entire challenge of instrument flight was still in the future for the just-born commercial aviation enterprise that existed in 1929. The first instrument flight check would not be given until 1933.

The gyro horizon would provide the pilot an accurate reference to the geometric plane tangent to the earth directly under his plane. In instrument conditions with no horizon (one expression for this is "in the soup"), without visual earth reference, a pilot could quickly become completely disoriented. With the gyro horizon instrument, he or she was as well-oriented earth wise, as one would be on a clear day and much better off than on a hazy day or night, and infinitely better off than one would be in zero-zero instrument conditions without the device. The gyro horizon was the enabler that let the pilot proceed on an instrument flight plan. With the addition of radio navigation aids, the pilot could take off in poor weather, and land in poor weather, and control his aircraft during flight between airport ground events. Once reaching assigned altitude, the pilot could turn his plane's flight control over to Sperry's marvelous gyro stabilizer device. (The Navy *Privateer* patrol aircraft used the Sperry Mark 3 Automatic Pilot.)

These paragraphs reflect the state of the art of the instruments in instrument flying from the mid-1930s to mid-century. In later decades of the 20th century, electronics would advance the art. With the use of an autopilot and other advances, control of an aircraft during most of its flight profile would more and more become hands-off, with the pilot becoming more of an overseer of performance.

There are additional examples that can be cited in turning an aircraft over to full automatic control, from the beginning of takeoff to and including landing. As a naval aviator, I have participated in "drone" control flying, in which a full aircraft is taken off, flown, and landed, with no live pilot aboard. Grumman F6F-5K *Hellcat* aircraft were configured with Bendix P1-K autopilots, along with the radio command sets for control of such flights. Many thousands of drone flights have been made with few problems.

The next illustration shows an F6F-5K *Hellcat* drone, followed by two F8F-2 *Bearcat* chase planes. The drone has no pilot aboard. The Navy's Air Development Squadron Two (VX-2) had the early 1950s mission to control the drones as targets for Terrier missile test firings off the east coast of the United States. The drone is cruising on autopilot. In addition to 'wheels up' or 'wheels down' control, the chase plane pilots had 'throttle control,' 'rpm and mixture control,' 'stick and rudder control,' 'cowl flap' and 'wing flap' control of the drone aircraft. The drone's gyro-controlled autopilot took over and kept the drone flying in accordance with the last command received.

Illustration 9 - A drone with two chase planes

If the drone entered clouds in level flight, it would have flown steadily until out of gas. The chase plane pilots would have had to fend for themselves if they entered a weather mass. They had no autopilot and only first tier instrument capability. First tier means no backup electrical systems, no extra radio receivers and the like. Those F8F chase planes had been built to counter the Kamikaze in the Pacific, were intentionally unstable in flight, and could climb to 10,000 feet in record time in their World War II sorties to intercept the Kamikaze pilots. For all-weather flying, even though the chase planes had pilots aboard, they were not as well configured as their pilotless companion. (Later drones had the letters "NOLO" for "no live operator" painted on the vertical stabilizer so that local Fire Departments would not attempt to save a pilot in the event that the drone crashed returning from a mission.)

The aircraft in the illustration were not participants in the transition from VFR flight to IFR flight. As pictured, the point intended here is to emphasize the ability of the autopilot equipped drone aircraft to fly straight and level irrespective of clouds and visibility.

By the onset of World War II, the gyro technology in use in U.S. aviation was about 10 years old.

The German Luftwaffe, with its glider bombs, demonstrated not only gyro stabilized flight but remote control of the entire flight system of the glider bomb, by radio, from a parent aircraft. They were repeatedly successful in their attacks on Allied vessels with the HS-293 glider bomb in the Mediterranean in World War II in 1943 and early 1944.

Chapter 4 - The 1930s: Instrument Flying Takes Hold

A career that attracted many World War I aviators, and especially the young enthusiasts who had learned flying from them, was a career flying for an airline. The first U.S. airlines began flying in the United States in 1929 and 1930. The opportunity to be involved in building a new enterprise was not lost on young pilots who became excited that their newfound flying capability, which they treasured, might also offer career employment.

The airlines that formed and grew as the 1920s moved into the 1930s were caught up in the excitement of the transition from novelty to early maturation. Their aircraft and pilots, the route structures they pioneered, and the schedules and markets they established formed the foundation for the air transport business we know today. Developments in instrumentation, navigation, communications, ground support, and the pilot proficiency that made instrument flying possible, all took form in the 1930s.

The Triumph of Instrument Flight

While this period produced no breakthrough advances in airframes or engines, reliable aircraft were becoming available for airline use in the early 1930s as the result of more system choices to match airframes with of engines. The system of pilot(s), engine(s) and airframe with enough seats to produce adequate revenue for a given route structure developed from what might be characterized as the cut-and-try method, optimizing from choices.

With the engine and airframe performing to satisfactory safety and reliability standards, on-board flight instrumentation was needed to make flight in instrument conditions controllable. Radio navigation equipment in the plane and on the ground would need to team up to provide a second essential factor, navigation from one point to another. The clinching factor would be the pilots' advance in capability to be able to successfully conduct an instrument flight. The barrier of blind flying had to be overcome not just as a novelty, but as an every day capability.

Safe flight on instruments, after the Wright brothers' first flights and the solid achievements that VFR flying made in its first three decades, became aviation's most formidable challenge. The Boeing 247 of 1933 and the Lockheed *10 Electra* of 1934, as introduced to the market, were instrument equipped and were successfully put in service by airlines. The 247 came with autopilot and a pneumatic de-icing system. Aviation was poised to expand its degrees of freedom in all dimensions. The years 1933, 1934 and 1935 saw the instrument flight barrier overcome.

The Douglas DC-3 was introduced in 1935. For quite a few years (many are flying today) the DC-3 provided the best configuration of flight capabilities matched to airline flight profile needs. Two pilots, a stewardess, 21 or more seats for paying passengers, and two Pratt & Whitney R-1820 engines proved to be a good combination. The radial engines fitted with the N.A.C.A. (National Advisory Committee for Aeronautics, forerunner to NASA) cowl, controllable pitch propellers, good basic IFR instrumentation and the right payload made the Douglas the airplane of choice for many airlines.

The N.A.C.A. cowl deserves its place in aviation progress. Aerodynamics researchers at N.A.C.A. had determined in the 1920s that the protruding cylinders of the radial engines produced drag. The cowl they designed was the answer, not only reducing drag by streamlining a fairing over the protruding cylinder heads, but ultimately in providing some control over cylinder head temperatures. This came with the later evolution to the retractable cowl flap, closed to retain heat or opened to cool the cylinder heads. The cowl development was akin to the discovery that the fixed wheel sets created drag. At first there were wheel fairings, and eventually retractable wheels.

William Lawrence's radial engine design, the J-1 of 1921, the faith of the United States Navy in the design, and the upgrade to the J-5 made possible by British engineer S.C. Heron's cylinder redesign, led to performance and reliability. Finally, with the impatience of engineer Frederick Rentschler, who split off from Wright to form Pratt & Whitney (P&W), the economics of cost savings in manufacturing were realized in a series of highly successful P&W Wasp radial engines.

Increases in engine power, and engine reliability, were important, but aerodynamics designers were also essential participants in progress.

The airframe/engine choices were essential for range and reliability and revenue. The crowning achievement was the advance in instrument flying equipment, along with the pilot proficiency necessary to put cost-effective, reliable, aircraft into the skies irrespective of the weather. On schedule.

Pilot proficiency, in partnership with electronics in the air and on the ground, provided the ingredients for all weather airline success. A word coined to represent electronics equipment used in aviation was, "avionics." The electronic component of aviation systems lowered weight, improved response times, and added reliability.

At the outset, there was little formal definition of a set of detailed objectives to be met by an aircraft equipped for pilot-controlled flight in instrument conditions. The new instruments came to the instrument panel. Pilot feedback recommendations on positioning, lighting etc. were worked out by aircraft panel designers a step at a time. But for the basic step, my conclusion is that the instrument designers pretty much "got it right the first time." De-icing solutions, by contrast, took more than one step..

Public need, investment community interest, and the U.S. spirit of competition found common focus in the growth of the U.S. airline industry. Safety of flight was the first goal.

Early government sister agencies like the Civil Aeronautics Administration - CAA, and the Civil Aeronautics Board - CAB, were formed. Standards were set. Much later, with modified responsibilities and authority, the Federal Aviation Administration, FAA, and the National Transportation Safety Board, NTSB, replaced CAA and CAB. Generally, the government wanted a hand in the progress of aviation and in the protection of the flying public. For its part, the investment community would prosper if flight was safe and suffer if it proved unsafe.

Airlines became public companies, turning to the market investor for the ever increasing sums required to buy and to maintain transport aircraft. The airlines themselves could foresee expansion if they served the public, safely and economically. Aircraft accidents and incidents were news that made folks stop and think before they signed on as passengers. The government began to tabulate data on flight safety, and an airline's performance could be compared with its competitors.

Passengers, pilots, the aircraft builders, and the airline corporations had critical stakes in the safety issue. Unsafe practices were gradually rooted out in a business in which the number of watchdogs multiplied as the air traveling public multiplied, and that was pretty fast. Correctives did not eliminate all accidents. The human was part of the equation. But, compared with competitive forms of transportation, aviation's focus on safety has paid off. It evolved from an emphasis on safety not heretofore practiced in other forms of public transportation. One clear motivation: heavier than air flying machines were not underpinned by terra firma. Aviation's failures, its accidents, were given increased attention, and increasingly validated findings as to the causes of failure led to correctives.

Communication, "on" at all times, became an early safety of flight requirement. In aviation's formative years, aircraft were not fitted with data or cockpit voice recorders. The voice recorder "black box" of later flying days emphasizes the importance that accident investigators have put on reconstructing all the voice traffic that the pilot was engaged in or should have been engaged in. But, quite early in air transportation, pilot/controller voice communication was stressed. Recorders went into ground facilities as soon as the technology permitted. The early wire recorders were quickly replaced by the vastly better tape recorders.

Since many of the communication requirements were common to all the air carriers being formed in 1929, important radio services were contracted out to an organization supported by the airlines but which operated independently. From the beginning, that key organization providing radio communication services was Aeronautical Radio Inc. Founded in 1929, it is now known as ARINC. In many airports, during a substantial early part of the past seventy years, one might pass a small office in an air terminal whose entry door bore a tiny, low key, sign, "Aeronautical Radio Inc."

"ARINC develops and operates information processing systems and services that are essential to ensuring the efficiency, operation and performance of the aviation and travel industries. The company operates global networks that use both airline proprietary and standard open protocols. ARINC supports the aviation industry with voice and data radio communications through the shared use of the assigned frequency spectrum and radio facilities, as well as satellites." The quote is from ARINC's web site in 2002.

Each of the military services of the U.S. maintains extensive aviation communication networks. The civil airlines maintain extensive communication networks for direct contact with their stations and aircraft. These networks would be even more effective if they had the capacity to work together. It was an important recognition that led the early U.S. airline industry to initiate and support the cooperative effort that became ARINC. By 2003, this had become a $600 million dollar revenue company with 82 offices and 3000 employees. It is owned as a cooperative by the airlines it serves; these now include international airlines as well as U.S. domestic airlines.

Understandably, pilots have great motivation to achieve safe flight. Their jobs depend on it. Their lives depend on it. Training and certification of pilots became a top priority. Regular pilot re-certification was instituted. An annual flight physical by a licensed physician became a pilot certification and recertification requirement.

Engaging in instrument flight heightened the need for aircraft reliability. Scheduled maintenance programs for airframes and engines were put into practice. An aircraft whose pilot was struggling with component failure was less likely to make a survivable landing when operating under restricted conditions of visibility.

Aircraft schedules that could be maintained under almost all conditions of flight, pilots that could perform under varied conditions, and an airline operation that could be sustained in all weather conditions all came together in the United States in a short period, 1933-35. For the airline group and for general aviation and the military, there was no single day in that period to mark the transition.

Some railroads had taken their passengers for granted. Others linked up with new air transport companies. A new generation of field salesmen wanted to go eyeball to eyeball with customers who were too many railroad-hours away. Life speeded up.

The airlines began as very small enterprises. At first, route structures were limited compared with the high-density routes that resulted from passenger demands that cascaded later on. In the early years, air transport expansion was done with the zeal of pioneers who surprised themselves and their early passengers with the pace of commercial aviation progress. Though the transport aircraft available at the outset had limited cruising ranges, the competitive modes of transportation were filled with the impediments of land, and what man had contrived to put on that land. In those days, the airspace had few impediments. To compete with scheduled land transportation like trains and buses, airline pioneers saw that reliable flight schedules were needed. That was the first order of business and it was a big challenge.

The air transport operators were not alone in new enterprise challenges. Building aircraft for them was also a new business. Power plant development was a new business. Each proceeded almost independently with just a broadly defined consensus. This occurred well before airline executives became sufficiently powerful to define in advance what airframe and engine would best suit their business. The airline business developed in the beginning on routes that available equipment and a potential passenger base would support. It was also good if the plane got to its destination before nightfall.

Other groups of visionaries saw that airports, radio aids to air navigation and a communication and control infrastructure would be needed. The powerful rotating light beacons used in the very early days to help early mail pilots find their way from point to point across the United States did not penetrate very far into the clouds. For cloud penetration, not just an instrumented aircraft and a qualified pilot were needed, but proceeding with assurance from one airport to another required navigation equipment and two-way voice communication.

Despite the acknowledged risk of flying, pilots were eager to sign on to the new challenge of scheduled flight with paying passengers. Those pilots found partners willing to share those risks in marriage. The family man pilot, a breed different from the record setters and the barnstormers, needed a regular salary. Along with risk-taking investors, these aviators collaborated in the birth of an entirely new business opportunity, which came to be known as an airline.

The early pilots of passenger aircraft also proved, to themselves initially, that Contact Flight Rules, CFR, the rules for proceeding from one point to another by means of visual sighting of recognized earth landmarks below, were not going to be sufficient to build an air transport industry.

Part 43 of the Civil Air Regulations (those existing at an early period of U.S. aviation) dealing with General Operation Rules, and Part 60 on the subject of "contact flight rules," illustrate how government was dealing with a new challenge.

Examples of the early rules for the new solo pilot: "You are not permitted to pilot an aircraft carrying a person except a private, commercial or airline transport pilot..." "The minimum proximity of aircraft in flight is 500 feet (except by pre-arrangement of the pilots)." "Experienced pilots consider it unsafe to indulge in aerobatics at altitudes less than 1,500 feet." The parentheses involving the proximity exception based on pre-arrangement gave the military a sufficient relaxation in the rules to permit formation flying.

With the growing number of flights in the airspace, a set of rules of the road was needed. Early flying rules were patterned on rules of the road at sea. Powered aircraft had to give precedence to powered blimps and dirigibles. Those in turn had to give precedence to gliders and these in turn gave right-of-way to manned balloons.

What became known as general aviation dominated early flying. In the earliest days, the FBOs (Fixed Base Operators) at the local airport supported pilots who took off, flew locally and landed at the same airport. Some FBOs operated flight schools and some leased space to others who ran flight schools.

In the earliest days of aviation, pilots "learned by doing." The idea of accumulating experiences and putting them into a program of "learn before doing" took hold early in aviation. Ground schools and flight schools were an aviation idea long before driver training schools for automobiles.

The first practical simulator for flight was the Link Trainer. This simulation device skipped basic flight training (it assumed the student knew the basics) and went directly to instrument flight training. It evolved from the efforts of a man whose imagination was stirred by need. The need inspired Edwin Link to borrow technology from his father's organ company in Binghamton, New York. He defined the need he had perceived in his own early pilot experience to provide a realistic experience separate from actual air time, for the relationship between an aircraft's controls and its instrument's indications. Edwin Link had concluded that it was prohibitively expensive for instrument flight students to gather all the proficiency they would need from instrument training in actual flight. He put an organ builder's experience into developing a ground device to respond to the need. He saw how the pneumatically powered actuators for mechanisms in an organ could be adapted to a training device that would help pilots learn how to fly successfully with no visual horizon. The next paragraph contains a description of what a Link Trainer student saw before getting into Link's device.

Mounted on top of a pedestal was a small model of a single seat, mid-wing, aircraft. The model looked realistic except that it had no propeller and no wheels. The pedestal, with access steps on the outside, provided an enclosed compartment for pump and valves. For a canopy, the little plane had an opaque clamshell that opened on one side and was hinged on the other. Even that small detail of the clamshell showed Link's imaginative bent. The fuselage of Link's trainer could roll, pitch and yaw. There was room for one student on a seat under the clamshell. In front of him or her was an aircraft instrument panel and between the student and the panel was a control yoke. Under the instrument panel there was a recessed space forward and in that space for each foot there was a rudder pedal. There was a throttle lever available to the left hand. When the canopy swung down over the seated student, it was dark inside. Very dark.

Although lot to lot changes occurred in the trainers, the central grouping of panel instruments always included a directional gyro, a gyro-horizon, altimeter, airspeed indicator, and turn indicator.

The radio in the Link Trainer had a tuning knob and provided an aural signal in its headphones. The tuning knob was for the student to tune the correct station. The correct station came in at the frequency shown on the tuning dial and was corroborated by the station's aural "call signal identifier," just as in the aircraft itself. The station identifier was repeated at intervals but did not interfere with the radio range signal covered next. Once the station was tuned and identified, the student's attention turned to the radio range signal sent out by that radio station.

The radio range signal, decoded, was the Morse Code letter "A" (sounded as dit-dah), or the letter "N" (sounded as dah-dit), or a steady tone. The steady tone marked a merging of the A and the N signals so that neither A or N would be heard in the headset earphones but rather a steady tone. It told the student that he was on one of the "beams" of the radio range station.

When approaching a non-directional beacon (NDB) located on the beam of the radio range station, the radio range station being simulated would be interrupted with a third simulated signal, a fast rising aural signal of the call letters of the beacon, followed by the rapid decline in sound after passing it, and then resumption of the A or N or steady tone signals from the low frequency airways station being tracked. Though off-frequency to the radio range station, the NDB would momentarily overpower that station's aural signal. A direction finder needle, tuned independently to the NDB, would swing from pointing dead ahead to dead astern as it was passed.

The inset photo at lower left in Illustration 10 shows a Link Trainer, mounted on its pedestal, with canopy closed. The unit is on display in the passenger lobby of the Binghamton (New York) Regional Airport. The airfield there takes its name from inventor Edwin Link.

The larger part of Illustration 10 shows a Link Trainer with a student. The student has his headset on. When the door is closed and the overhead clamshell comes down, the student is in a darkened cockpit ready to begin a simulated instrument flight. The Link trainer's interior illumination lamp housing is recessed in the door. When the door and the overhead clamshell are closed, that lamp is the only relief from total darkness.

The Link Trainer operator, not pictured, is outside at a desk on which is located a tracking device. That device created a continuous tracing of the student's flight track. The Link operator took on the role of an air traffic controller, giving voice radio commands to the student and setting the student up on a radio range station beam appropriate for the flight "problem" being simulated in a particular session.

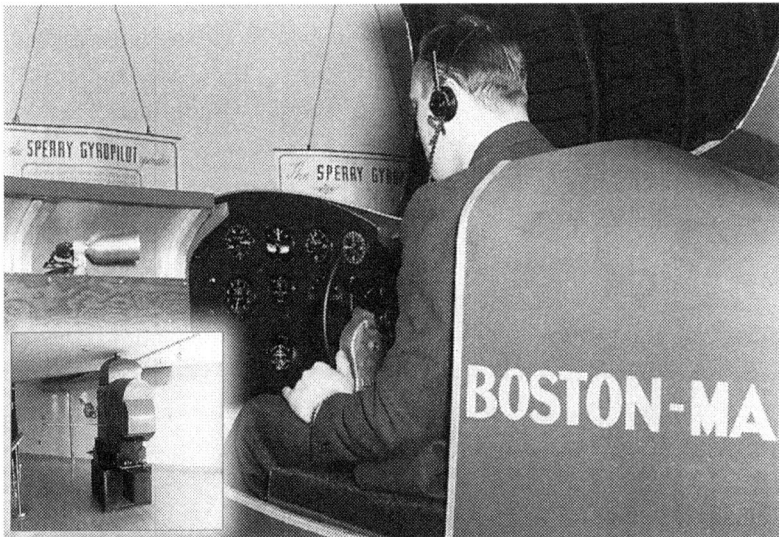

Illustration 10 - A Link Trainer Session

Most often, the "aircraft" began the flight problem by proceeding from one point to another on airways. The student would fly "on the beam," using direction controlling aileron and rudder changes to get back to the beam whenever the track seemed to drift off. The Link operator could, for example, insert a wind force and direction. Then, the student would get a realistic challenge in learning to maintain flight on the beam by having to compensate for wind drift. This might mean maintaining a course heading different from the geographic beam heading as the aircraft "crabbed" into the wind. Turbulence could be introduced to make the student use the elevator flight control to keep to the assigned altitude. When the student received en-route directions and changes in flight plan through the earphone from the Link Operator, the radio beam could still be heard in the low background. It was an excellent simulation of reality.

Edwin Link's contribution, not visible on the exterior of his Link Trainer, began with a suction pump in the base under the step the student used to get into the Link Trainer. The pump fed control valves operated by the stick and rudder. Pneumatic bellows borrowed from his father's organ business served as actuators. Another motorized device could introduce attitude disturbances, simulating weather turbulence. For flight control, the student relied mostly on a gyro horizon, a directional gyro and an altimeter. There was a turn indicator, and a rate of climb/descent indicator. The tracing made by the operator's recording device could present evidence of an untimely end for the simulated "flight," a great embarrassment to the student. It was probably an unintended consequence of the design, but when the student was working the controls a little overtime, the suction pump too worked overtime and emitted the shimmering sound and feel of an aircraft caught in a downdraft.

After an hour or so in the trainer, the student and operator could then go over the flight track that the student had actually simulated in the exercise. The student could see by the tracing on the paper where he or she had done well and where hesitancy or a little panic might have caused a glitch or two in performance. Edwin Link's device saved a lot of aircraft and a lot of pilots. Link Trainer proficiency proved to equate to hands-on instrument flight experience. Its economies versus the high cost of actual flight time were very persuasive. And in World War II, it was not only dollars saved. The time efficiency of the Link was far superior to actual flight. The "overhead" hours in the use of the Link were almost nothing compared with the pre-flight, post-flight, ground run-up time, etc. of an actual aircraft. In addition, for this comparison, a lot of in the air flight time could not be used for instrument training. The Link trainer had no startup and no shutdown time losses. There was not even a takeoff or landing.

Introduced into some U.S. military flight schools by 1935, the Link Trainer, Model C-3, proved to be much more than a learning aid to student pilots. It helped shape in-flight instrument flight training programs. The episode of the disastrous re-introduction of the Army Air Corps pilots to flying the U.S. mail stimulated the first order for the trainers by the government. The introduction of the Link Trainer preceded establishment of dedicated instrument flying schools by the airlines and the military.

Pilots progressing toward instrument flight proficiency passed the first certification tests promulgated by the U.S. Civil Aeronautics Administration. They learned to fly observing Contact Flight Rules, CFR. Gradually, VFR, for Visual Flight Rules superseded CFR as the operable term. "Contact" had derived from maintaining contact with the ground. "Visual" incorporated the ground contact responsibility but added the responsibility to maintain visual contact with other aircraft in the air space when flying VFR. The subtle differences were a challenge even for those in the profession to distinguish. For all pilots, then and now, what the human eye can see from the cockpit has never diminished in importance.

Instrument flight, conducted under IFR-Instrument Flight Rule conditions, meant that a plane and its pilot did not have to descend every time clouds were encountered in the sky.

By the middle of the 1930s, proficient, safety-minded airline pilots were increasingly supported by increased aircraft systems reliability. Backup capability, having at least two ways to achieve each essential element in safe flight, became the norm. The term, systems, began to include electronic and hydraulic systems in addition to basic muscle-operated mechanical flight control systems. The field of aviation, increasingly a composite of commercial enterprises, was here to stay.

The Triumph of Instrument Flight

Along with the introduction of radio aids to air navigation, the thirties saw air traffic control systems installed across the United States. The nation's civil airways system was created. If one considered the earlier array of light beacons as an airways system, then civil airways were being re-created using electronics technology as the essential component. The impetus for the establishment of air traffic control systems was the safe conduct of aircraft in instrument flight conditions. By World War II, airways had grown to north-south and east-west patterns in the United States.

The cloud challenge gradually faded. The challenge has shifted to the flight density of aircraft in the skies. Even if the United States atmosphere were perfectly clear of all clouds and smog every day, the volume of commercial flights in 2003 would have demanded an air traffic control system comparable to or even better than the system in place.

Radio communication was essential. Just as vital were other navigation aids for flying. Jeppesen is the name of the leading publisher of airways and airport approach and let down charts. Jeppesen's ultimate customers are pilots and navigators, civil and military. Jeppesen currently (2003) is part of the Boeing Aircraft Corporation.

Navy pilots carried H.O. 510, for Hydrographic Office Publication 510, a loose-leaf booklet of the up to date charts necessary for flight over land or over water between land stations. A visible companion of the airline pilot was a bulging leather briefcase. Notams, for Notices to Airmen, would be issued as immediate advisories when a ground facility was being added or one was being put out of service. Or, for example, when bombing or strafing was going to be conducted at a military bombing range. The Notams for anticipated activity, or activity still in effect from prior months, were incorporated into new charts and re-issued to Navy pilots on a regular basis. In naval air squadrons, the practice was to turn the old set in order to get a new set. This avoided inadvertently going aloft with outdated information.

The 1930s: Instrument Flying Takes Hold

The move to implement instrument clearances for all airline flights required improvements in weather forecasting and current weather reporting. Commercial aircraft capable of passenger-practical flight above 10,000 feet were on the way. That increase in the flight profile options would require state-of-the-art improvements in aircraft cabin pressurization and better engine performance. One payoff was that extreme turbulence weather situations would become avoidable.

Weather forecasting and increased flexibility in the radio range route structure combined to permit weather avoidance in more and more situations. This was especially true when high frequency radar became available at the end of World War II and the higher frequency radio navigation systems like omni-range superseded the original radio range networks. It became possible to vector even lower altitude air traffic around the worst of the in-flight weather hazards even before the advent of modern jet powered, pressurized aircraft, moved commercial flights into the upper reaches above 30,000 feet and above most weather. The foregoing thoughts related to pressurization and higher altitude flight profiles have been introduced here for perspective only. The challenge of instrument flying was met and won at altitudes below 10,000 feet.

Weather reporting for flight purposes developed into regular broadcasts. An airfield's "ceiling and visibility" broadcasts found the pilot's ear especially receptive. Even with advances in instrumentation, CAVU, for Ceiling and Visibility Unlimited, was always a welcome condition.

The many ways in which variations in visibility can influence a pilot's judgment are important to the story of instrument flying. The most welcome visibility condition, and the one in which aviation was first practiced, was daytime, without fog or rain, and before smog began to obscure major population areas. A second condition occurs in morning or evening twilight where visibility can be hampered by something as innocent as a blinding sun or localized ground haze or fog. The third broad condition of visibility occurs in night hours, again in clear weather. Until the human eye is fully acclimated, darkness can be an impediment to an immediate grasp of a visual horizon. Night flight under good visibility conditions is more of a challenge to the inexperienced pilot than flight in daylight. Night flight over areas with ground haze can lead to disorientation if the pilot fails to keep a respectful grasp of what his instruments are telling him or her.

The stars above, in a cloudless night sky, help establish a visual reference. A descent into haze loses that night horizon reference and adds the challenge of lowered forward visibility. There still may be lights on the ground below to help give the pilot sufficient reference. If the descent is into haze over water, with no ground lights, visual reference *above and below* can be lost. Instrument flight is the only recourse. Attempting to shift to instrument reference may come too late and the pilot can become anxious, distrustful of all information, and then completely disoriented.

The term "instrument conditions" introduces a broad spectrum of flight situations. Generally, for level flight at altitude on instruments, the condition of darkness does not add much to the challenge for the experienced pilot. In an approach to landing on instruments, the changeover phase in which the pilot makes initial visual contact with the ground can present a different challenge in darkness as compared with daylight. Among the factors are: the pilot's forward visibility at the field; whether clouds present a well defined or a ragged ceiling; the horizontal and vertical geometry of the instrument approach patterns; the profusion of structures and their lighting in areas immediately adjacent to the airfield. All play a part in determining whether a given day or night can present the more challenging condition for pilot judgment. The instrument pilot must take all these conditions in stride. With experience, he or she does not consciously make these distinctions one by one. Conditions are what they are, and the pilot must be able to create an accurate picture, a composite of the airspace and ground space under it.

An airline once provided even its most experienced pilots a familiarization trip over a route before assigning the pilot to a route that he or she had not flown before. The "fam" flight has all but disappeared according to recently retired Delta Air Lines Captain Robert E. Mitchell. It is still in practice for the first flight across an ocean. For a time, flight situations at some airports led to a pilot requirement to examine 35mm slides of its terrain and approaches, but that is no longer required. Mitchell, who flew for Delta for 31 years, and the Navy before that, stated that after an initial qualification in an aircraft based on simulator time and flying the aircraft, and a so-called "mother-in-law ride," no further familiarization flights such as route familiarization flights are assigned.

The ceiling at a United States airfield is a number in hundreds or thousands of feet that defines the base of the cloud cover. In flat-structured stratus clouds, this ceiling, or base of the lower clouds, is quite uniform and the number that is broadcast is conservative, that is, the lowest ceiling is defined rather than any attempt to present an average height of the base of the clouds. At one time, a weather balloon would regularly be released from a ground station. The U.S. government, with the Air Commerce Act, commenced use of balloons in 1909. Knowing the balloon's rate of ascent, the ground station could calculate the ceiling when the balloon disappeared in the clouds. In later times, automatic and continuous measurement of ceiling, by means of optical ceilometers, has nearly eliminated the use of balloons.

There are times as when an aircraft proceeds in and out of clouds that it is experiencing what is called a "ragged" ceiling. A related but not as potentially confusing a situation occurs when the aircraft is flying in an out of the "tops" of the clouds. The practical impediment is a visibility condition. When the aircraft is in clouds, whether in a solid overcast with a well defined ceiling below or in a ragged overcast in and out of clouds, the operative forward visibility should be considered to be zero. Passengers or non-flight personnel may be able to intermittently see the ground below but that information is not useful for a pilot flying a conservative flight pattern in instrument conditions, especially during an approach to a landing field.

The Triumph of Instrument Flight

Lighting has played an important role in air transport progress. In the 1920s, night pathways of light beacons were constructed across the United States. A pilot making a flight at night under visual flight rules could derive navigation information from these lights. Maps were available to give the airman a defined location for each beacon. Knowledge of the beacon's characteristics could help a pilot determine whether he was proceeding on his intended course.

For landing at a field, the approach end of a runway has long been marked by a series of required green lights in a line directly across the approach end of the runway. Almost flush to the ground, along both sides of the long axis of a runway, a series of white lights defined the runway in use, often called the "duty" runway at an airport. In the early days, these were called CAA lights, for Civil Aeronautics Administration, lights. These lights were early requirements for airports serving commercial passengers. Private airports of any size would also show these standard lights. Operators flying passengers on a chartered (non-scheduled) flight would plan whenever possible to use airfields with lighting consistent with established airports.

Later, some airfields, particularly those anticipating regular use for instrument landings and takeoffs, installed additional lights called Bartow lights. These were much brighter than CAA lights, and their intensity could be controlled through five levels. The fact that a pilot could ask for, and almost immediately receive, a *change of light intensity*, helped direct the attention of the pilot's eyes to the outlines of the landing surface, especially when visibility was restricted.

Bartow lights in the 1940s were not flush with the ground. In a tight situation, for an aircraft that no longer had an option to reach another suitable landing field, the risk of knocking off a few light stands was considered acceptable in the tradeoff for a successful emergency landing. As instrument flying developed, certain runways at an airfield were configured as "instrument" runways. For these runways, lighted extensions in both directions came along a bit later. These give the pilot confidence that he was on the correct path before he reached the approach end of the runway.

Category III airports have airfields where the most advanced lighting and electronic aids are available. There will be more about such airfields in the final chapter.

With the advent of Air Traffic Control (ATC) and an "instrument flight clearance," the category of flight under instrument conditions had arrived. The flight need not be proceeding under actual instrument conditions but can be proceeding under the assumptions that instrument conditions existed. A flight that proceeds on an instrument flight clearance from an air traffic control authority and is subject to deviations from plan ordered by that authority is a flight under instrument conditions. The flight may have begun in clear weather and may even have clear weather forecast for its entire route. But, such flights can be rerouted for air traffic control purposes. Here, the pilot does not control (though may influence) any subsequent routing. He or she must be prepared for instrument flying. As the practice for airlines developed, an instrument flight plan was filed for all flights.

Next we will look at some of the early days of the last trunk airline to be formed in the United States.

The Triumph of Instrument Flight

Aviation Humor

There are old pilots,
and there are bold pilots,
but there are no old bold pilots.

Origin unknown.

Chapter 5 - An Airline is Born

I t took a special breed of pilot to sign on in the first cadres in the creation of an airline. There was no human resources department to screen and interview the applicant. There was no specialized media in which to advertise for personnel. Word of mouth and perhaps a news story that an airline was being formed would heighten interest among the relatively small number of pilots that formed the pool of available pilots in the early 1930s.

This chapter will take a brief look into the lives of men, and a few women, who were involved in the decision to create something new, and who worked together to achieve the result. The airline to be examined here was not in the very first group that made history in U.S. air transport. Nor did this airline ever approach the size of airlines like United Airlines or American Airlines.

Northeast Airlines in other ways did not fit the mold of other early airlines. It did not partake of the rail-air, rail by night and air by day, experience. In contrast with a substantial segment of executives in the passenger train business that saw no threat from air travel, Northeast was founded by rail executives who felt that passenger travel by air was a reasonable business prospect. In its startup mode, the airline they founded was supported by their railroad, the Boston & Maine (B&M). B&M was a relatively small railroad serving northeast states so perhaps their management was "out of the loop" of major railroading and could be excused for their naivete.

As a source of airline experience, this last trunk airline to be formed in the United States teaches what it took to get a foothold in the passenger-carrying air transport business. Northeast did not begin with the national ambitions implied in the term, trunk airline. It did not actually begin as Northeast Airlines. It began strictly as a regional airline serving the northeast, from Boston north, under the name, Boston & Maine Airways. Then, years later as Northeast Airlines, it became the first of the trunk airlines to be bought out (by Delta Air Lines eventually, following intermediate ownership), in a period that eventually saw many buyouts.

The airline's aviation learning years began with its first hastily arranged flights using Stinson *Trimotor* aircraft in August 1933. The area it served had flight conditions that influenced its Pan American Airways predecessor decline to pursue further operations after shutting down New England service for the winter with the onset of late fall fog in 1931. Northeast's first pilots made the transition to flying by Instrument Flight Rules (IFR) when, as Boston & Maine Airways, it obtained Lockheed *10 Electra* aircraft to replace the *Trimotors.*

The factual source for much of this material came from experiences told in a wonderful book, *Adventures of a Yellowbird*, by Captain Robert W. Mudge. In 1969, Branden Press, Inc., a Boston publisher, published the copy used for reference here. Branden's arrangement with author Mudge was terminated many years ago and the book is out of print.

"Yellowbird" is a term that stuck with Northeast because of the use of the color, yellow, in some aircraft indicia and advertising graphics intended to catch the attention of the flying public when the airline won coveted route authorization to Florida, and Florida's sun. Even the dishware, in those wonderful days when dishes were used to serve meals to passengers, bore the reminder.

Robert Mudge chronicled events in which pilots who had joined Northeast just a few years earlier than he, made aviation history. Those pilots treated their flying events as all in a day's work. To them, the experiences were the ordinary things one had to do to make an airline into an economically successful enterprise. Those efforts did not make headlines. Exploits in the air in connection with scheduled airline operations were not conducive to attracting passengers.

Mudge's title, Captain, reflects the position he held with his airline, a "left seat" pilot. Left seat pilots did not exist from the beginning. The small 1933 fleet operated by Boston & Maine Airways, were Stinson *Trimotor* aircraft. This three-engine plane carried 10 passengers but just one pilot who sat forward in the pilot's section of the cabin behind and to the left of the center engine in the nose. In the early days of transport aviation, news media carried pictures of Fokker *Trimotors* and Ford *Trimotors*. Although the Stinson family was well known in aviation design circles, news media were even then celebrity-oriented so the Stinson *Trimotor* was not as well publicized as aircraft bearing the names Fokker and Ford.

One photograph in Mudge's book shows the interior passenger cabin of the Fokker *Trimotor*. Two struts, in the shape of the letter, A, without its middle bracket, were used to stiffen the interior fuselage of the Fokker. One had to crouch down to pass under these struts when moving fore and aft in the cabin.

The Stinson pictured in the next illustration is from the collection of Robert Mudge. Close examination of the illustration reveals that there are chains on the tires of this aircraft. Chains fit the airplane-as-transportation picture in the northeast winters of the 1930s. The autograph is that of the pilot Hazen R. Bean, wearing galoshes, standing in front of his aircraft.

**Illustration 11 - Stinson *Trimotor*, Boston & Maine
Airways**

Snow on the runway or snow on the landing surface was almost
a certainty in northern New England winters. Pilots were expected to
find those white runways on white backgrounds, put their skills to
work to land on the earliest available part of the runway or landing
space available, and then to use caution in applying brakes. It would
be a few years before airports had ground personnel check the
landing surface conditions and then respond to pilot queries on
runway conditions. It took a few more years for the runway
condition to appear with the 'ceiling and visibility' in broadcasts.
When full instrument approaches using radio range letdowns became
the practice, a helpful tower would inform the next plane to land

what the most recent pilot's experience had been concerning runway conditions. The tower "advisory" would take the form of "braking action poor." Or, "fair," or "good."

Early pilots with Boston & Maine Airways earned their Captain designation when the airline acquired the twin-engine Lockheed 10A *Electra* passenger planes. These were Boston & Maine Airways' second generation of planes and replaced the Stinson *Trimotors*. The *Electras* were configured for two pilots. In early twin-engine, dual control aircraft, the protocol called for the command pilot to be known as Captain and fly from the left seat with a Copilot in the right seat. Perhaps, the American car and its road customs triumphed over the British motoring experience. Even more important, the *Electra's* instrument panel revealed the basics for instrument flight.

That lone Stinson *Trimotor* pilot had a lot of eyeballing to do. In general aviation as well as in commercial air transport flying, "see, and be seen," became the eyes-alert motto for safe flying insofar as aircraft to aircraft collision avoidance was concerned. Cockpit visibility was never good enough for total reliance on that nostrum. Jet-age speeds have further cut into its value. Though not sufficient to eliminate the possibility of mid-air collision, "see and be seen" is still necessary.

The pilot had to be an acute listener. It was listening that informed him of the health of his engines long before engines were fully cockpit-instrumented. In the very early days, sound was an indication of low airspeed and helped predict the onset of a stall. In another example of information that did not come from an instrument panel, early engine instrumentation was attached to the engine itself and the pilot had to look outside the pilot enclosure to get instrument "readings."

Illustration 12 includes the instrument panel of an early Lockheed *10 Electra*. The source photo is in the Walker Transportation Collection of the Beverly Massachusetts Historical Society.

Illustration 12 - Lockheed 10A *Electra* instrument panel

The *Electra's* instrument configuration can be seen in the panel. The radio frequency controls, the flight surface indicators and controls, and various engine controls and performance indicators present a baffling panorama to the student pilot who first beholds them.

Indeed, this panel, upon initial examination by the experienced pilot, might suggest a crazy quilt growth pattern. After a period of reflecting on what is there, the more practiced eye begins to find what it needs to see. In later years, groupings of instruments were more carefully arranged and copilots had a complete set of essential flight instruments. For focus, in this panel, the turn indicator is dead center.

The pilot and the copilot are equipped with identical wheels for aileron and elevator flight control actuators. While not perfect circles, and supported inside their rims with radials that formed a Y, (in the illustrated cockpit, the Y is inverted) their rotation moved the aileron controls and forward and back motion moved the elevator controls.

Above the levers on the power pedestal in lower center of the picture, are several instruments of note, all available to a sight line for both pilots. At the top left of the three-over-three array, is the gyro horizon. Centered in the top row of three is a compass indicator, partially hidden by a knob in the picture, but visible to the two pilots. Directly underneath the right-hand top indicator, in the lower set of three, is a rate of climb or descent indicator. Centered in the bottom row of three, as noted, is the turn indicator. At the left is the airspeed indicator. Above this array, at mid-windshield, is the magnetic compass indicator. Above the magnetic compass is a larger round dial with a hand crank. This is the "homer," a device to determine the bearing to a low frequency radio range station on the ground. It is part of the air navigation equipment in the *Electra*. Showing through the upper right segment of the copilot's yoke, on the instrument panel, is a carburetor air temperature indicator.

For multi-engine pilots, the power controls on the pedestal in the bottom center of Illustration 12 remained in this configuration for many years, with fuel mixture ("rich" or "lean"), throttle and rpm lever arms, one for each engine, disposed in pairs.

Setting aside the matter of wing and propeller anti-icing, the panel in Illustration 12 shows this aircraft to be equipped for instrument flying. In later years, the grouping of indicators on aircraft instrument panels was improved with each generation of aircraft.

Robert Mudge began Chapter One of his book, *Adventures of a Yellowbird*, with a compelling sentence.

"It is perhaps the world's good fortune that the road beyond our dreams lies obscure before us as we start out along the path to fulfillment."

In its *Summa Simplified*, the Confraternity of the Most Precious Blood introduces the words of Thomas Aquinas as follows:

"The road that stretches before the feet of a man is a challenge to his heart long before it tests the strength of his legs. Our destiny is to run to the edge of the world and beyond, off into the darkness: sure for all our helplessness, strong for all our weakness, gaily in love for all the pressures on our hearts."

One can see that Mudge approached the subject of flying, and St. Thomas the subject of life itself, with respect for the unknown and faith in the future.

Here is a passage on pilot judgment from Mudge's remarkable book. The parentheses in the following paragraph are mine.

"Flying was news in those days. (1933) It was explained carefully (in the news) that the Boston & Maine Airways had rules of safety which forbade flying in such weather. (fog) It was comforting, of course, for the public to feel the airline was governed by such a rigid set of rules; but this was far from the truth. Rules, of course, did exist; but they were simply the rules that each pilot, individually, had learned by himself. The airline was run on pilot judgment - and that was all. Rules would come, but only slowly and as experience demanded. For now, today, the rules of operations were only vaguely outlined in the minds of Anderson and Bean. Vague though they (the rules) may have been, they worked."

Anderson and Bean were the first 'hires' made by a pilot named Collins. The latter, as the first pilot hired, could be regarded as a founder of Boston & Maine Airways.

In the early pages of his book, Mudge introduced two water-caused events, each of which culminated in emergency landings by a Stinson *Trimotor* belonging to Boston & Maine Airways in its founding year of operation. One shut down all three engines and the pilot made immediate and successful preparations for an emergency landing on a farm field. The culprit was carburetor icing. It can occur in clear air on an ideal day and in any and all forms of cloud condition. There was in Boston & Maine Airways' formative years no answer for carburetor icing with the Stinson *Trimotor*. The ultimate solution for Boston & Maine Airways was to add an important requirement to the list of mandatory features required in any replacement aircraft. The feature was "carburetor heat." That came later with the Lockheed *10 Electra*.

A second emergency landing brought to light a problem that caused a B&M Airways Stinson to lose two of its three engines. In this incident, another farmer witnessed a bumpy, but safe, landing. The diagnosis: contaminated fuel. These early airline pilots knew where their pay came from. The men were frugal. Their sustained employment depended on keeping revenues above costs. The pilots often saved money by running aviation fuel from the main tank for takeoff, and switching to automobile fuel from another tank when leveled off in a cruising flight condition. In this emergency landing incident, there was no way to determine where the contaminated fuel had come from. The airline immediately instituted a new practice. The two full containers of aviation fuel kept in the red painted barrels at each of the served airports were dumped and refilled every six months.

Even a fresh load of fuel can have some water content. Usually, engine-stopping contamination came from water that had condensed over time and collected in the bottom of a fuel tank. As long as the fuel used by the engine did not get drawn exclusively from the bottom of the tank, engine stoppage would not occur. Later on, mandated regular pre-flight checks involved "draining the sumps," jargon for letting a small amount of water and fuel drain from the bottom of the fuel tank.

The Lamp is a publication of ExxonMobil. The Spring 2001 issue contained some eye-opening numbers. Exxon was supplying one fifth of the world's consumption of aviation fuel on any given day. 700 airports in 86 countries! 25 million gallons sold every day! From 45,000 gallons of jet fuel in one Boeing 747, to 5 liters of aviation gas in a 1909 *Bleriot* for an air show. A picture caption on page 6 of that issue of *The Lamp* was quite revealing. "Crew Chief Mario da Silva runs a fuel-quality test at Guarulhos Airport in Sao Paulo, Brazil, the busiest airport in South America. He matches a color code on the card with the color of a jet fuel sample." In the photo reproduction, the colors being compared all look gray. The color swatches on the card look, respectively, more gray, less gray, and hopefully, just the right gray. This is the end of a sophisticated fuel delivery chain, so the crew chief was really looking for an outlandishly wrong color. The other data in the article are much more reassuring, such as "less than 1 milligram of solids per liter and less than 30 parts per million of water." Those are measurable contaminants without depending on any one human being's color perception capability.

Robert Mudge wrote in *Adventures of a Yellowbird* that Boston & Maine Airways' year of 1933-34 was by far its most crucial. There was 'a north of' Boston, 'south of Boston' dichotomy. B&M Airways had pledged its future to passenger traffic generation north of Boston, at first to Portland and Bangor in Maine but eventually to a comprehensive route structure serving northeasterners who were willing to take some extra risk to make their time more effective.

Robert Mudge's book includes anecdotes of how the new airline attracted passengers. Amelia Earhart was an important operative for Boston & Maine Airways in attracting early passengers. Interestingly, she did not fly for B&M Airways, but she did promotion for them.

In the next photo from the Beverly Massachusetts Historical Society collection, we see Amelia with a number of ladies. She would accompany such groups on short flights over the then short routes of Boston & Maine Airways. If she helped the ladies become comfortable with flight, the ladies would then approve flight for the family breadwinners, the husbands. Completely logical thinking on the part of all those ladies, including Amelia whose idea it was.

Illustration 13 - Ladies fly, including Amelia

The photo was taken at Bangor, Maine on August 12, 1934. Amelia Earhart is standing at the left. Dispatcher Thomas Gore of Boston & Maine Airways is the man in the picture. The aircraft is the Stinson SM-6000, the *Trimotor*.

It is instructive from Mudge's story to learn how the airline kept its growing trickle of early passengers coming back. He emphasized the reliability of the flight schedule. The airline introduced delays when it was prudent to do so to await improved weather conditions but they did not cancel many flights.

As noted, the first pilot employed by the airline was named Collins though he did not fly for Boston & Maine. He had earlier been a contract mail pilot. The next hire was a pilot named Anderson. Collins became the pilot in the front office and Anderson's role was to be the pilot in operations. To Anderson fell the responsibility for learning, followed by teaching, followed by insisting on the practice of, safe procedures. To Anderson also fell the challenge to recognize change and to make the proper accommodations to change. Anderson had to confront New England weather, its land originating challenges and its sea originating challenges.

Larger airlines operating to the south of New England were buying new, twin-engine, all metal construction aircraft with retractable landing gear, landing lights, radios and flight-in-cloud instruments. And these new aircraft had carburetor heat. Those were the early Lockheed *10 Electras*. Configured with their advanced features, *Electras* found a welcome from the airlines.

The Stinson *Trimotors* flown by Boston & Maine Airways dated from an earlier aircraft generation. While the Stinson pilot's instrument panel was beginning to have part of the set of flight instruments needed for instrument flying, the ground over which they would fly had no radio aids and north of Boston their landing fields had no lights. Many fields had only a grass surface. North of Boston, not even a light beacon system had been installed. Boston & Maine Airways was a daytime operation. Its planes were configured for the environment the airline had chosen to make its own. Fortunately, the *Trimotor* proved adaptable to the special conditions encountered because en route and destination weather forecasting, and the communication of existing weather conditions, were both still in a primitive stage. As Mudge tells it, a major decision was to operate both summer and winter.

Captain Mudge put it this way in his book: "The Boston and Maine pilots were professionals who had learned to approach New England weather slowly and carefully. At first they retreated, and watched and thought. Then they began to approach more closely, observing all the while, not getting too close, for it might kill them - but as close as they felt safe - to see what made it tick. They learned to probe, while in their back pockets they kept in mind a sure way of getting out if they had to…Good weather flights became practice missions for bad weather."

An Airline is Born

New pilots had to be checked out in the airline world of 1934, and checked out over a route to be flown. Not many pilots got their Boston & Maine Airways check flight on a trip quite like that experienced by Stafford A. Short. He had flown with Hazen Bean in an earlier flight enterprise. Short elected to get his checkout with Bean on a run from Boston to Burlington, Vermont. With 100% cloud coverage and limited visibility, Bean elected to take the Stinson *Trimotor* off from Boston's airport, heading east into a wind off the ocean. Short crouched just behind Bean. As the plane ascended, it flew into solid fog. The only option Bean had was to try to get some altitude

The situation now involved two pilots, neither instrument qualified, in a plane that was not instrument qualified. The *Trimotor* had flown into solid instrument conditions. As pilot, and author, Mudge described it: (again, the parentheses are mine)

"He (Bean) hung on as best he could-trying not to turn either way and keeping his eye constantly on the turn (needle) indicator in the center of his panel. He really didn't trust it very much; it was a new instrument he had never really used before; but at a time like this, it was all he had. Slowly and gently he eased the wheel back to gain precious altitude."

"Bean had concentrated intently on the new turn indicator, and managed to hold a straight course. After a rather short climb, he had broken out on top of the fog. There were no breaks in the clouds visible anywhere…Turning north, he steered a compass course toward Concord (New Hampshire) in hopes that he could find some breaks in the clouds near there. After about 35 minutes of flight, he figured he should have been over Concord, but he saw nothing, so headed for White River Junction (Vermont). Holding this course about 30 minutes, (there was) still no sign of the ground. Turning right to a north heading again, he flew toward what he hoped would be Montpelier (Vermont). A few minutes after making this turn, he saw a break in the clouds and spotted a town…(he) recognized it as Middlebury (Vermont)…"

Concluding this flight meant dropping down beneath the overcast and making course toward Montpelier where they landed. That wind must have been pretty strong. Looking for Montpelier and finding Middlebury is a testimony to Bean's confidence in his ground recognition. While the distance covered was checking out reasonably well, the angular divergence between Montpelier and Middlebury from White River Junction is over 30 degrees!

The final line of Mudge's account of this flight episode states, "Short was now qualified over the route."

On page 84 of Robert Mudge's *Adventures of a Yellowbird*, one finds a 1934 tabulation of instrument flight landing minimums for Boston, and its Maine destinations of Portland, Augusta, Waterville, and Bangor. If runway lights were available, a night minimum was published. For Boston, in daylight hours, the minimums were ceiling 300 feet, visibility 2 miles and at night, ceiling 600 feet, visibility 4 miles. Boston & Maine Airways was not at that time instrument-equipped. Those numbers were for aircraft and pilots that were instrument qualified.

By the late 1930s, Boston & Maine Airways had aircraft equipped for instrument flying. According to Captain Mudge (in a November 2003 conversation), Northeast was conducting formal instrument training in Boston before the end of the decade. In 1941, its instrument training was moved to Burlington, Vermont. By 1942, Northeast had a full fledged ground and flight school dedicated to instrument training there. Mudge's copy of its instrument flight manual carries the notation, "Revised July 1943." Mudge is one of its eight authors, and is credited as the meteorology contributor.

Hazen Bean, by his self-taught, on-the-job performance, had demonstrated that he was instrument qualified for takeoff and for en-route flight. He would need a better aircraft, with better instrumentation and radio navigation ground aids to complete the destination part of the instrument qualification. To get to a landing at Montpelier, Bean had called on his earlier skills of detailed recognition of ground features and their geographic relationship to each other.

It was clear from the Hazen Bean story that instrument advances were coming to the pilot's instrument panel. These became available in aircraft in one brief period. The first addition was the turn needle. It was a flight control instrument with an accurate response to a turn motion of the aircraft but one that required a very considered interpretation of what it did and did not tell the pilot. Almost at once, the needle indicator was combined with a ball in the lower arc of the round indicator, into an instrument called the turn indicator.

The turn needle indicated if an aircraft was turning. If one kept the ball in the bottom of the instrument centered by proper application of rudder, the turn of the aircraft would be aerodynamically coordinated, that is, no "slip" and no "skid." In a flight fully obscured by clouds, where the pilot had no visual reference, the pilot could keep the aircraft from turning by keeping the needle and the ball centered. Or, one could use aileron to make an intentional turn, say a "one needle width turn," holding the ball centered with rudder application for coordinated flight. A pilot experienced in the use of this turn needle information could maintain a modest turn rate. Maintaining a constant altitude, during a turn in clouds using the turn needle, requires keeping track of other instruments, especially the compass, the rate of climb/descent, the altimeter and the airspeed indicator.

The turn indicator was actually the first instrument installed on the pilot's instrument panel whose intelligence was derived from the gyroscope. As noted, its function depended on a gyro force called "precession." The pilot did not need to know that. He or she did need to understand that the use of the needle in instrument conditions to maintain level, controlled flight on one heading, required extraordinary concentration and an ability to steadfastly disregard false interpretations that might derive from what the human body might "feel" was happening.

For a controlled turn in level flight, the pilot not only had to maintain a constant offset of the needle from center, for example a "one needle width turn," but needed to keep the "rate of climb" instrument averaging no climb or descent. This maintenance of a steady altitude had to be corroborated with a steady altimeter and steady airspeed.

Needle-ball control takes concentration. It was and is a challenging method to conduct flight even in clear conditions. It was not a panacea, and it did not encourage pilots to use it for a planned instrument flight. For most pilots of the early 1930s, the fact that the turn indicator could enable safe flight in the event of unplanned entry into clouds was almost as obscure as the cloud condition itself.

The use of the turn indicator for flight control was occasionally simulated in ground instruction in the Link Trainer. It was a test of the pilot's reaction to loss of the gyro horizon. With an air driven gyro as the basis for the information relayed to the pilot by the turn indicator, along with an altimeter, a "rate of climb" indicator and an airspeed indicator, most pilots could demonstrate flight control in clear weather.

Interestingly, the foregoing are the instruments which early flight students, including World War II student pilots, became most familiar with during primary flight training. With emphasis on takeoffs, landings, acrobatics, and drift control practice in a concentrated flight program, the flight instructor of the 1930s and early 1940s was not likely to take much time to educate the students on how his or her instruments were powered. Or even to try to teach the student everything the instruments were telling him.

When the gyro horizon instrument came into general use, the use of the turn indicator as the aid to controlled turning, a challenging process at best, faded into history for most pilots, though keeping the "ball centered" remained good technique. Back-up a/c (alternating current) power, for example primary and secondary generators and then alternators, had become standard. Suction pumps were standard. The importance of the gyro horizon became recognized and the back-up for the gyro horizon was another gyro horizon powered from a different source. The turn indicator as a back-up for the gyro horizon was taken much less seriously as back-up gyro horizon instruments with independent energy sources were added.

In addition to its indication of *the wing down* condition of the aircraft from which the pilot could infer that a turn would commence, the gyro horizon provided *a second piece* of essential information. The device told the pilot whether his aircraft *was nose up or nose down*, and by inference, whether it was climbing or descending. This essential information was quite difficult to pin down when engaging in turn indicator flying. Before the availability of a gyro horizon, as noted, one had to use two other instruments, the altimeter, and the "rate of climb" indicator, to infer gaining or losing altitude. Rate-of-climb devices had very jumpy needle indicators. Pilots do not like jumpy needles.

The airspeed indicator had come much earlier. It improved dramatically on the pilot's determination of airspeed, an essential piece of flight information. Before the airspeed indicator with its Pitot static tube sensor on the plane's forward fuselage or wing, one method to infer airspeed was by listening to the sound (pitch) of the wind past the wing struts. And when airspeed fell close to stall speed, the experienced pilot had to quickly recognize the feel of an aircraft entering the stall condition.

The ability to get from the vicinity of the takeoff field to the vicinity of the landing field while maintaining the aircraft in level flight improved day by day, flight by flight. Regularity of flight departures led to retention of dedicated passengers. Mail contracts, when added to passenger revenues, provided additional income from the U.S. Post Office Department. The combination gave the early airline a margin, though tight, of revenues above costs. Mail subsidies for airlines were a throwback to earlier transatlantic shipping days. Cunard Line ocean-going ships had made a priority of transporting His or Her Majesty's mail, taking on passengers only when the mail requirements had been met.

The pilots who transported passengers for pay were eager for their companies to obtain technical improvements, and then to upgrade their own flying skills, so that they could maintain flight under instrument conditions. They developed an acute appreciation for how their early disciplines for maintaining flight in clouds needed to be advanced. The earliest airline pilots set and met their own standards for meeting flight schedules while conscious of the need to reduce risk for passenger, pilot and aircraft.

When the fog rolled into an airfield, the early airline companies saw to it that a telephone connection to a telegraph system operator was available at both departure and destination airports. The pilot eyeing his scheduled departure time could be notified in sufficient time to delay his departure until arrival airport weather conditions improved. There was someone in charge in actual practice even if there was yet to appear a man with a title and full details of his responsibility spelled out on paper. The early pilots with a healthy respect for weather impediments to safe flight were smart enough to heed the advice to delay. Those that were not smart enough to respond to cautionary signals became casualties. The process was self-cleansing.

The complete mastery of all but the cruelest weather conditions came rapidly for the newly named Northeast Airlines, successor to Boston & Maine Airways. By December 7, 1941, this airline, with its extensive experience in northward flight, had become a leading airline in all aspects of instrument and cold weather flight operations. As part of this experience, Northeast undertook contract flights for the military, added new planes equipped for weather and instrument flying, and became an experienced north Atlantic rim airline.

Mudge's fellow pilots who had originally signed on with Boston & Maine Airways would be among the first to conduct regular flights across the North Atlantic rim. These pilots and crewmembers accumulated sub-polar flight hours on flight schedules intensified by war preparations and then during war itself.

There was no one day when general aviation, the air transport industry, or the military could proclaim the subject of instrument flying solved. But, from 1935 on, practicing some prudence, flight plans could be executed successfully and schedules met. The icing hazard still took a toll, but icing condition avoidance and the gradual improvement in anti-icing equipment and its use reduced the adverse outcomes.

Tragic and unnecessary outcomes still occur to the time of writing this story in 2001-2003. From Colorado to Minnesota to Massachusetts, fully equipped charter and private aircraft with whole families, or groups of executives, or politicians or teams of athletes have gone down in weather that proved too much for the judgments of those electing to fly.

By the late 1930s, the air transport industry was beginning to squeeze out pilots who could not learn to cope with instrument flight discipline. Qualified pilots and forecasters and "by the book" operations departments became dominant in the decision chain. This expertise was applied during preflight and in-flight operations.

The military learned from airline experience, and from evaluation of operational flight data, to add extra oversight at all stages. One difference is the duty rotation that was part of a military pilot's career planning. It adds to breadth of experience but detracts from depth of experience for given locales and flight routes.

Boston & Maine Airways had begun its life in commercial aviation, flying out of cities like Boston, Massachusetts, Portland and Bangor in Maine and White River Junction in Vermont. Then, returning the favor of the World War I pilots who had inspired and instructed its early pilots, Northeast Airlines as successor to Boston & Maine Airways, under contract, extended its air transport flight capabilities to Nova Scotia, Newfoundland, Labrador, Greenland, Iceland, and Prestwick, Scotland. This all came in preparation for U.S. participation in World War II.

In the last Navy aviation squadron to which I was assigned, with duty as Instrument Flight Instructor (IFIS), at NAS South Weymouth, Massachusetts, a number of the "weekend warrior" reservists were senior Northeast Airlines pilots. I have saved the record of my final Navy instrument flight-check. It took place in a P2V-5F Lockheed *Neptune* aircraft. As a qualified PPC, I flew the check flight in the left seat. N.E. Marston, a Northeast captain, conducted my instrument check.

Aviation Humor

From "Will Rogers: A Biography" by Ben Yagoda.

Charles Lindbergh's advice to his friend and aviation travel enthusiast, Will Rogers:

"I'm glad to see that you're riding the airlines. I hope you keep out of single engine planes at night."

Chapter 6 - Radio, Airways, Weather and Good Practices

Businessmen involved in early airline building, and the pilots they hired, had been train travelers. One indelible impression of train travel was, and still is, the Conductor hanging on the bottom step of a passenger rail car looking at a large pocket watch, and waving his arm, or a lantern if at night, to the engineer up forward that it was time to leave the station.

The schedule, especially the departure time, became an early airline imperative. When weather turns violent or destinations and alternates are below weather minimums, airlines may delay flights but they rarely cancel them outright.

After several decades of flights so regularly on time that they were taken for granted, airline flight cancellations began to rise as the twentieth century gave way to the twenty first. Airlines and their pilots in the last decade of the 20th century faced dense departure schedules that the U.S. air traffic control system could barely handle. Any system delay exacerbated the problem. Weather, blame it on El

Nino or La Nina, plus all-time records for numbers of flights and passengers, an aging U.S. air traffic control system, and too few gates and runways at airports, added up to an air traffic control system that had become overloaded. Long departure or takeoff delays or outright cancellations increased in frequency.

This more recent flight delay record should not detract from the on-time performance that U.S. airlines were able to maintain over a fifty year period from 1945-1995. Airline pilots and other flight crewmembers have not had the option to decide that flying on a particular day to a particular destination was something they did not care to do.

Keeping to the schedule has involved a passionate commitment in commercial airline operations. The high faith of a small number of early air travelers was recognized as the essential building block for the future. The schedule became the focus of the organization, and the responsibility ultimately of the pilots. Prior to the availability of radio aids to navigation on the ground and in the aircraft, an early aid for maintaining schedule required the pilot to memorize every detail of the surface over which the flight had to be conducted to reach its destination. Call it an early form of "instrument flying." Such characterization might raise eyebrows from those who later participated in more rigorously defined and technologically implemented instrument flight.

Pilots of those early airline flights used their studied, encyclopedic memories of terrain, lakes and rivers, buildings, farms, and railroad tracks as their radio beam. And they became able to function at night as well as in the daytime. This night capability was not trivial. Ground features at night involved a different memory map than ground features by day. Once the night became the pilot's friend, it was actually easier to track ground features at night than during the day.

Still, schedule delays were frequently necessary before the radio beam became available to act as a precisely defined flight path in its constantly "on" condition.

Airways as pathways in the air for aircraft did not become widely available in the U.S. until reliable radio aids to air navigation and to air/ground communication became broadly implemented well into the 1930s. Before dealing with airways navigation, let's review the progress in air to ground and ground to air communication.

There are many supporting players in the cast that made the transition to instrument flying so successful that it has been completely absorbed into our flying culture. Flight through instruments is now totally un-remarked for the freedom it gives to move about.

An aircraft flown by many student pilots preparing for World War II, the Stearman bi-plane, had no voice communication equipment except for the "gosport" used for intercommunication (the human voice, loud enough to be heard over engine noise) between instructor and student. This was an "aid" the instructor in a one-way communication to a pilot in training, and certainly meets any test of the term, "voice communication," but it was not going to be of assistance in the air/ground communication needed for instrument flying.

There were other early aids to communication. The landing direction in use for landings on the landing "mat" at many primary stage pilot training facilities operated by the military was indicated by tower-mounted rotating light beacons with white and green sectors that could be pulsed in enough different sequence "codes" to provide the pilot a landing direction. It helped if the neophyte pilots looked for the windsock, or wind tee, or tetrahedron, one of which might be the local field's visual aid from the sky for the pilot in the air to determine ground wind direction. It also helped if the student pilot took pains to observe what other air traffic was doing.

The tower represented "authority" at an airfield. Hanging from a ceiling in the tower operator's space, on a flexible arm, was a special Aldus type lamp (a round barrel, perhaps a foot long, from which a focused light could be turned on and off with a trigger). It could flash red or green. The lamp could flash red in the direction of a trainer aircraft coming into the airport approach pattern on a landing-prescribed flight path as a caution to the aircraft to stay in the air until some impediment on the runway or landing mat was cleared by airport ground personnel. A green beam confirmed to the pilot that what he was doing was approved.

In my own experience as a military flight training student following primary training, aircraft in use had a voice radio receiver/transmitter known as a coffee grinder. The pilot used a handle on the device to rotate a dial until the right frequency was set. Some frequencies used were 1,000 kilocycles or more, in a band above the AM radio spectrum. Using voice test transmissions, it took a few tries to get centered on the best frequency with the coffee grinder. "North Whiting Tower, this is flight Student One, how do you hear me?" The response, when everything was set right, was "strength five, modulation good."

Later, military aviation voice communication was moved to Very High Frequency (VHF) radio equipment in the 112-135 MHz range. By this time, the aircraft's assigned frequencies were controlled by a button selection from a few crystal controlled frequencies. No coffee grinding necessary. If one setting did not work, there was a secondary frequency on another push-button. Still later, the VHF spectrum got crowded with aircraft-related voice transmissions and the military were "shooed upstairs" to the Ultra High Frequency (UHF) range, 225-400 MHz. Again, it was punch the correct button, and these very reliable units would put you immediately on the appropriate Air Traffic Control, or Tower or Ground Control frequency.

The foregoing paragraphs are introduced to emphasize that instrument flying required voice radio communication, "on" at all times. The assigned frequency might change, but pilots and air controllers quickly confirmed communication on a secondary frequency assignment. A pilot's communication requirements today can cover Air Traffic Control, Approach Control, Ground Control, Tower, and for the airline pilot or the charter pilot, his or her own organization's operations department.

Radio, Airways, Weather and Good Practices

In Charles and Anne Lindbergh's 1931 flight to the Orient in their twin pontoon aircraft, *Sirius*, Anne Lindbergh who had just become a qualified pilot had to master the use of Morse Code. The aircraft had no voice radio. She had to develop finger dexterity on the transmitter "key" to send Morse code to a ground station. Communications, essential while *Sirius* approached Japan southbound along its island chain, meant composing, transmitting, and waiting while a Japanese operator at the ground station deciphered her Morse Code into English, translated into Japanese, composed a reply, translated back to English, coded it in Morse code and transmitted it to *Sirius*. Voice radio would not save all those steps but when voice transmitters and receivers became available, thousands of pilots were spared that transmitter key. Instrument flying was a huge beneficiary of voice radio.

The radio "beam" was the navigation bridge. Voice radio was the human communications bridge. Combined with new instrument panel indicators that provided aircraft attitude information, the advances took air transportation from formative years to growth years. When point to point flights could be scheduled and execution taken almost for granted, growth in traffic resulted.

Radio beam technology came into being using low frequency transmissions in the 200-550 kilocycle frequency band (excluding 500 kilocycles, long used as the emergency distress frequency by mariners). These transmissions were made from broadcast stations that became known as "radio range" stations. A series of these relatively low-power ground broadcast stations separated by 75-100 miles defined what became known as airways. "Relatively low power" was 1000 watts or lower. This was comparable in power to many commercial broadcast radio stations in the AM band in the 1930s and a fraction of the power of the 50,000 watt "clear channel" radio broadcast stations authorized for some early AM stations in the United States. "Radio range" and "radio beam" are loosely interchangeable terms.

Let me add an appreciative note on the AM radio stations. Aircraft -installed direction finders of the low frequency radio beam era could tune in the AM radio stations. Pilots used this capability to cross-check other navigation information. Occasionally, a low frequency radio beam station along the airways route might not be functioning and the use of a local radio station to provide navigation information was available to the pilot, and was used.

The low frequency, hundreds of kilocycles, radio range station, with its four beams, became the navigation mainstay of the nation's airways system. It remained so until a system based on frequencies in the megacycles began to replace it, but the concept of airways and airways support aids did not change. With the pilots who quickly learned to use the radio range tool, in conjunction with the new instrument panel indicators, the United States' domestic airline business was finally transformed from daytime operations in clear weather to all-weather, 24-hour capability.

The next illustration bears the notation that it represents a stylized or typical low frequency radio range chart. The depiction is labeled stylized only because the beams are arbitrarily aligned in the illustration by chart convention, North, East, South and West. As implemented in actual practice, the directions of the beams were chosen to fit local terrain features, and a local airport if one was specifically served. Only occasionally were adjacent beams exactly 90 degrees apart.

In Illustration 21, later in the story, the reader will see how the radio range station was adapted for instrument letdown and approach to an airport.

The actual radio transmitting towers are not shown in the illustrations but are physically located where the radio beams narrow and cross.

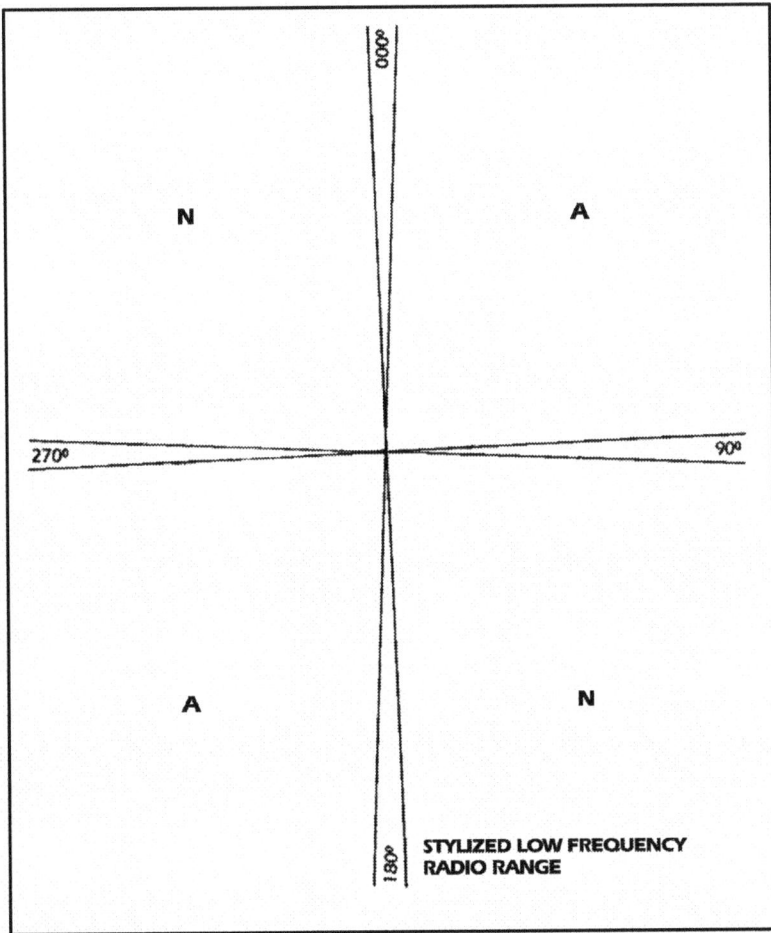

Illustration 14 - Low Frequency Radio Range

Four transmitting towers, arranged in a square, carried the four antennae of the radio range stations. The technology was based on "Loop," or "Adcock," design. The technical difference between them was small and something that did not need to concern the pilot. What is important is that these radio transmitter stations served for well over a decade as primary aids for both airways navigation and for instrument approaches to an airport. They were the essential installations on which the founding years of domestic instrument flight navigation depended. With the addition of other non-directional radio wave transmitters, the four-beam transmitting stations also served as airport letdown-to-landing aids and as climb-out aids. Some did double duty, both to define an airway and also to provide an approach and letdown path to a given airport.

The radio range transmitters were first located along flight paths between the larger U.S. cities. Each had a basic broadcast (carrier wave) frequency in the hundreds of kilocycles, in the same basic band as the AM radio stations, but just below that band in frequency.

The Morse Code letter, A, a "dit dah" sound in the pilot's earphones, and the Morse Code letter, N, a "dah dit" sound in the earphones, were broadcast into alternate quadrants by each pair of the set of four antennae at the transmitter. The pilot or copilot tuned the aircraft receiver to the station's basic, published frequency known as its "carrier" frequency. When the pilot could hear a steady tone in his headphones, he or she knew it was the merging of the dah dit sound and the dit dah sound. The steady tone meant that the pilot could no longer hear a discrete A or a discrete N, confirming that the aircraft was right on one of the four "beams" defined by the station.

With the term "beam" borrowed from usage such as light beam or headlight beam or searchlight beam, pilots gained confidence that if they flew the steady tone, they were on the beam. The beam represented a path in the sky directly over an invariant and known path on the ground. Further out from the transmitter, the beam was wider, and further in, the beam narrowed, until over the station itself, it converged to a point. Those radio beams created by the set of four antennae, functioned as "memory" that would be superior to any human memory of visible earth features even when the pilot could see those features. That invariant path existed whether or not the pilot could see the earth below.

A critical element of the low frequency radio range broadcast was its station identification. After tuning to the correct frequency, a pilot would confirm that he was tuned to the station he needed by listening for its "call letters." This consisted of a repeated Morse Code aural broadcast of three alphabet letters, an identifier feature of all the under-550 kilocycle airways radio stations of that era.

Some ground radio stations in that low frequency band were used for communications alone, others performed as non-directional beacons (NDBs), and still others were airways radio range stations, as just discussed, with their four beams.

A very early example of call letter identification in the nation's authorized low frequency radio transmitters was Radio Annapolis, with its call letters NSS. In Morse Code sounds, that would be dah dit, dit dit dit, dit dit dit. Radio Annapolis was a Navy communication station and not an airways radio range station. All of the foregoing types of low frequency radio stations would periodically broadcast their call letters for identification purposes. A sectional map (now called the "Sectional Aeronautical Chart") showed the geographic location of these transmitters. The United States is completely covered by a set of these sectional charts that overlap slightly.

The pilot who had learned to fly the radio beam from one station to another had part of the challenge already mastered for using a radio beam in the slightly more complex procedure of letdown and landing approach to an airfield. We will cover that situation by examining an actual instrument approach procedure later in the story.

As aviation grew, an operational control apparatus grew along with it in the United States. Generally known as the air traffic control system, it consisted of airways, radio aids, and weather forecasting and reporting. Over the years, many U.S. government departments have been involved in handling each of the three essential components, radio, airways and weather. It is an important part of history that these all worked together. The pilot was rarely aware of what department of the U.S. government was furnishing the service he was using. For most pilots on most flights the air traffic control system worked so well that it was hardly ever mentioned in news media.

Very early in U.S. aviation, a system of regulation began and the regulation grew with the system. Not always in perfect step, but consistently in a constructive direction.

Radio stations are licensed by the FCC, the Federal Communications Commission. For an essential growth period in flying, weather was handled by the United States Weather Bureau. The United States Weather Bureau was active before the air traffic control system took shape. It began in 1870 with the Department of the Army and in 1891 was transferred from the Signal Corps to the Department of Agriculture with an emphasis on helping farmers.

In the present day, using technology such as satellites and doppler radars among its tools, we now have a National Weather Service (NWS) and The National Oceanic and Atmospheric Administration (NOAA).

Airway designations, and air traffic control, including towers and radar facilities at airports, are run by the Federal Aviation Administration (FAA). Accidents are now investigated by the National Transportation Safety Board (NTSB), an independent Federal agency.

After September 11, 2001, the airlines relinquished baggage inspection responsibilities, and this burden was taken over by a newly formed Transportation Security Administration, part of the new U.S. Department of Homeland Security. Yet another player had joined the long history of federal agencies involved in U.S. aviation.

Sometimes the public discovers that one of these agencies is openly at odds with another. Generally, the open debate is constructive and the United States air traveler is a beneficiary.

All of the "regulation" discussed here involves the *operation* of flight. It does not get to the *business* of flying. The United States deregulated the business of flying in the same general sequence of change in which power generation and transmission were deregulated. After giving sufficient notice beforehand, airlines have now been authorized to add flights on segments, to remove flights, to buy, sell, lease and sublease "gates" at airports, and even to swap "slots" for landing and taking off at airports. That is another story entirely. It has an impact on aviation, on the health of airlines and airports, and on the convenience or inconvenience of the flying public.

An airline pilot must file a flight plan and must adhere to it. The pilot or a controller in air traffic control may introduce a modification en route. The pilot can initiate a request for change. Unless a pilot declares an emergency that he and his aircraft are constrained from normal options, air traffic control has the final word. The words here apply as well to military pilots and general aviation pilots using the airways.

A pilot qualified to take an aircraft aloft at an airport can take off without filing a flight plan. That is an exception to the regulation and control of air traffic. Since its inception, air traffic control, and the participating pilots, be they civil air transport pilots, military pilots or general aviation pilots, have created an enviable U.S. safety record.

Before the installation of the early radio navigation aids, and the airways system that the radio range stations defined, pilots had to maintain Visual Flight Rules and detour around clouds. If flying over land, above which the sky was partly overcast, pilots might get only an occasional glimpse of landmarks below if maintaining a flight altitude above a cloud layer. That brief glimpse had to supply vital information. If that undercast had fewer and fewer "breaks" in the clouds through which ground contact could be reaffirmed, the wise pilot would go down through one of the breaks and fly 100% in "contact" with the ground. The main recourse before unacceptably low altitude flight became necessary was to find a landing field.

With early voice radio equipment, pilots had been able to call in to manned stations, for example airport towers, in the days before air traffic control became a reality. Pilots could get local weather observations, one element of which was "cloud cover." A cloud cover of "five" meant an overcast in which five tenths of the sky was obscured. Hearing that a station, possibly at an airport ahead, had a cloud cover of five or above, the pilot might not wait to gamble on catching one final break in the undercast and begin to consider getting down underneath the clouds.

The United States Weather Bureau initiated a system of collating weather information coming in from its observation stations and packaging it into regular interval broadcasts of weather. An important addition was the teletype (short, for teletypewriter), a machine that would convert the transmission reports of weather information at many stations from coded transmissions, and print them out in human-readable form on paper. In pilot jargon, these schedules became the "skeds." With this service available, a pilot could obtain weather information beyond direct local observations from a station with which he was in voice communication. An operator at that station could look at the skeds coming out of the teletype and provide weather information for other stations along the route of interest to the pilot. This service was invaluable to a pilot faced with determining which alternative airport might be available for landing in case his scheduled destination went "below minimums." The skeds also were put to use when a pilot was doing his pre-flight planning at an airport. Skeds for prior periods would be hanging on a clipboard underneath the most recent one in the weather briefing room and a pilot could evaluate trends in the weather at stations of interest.

The teletype was an electromechanical marvel of its time. These units had a typewriter style QWERTY keyboard with typical, and some atypical character choices. Even though these had keys, most were used as receiving printout devices. The teletypewriter advanced its roll-fed paper over a roller just like a typewriter. It printed by electrically blasting a smudgy looking dull yellow coating off a black carbon under layer. Early units had a 64-character alphabet.

All states of water, for example droplets suspended in air in cloud form, or frozen, in various forms of snow or ice, were encountered by early pilots and identified as potential hazards to an aircraft in flight.

Icing on the wings, and on the propellers, leads to loss of lift, and thrust, respectively. The aircraft pilot is forced think about landing options unless a zone of warmer air can be found. No answers were immediately at hand at the beginning of the 1930s. Icing on the wings, if not observed visually by the pilot, would quickly become noticeable on the flight controls. Propeller icing resulted in loss of thrust and its effect was additive to the effect of wing icing.

For aerodynamic surface icing, visual monitoring of those surfaces that can be seen from the cockpit or cabin helps a pilot determine severity and hastens a decision to change the flight profile. Before anti-icing systems were added to aircraft, getting out of the icing condition was the first consideration. For aircraft equipped with controllable pitch propellers, if propeller icing developed, rapidly increasing and decreasing the rpm (revolutions per minute) of the propellers would help temporarily to throw off ice.

Maintaining higher airspeed by adding engine power was an initial recourse for the loss of lift due to wing icing. Rime ice, a thin coat of granular frosted snow, can be tolerated for brief periods. Clear ice, usually accumulating from rain freezing on cold surfaces, builds up fast and presents a greater hazard to flight. The classical weather knowledge response to clear ice, absent a fast corrective in flight plan under the control of an air traffic control facility, is to go up in altitude while the aircraft still has the ability to ascend. The rationale is that the rain has to be coming from above where the atmosphere must be warmer. Also, a cloud mass may consist of liquid droplets just on the verge of becoming ice or snow and a cold body like an aircraft may be all that is necessary for the water to change from the liquid form to snow or ice. Outside air temperature is an essential piece of knowledge for all flights and is critically important information for an aircraft encountering ice. If the air mass is already in snow form, the aircraft generally has little problem.

Before discussing engineered solutions to icing, two other water situations are worth mentioning as early hazards to flight in situations where icing was not a factor. One situation found the upfront multi-engine pilot sitting in an enclosure that was sometimes called a "greenhouse." Early enclosures were put together in sections. The enclosures that may have seemed to have been air tight for thousands of miles of cruise flight were not water tight at all in cloudburst conditions. The enclosures literally "leaked like a sieve." The "wall of water" was distracting to a pilot trying to keep the wings level in strong turbulence. The other condition where moisture was a distraction came during landings. Wipers may go back and forth as designed, but a rain or snow condition can be so heavy that the pilot cannot see through the windshield. The PB4Y-2 (1944) had a sliding, indented, panel on the pilot's side that could be pulled back enabling the pilot to see forward on the left side and at least watch the left edge of his runway. These were two variations from the commonly encountered instrument conditions and were not first order imperatives in anti-icing or anti-fogging. Icing required carefully engineered improvements to help make instrument flying safer.

Loss of lift due to wing icing or loss of thrust due to propeller icing can become challenges that no amount of skill with engine or flight controls can overcome. Scheduled air transport operations faced a serious impasse if the sole solution to ice involved ascending to warmer air strata above. Prevention of ice formation was the only real solution. The technical answers to icing challenges came in four systems introduced over a period of time.

For the flight surfaces, these came first as wing and vertical stabilizer leading edge de-icing systems known as "boots." Later, heat applied inside the aerodynamic surfaces became the preferred solution that kept ice off the surfaces altogether.

For propellers, first came alcohol de-icing and later, electric propeller heat. Where relevant to a specific flight situation discussed in a later chapter, some of these solutions will be illustrated in examples taken from actual flight operations.

The pilot who intended to proceed on instruments needed assurance that *all systems* were going to continue working. Fuel management is one of those systems on which a pilot and especially the instrument pilot has a critical dependence. He or she wants to make sure that an engine does not stop generating thrust while primary attention is being directed to accomplishing an essential instrument flight procedure. Loss of power while flying in instrument conditions is a very challenging distraction. The first line of defense then and now: pre-flight check lists. Another general prudential observation is worth noting here. The first difficulty encountered in a flight is usually dealt with successfully by a prepared pilot. It is when a second and even a third unexpected flight hazard or equipment failure occurs that even the best of pilots can become overwhelmed. Removal of causes is sound practice.

With the advent of jet-powered aircraft, the airline industry and the military services found themselves operating a mix of conventional propeller planes, requiring aviation gasolines of various octane ratings, and pure jets or turbo-props that required jet fuel, a close relative to kerosene. Instances of aircraft being fueled with the wrong fuel did occur and a crash was an inevitable result. Even a reciprocating engine plane could be fueled with a non-optimum grade of aviation octane gasoline. Let me give a personal example.

One day in 1952, the author was assigned to fly an F8F *Bearcat* from NAS Chincoteague, Virginia to NAS Niagara Falls, New York on hurricane evacuation. Weather in the northeast was poor and the single engine F8F was not an instrument flight certified plane. It had no backup instrument systems. A VFR flight plan was filed. The flight proceeded north under a low cloud cover using ground references, cross checking with radio beams in rain-lowered visibility areas by constantly re-tuning the low frequency radio range receiver to stations ahead. After a positive ground check by visual identification of the Chemung County airport near Elmira, New York, the flight proceeded west to Niagara Falls.

Upon landing, ground personnel announced that the Niagara Falls Naval Air Station did not stock the 115/145 octane aviation gasoline (avgas) that the Pratt & Whitney R-2800 engine required. There was about a half tank of that "hi-test" fuel left in the main tank. The fuel truck crew was directed to fill the belly tank with

100/130-octane fuel and not to add gas to the main tank. The plan was to return to Chincoteague, using the unadulterated hi-test in the main tank for takeoff, without cross-feed. When leveled off at altitude, fuel management required a shift to the belly tank with cross-feed, letting the lower octane mix with the higher octane gas remaining in the main tank.

Two days ensued waiting for the storm to pass. A flight plan was finally approved for return to NAS Chincoteague, Virginia on a Sunday morning. Locally, the Niagara frontier had 10,000 feet of solid overcast. Clearance was obtained for a flight, "five on top," which meant climbing to 500 feet above the clouds, and then to proceed back to Chincoteague in the clear, 500 feet above any undercast. That was an approved clearance for those times.

The F8F climbs pretty fast. I was relieved to break out on top, a few minutes after takeoff. Then, fuel demand was shifted to the belly tank. This tank would give the aircraft just over one hour of flight in the level cruise condition. The airways routing to Chincoteague was fairly direct.

I had not done all my homework. Approaching Philadelphia, the undercast disappeared as had been forecast. Then, while the aircraft was almost directly over the Friendship Airport in Baltimore (now, BWI, for Baltimore Washington International) the engine quit cold.

On over water flights in the F8F, pilots were warned to manage gas so as not to risk losing power at low altitude because the R-2800 engine used up a bit of altitude while the prop windmilled the engine to a re-start.

I was fortunate that the "five on top" had put the aircraft up around ten thousand feet. The F8F dropped nearly four thousand feet before the engine restarted. Part of the time was used figuring out what had gone wrong. Which was, simply, that the belly tank was running the engine, *and* it was filling the main tank at the same time. The F8F did not glide very well. This flight did not have the contented hour plus minutes at cruise altitude that a belly tank would have given with a full main tank at takeoff. As configured, this flight had only an abbreviated, hour minus minutes, before the belly tank was empty.

In the few anxious moments after the engine was re-empowered, I looked around to see if anyone had been noticing. This flight returned to home base without broadcast of any kind. Early Sunday mornings in 1952 were still good times to be flying. Not too many folks around. The importance of fuel management was brought home to me. If that F8F had been in the soup when the stoppage occurred, the number of items requiring the pilot's attention might have been just one too many.

All pilots learn to be kind to their aircraft's power plant. The specified fuel, from a source that maintains that fuel in a correct environment, is of more than casual interest to a pilot. The discipline has come to the automobile. From a single dispensing pump, to low-test and hi-test, to several octane ratings, the automobile engine designers and manufacturers have taken a leaf from the aircraft engine book.

The consequence of poor fuel management in an airplane is a bit more punishing than running out of gas in a car. Optimum firing of the plugs kept the engines of both cars and planes running smoothly. From early days, the aircraft engine was given redundancy. One example was a dual ignition, with "right" and "left" magnetos to be checked before returning the "mag" switch to "both" for takeoff.

For instrument flight preparation, the pre-flight is worth going over a second time. Here are some pre-flight checks that served well in the propeller era. Drain water from the fuel sumps until you're sure it is all gas. Check oil sumps for signs of bearing metal (shiny) or metal particles attracted to the magnet on the inside of the closure device. Remove Pitot static tube cover. Remove battens from control surfaces.

Using the Pratt & Whitney R-2800 engine as an example, it was desirable for many engines and mandatory for the 2800 to pull the propeller through a couple of rotations by hand. The master cylinder was on the bottom and if oil runs by the rings and collects in the head chamber, the piston rod could snap, or in a less likely event the rod could go through the piston head. Both sequences were bad. The general term was called "hydraulic-ing," pronounced "hydraul-icking," and derives from the incompressibility of fluids. It occurred when the engine was started without first going through a manual pull-through procedure. The damage might not have shown itself until the plane took off. When the damage took effect on takeoff, the aircraft and its occupant(s) faced great danger.

Keeping the power plant functioning is just a bit more on a pilot's mind than on a motorist's mind. Making sure that the power plant keeps functioning during an instrument flight motivates a pilot to be just a bit more of a stickler as he or she confirms that each pre-flight item is conscientiously checked.

This is a good place to emphasize for the record the second of two aircraft systems that have been supportive of instrument flying. The first was fuel management. The second is pressurization.

Pressurization has many ramifications. It has enabled the aircraft and its human cargo to circumvent storm cloud build-ups and to fly above weather.

The proper amount of oxygen in the breathing mix keeps pilots alert, on top of their game. As a passenger in transport aircraft, I have appreciated pressurization. All of my pilot service in military aircraft required donning a "diluter-demand" oxygen mask. It was a hassle and often we tried to get by without it. Our pilot performance suffered.

With some of the early solutions to all-weather flying in place, U.S. aviation was ready to make the years 1935-1939 a period of growth in experience along with a remarkable extension of capability. Civil and military aviation improved with the volume production of new airframes; these came with engines of advanced performance.

A now revered aircraft, the Douglas DC-3, began a remarkable life in 1935. The aircraft served as a marker for the period. On time, schedule-keeping performance was the mark.

Illustration 15 - Northeast Airlines DC-3

The DC-3 in the illustration is shown taxiing out by the Boston Airport tower. The copilot and ramp manager are exchanging salutes. The dark front surfaces of the wing and empennage (the leading edge of the tail surface) reveals the anti-icing "boots."

Engine manufacturers prospered with a customer base that included expanding military and commercial air transport requirements. Airframe and engine design and manufacturing are capital intensive. Business risk was spread in the U.S. aircraft industry. The prime contractors wisely "subbed" the manufacture of many parts to avoid excess capacity and excess employee base if the next contract went to a competitor.

The third segment of U.S. aviation, known as general aviation, was also expanding and began to supply a growing cadre of pilots. While some aircraft had short production lives, small plane airframe and engine manufacturers continued to add to the strength of U.S. aviation. Fixed Base Operators, who risked their own money to be part of general aviation, in both large and small airport facility operations, proved an important resource to aviation. Their airport development efforts and management skills worked together to support growth in aviation, particularly in light plane aviation.

The airline industry needed a steady input of pilot and ground support expertise. Many who achieved success in aviation worked their way up starting in some aspect of general aviation operations. Today, executive jets of fully advanced design take to the air every day with all-weather pilots and flight systems, carrying passengers who can justify the extra expense over commercial flights. And with aircraft owner share programs, many frequent travelers can save both money and time compared with scheduled airline flying.

Unfortunately, the small airport, where so much of U.S. aviation's early history was created, is now represented more in aviation archives than in being. Four such airports were in operation at one time within five miles of where these lines are being written in western Massachusetts. These have all faded into history. The counties of western Massachusetts still have five general aviation airports operating, and after a downhill plunge in activity after September 11, 2001, a revival was in progress by 2003. VFR flying faces many restrictions in 2003 that did not exist in aviation during its birth years.

Modern interstate highways have no lanes allotted to the speed of a Model T. U.S. airspace no longer has a place for aircraft that do not have voice communication equipment and transponders.

Chapter 7 - Atlantic Air Transits: War in Europe

World War II contributed a huge second generation of war pilots. The U.S. World War II military pilots added millions of flight hours to the cumulative flight record of U.S. aviation. The military aviation hours were often accumulated off airways and quite frequently in foul weather conditions. While it was not a stated goal of military aviation to move the state of the instrument flying art forward, that was an important collateral result of their flight operations. What the military did in the air and in ground support advanced the art of instrument flight. In the North Atlantic, U.S. civil airline pilots and military pilots worked in concert to achieve war objectives. In early postwar years, the country was able to expand its airline routes and route densities with pilot proficiency as a given.

Student pilots in military flight training programs at the outset of World War II were often on their way to combat in just one year.

They went from aircraft with no voice communication, and navigation by recognition of ground highlights below, to aircraft with full voice communication, radio range receivers, celestial navigation domes with a ring to hang a navigator's octant, possibly an installed Loran system and even radar. Even the skilled airline pilots who were going to fly on contract to the military had to become comfortable with a subject like celestial navigation, especially for the long over water flight segments. There were no floating radio range stations. There were Loran stations, possibly on an island or peninsula, but that higher frequency radio navigation aid was only available in certain areas and it had a daytime distance from station fadeout comparable to the fadeout of low power radio range stations.

Navigation has always been a necessity for a pilot. Most of an aircraft pilot's over water navigation practices have come from the sea. The inshore seaman plotting his way along a coastline identifies landmarks and takes a set of bearing lines on them and where these lines cross, his position is determined. Interestingly, this has long been known as "piloting." The aviator maintaining VFR flight without radio aids uses a chart and identifies objects as the aircraft moves from point to point. This pilot does not generally take bearings because he has the comfort of clear layers of air beneath and does not fear rocks and shoals under a keel as does the mariner. Whether IFR or VFR, it was occasionally necessary for the air pilot to proceed by dead reckoning, DR, when out of sight of visually identifiable objects or out of range of tunable radio navigation aids. And again, for both VFR flying and IFR flying, long segments of dead reckoning had to be regularly cross checked and position updated with celestial navigation position finding. The Global Positioning System (GPS) using satellites has taken much of the skills challenge and calculation challenge out of navigation. One exception! It does not excuse the pilot from a requirement to navigate. It just changes the tools.

By 1939, the World War I military ranks in U.S. civil aviation had begun to thin out. Only the younger World War I pilots who had elected to cast their lot with aviation in some paying capacity were still actively flying. Those who had elected to help begin or join a new business venture called the scheduled airline, were the ones most likely to still have an active association with aviation.

Pilots who had signed on with airlines had surmounted many challenges. Among those were the challenges of fledgling businesses, of flight schedule maintenance, of night flying and finally of instrument flying. Their aircraft had grown more sophisticated. Use of ground and air instrumentation, and making a good judgment on when a weather front would have reached or passed by a given airport all demanded study and training. The 20 year olds of 1916 were in their mid-40s. Regular physical exams were now required. Pilots who qualified for the minimal physical standards of the 1920s might now require waivers or face voluntary surrender of a hard-won certificate known as the ATR-Airline Transport Rating.

As World War II loomed in Europe in 1939, progress in instrument flying had become the third rail for U.S. civil aviation. The advances made in U.S. commercial aviation in the decade of the 1930s benefited the future military pilots of World War II in many ways. First and foremost, the flight proficiency standards for military pilots improved as the experience gained in civil aviation was passed along.

With the onset of war, the nation was able to obtain some reciprocity on the support early military aviators had given to airline, airport and airways growth during the 1930s. It came with commercial aviation's unparalleled war effort. Many pilots who had learned their craft from World War I aviators would now repay that favor.

A group of younger men wanted to fly and chafed at the impediments to joining the U.S. military flight services. Some volunteered for the RAF in Britain or for the RCAF in Canada. Most became fighter pilots and many fought in air-to-air combat in the Battle of Britain. Later, with the U.S. in the war, the U.S. pilots in three Eagle Squadrons that the British had formed with U.S. pilots and British commanding officers were eventually absorbed into the U.S. Army Air Corps.

The experienced hands in the nation's still-developing scheduled airlines were about to put their more extensive flying skills to work directly for U.S. national defense. First, they would expand their capabilities and their nation's readiness by regularizing flight over routes that had earlier been flown only by a few aviation pioneers. The most important route extension was air traffic across the north rim of the Atlantic Ocean, via Newfoundland, Labrador, Greenland, Iceland and Prestwick, Scotland. There were many false starts in the early attempt to fly in this region, and lives were lost.

This story will get back to the all-important north Atlantic air transit challenge after being introduced to the passage of a military aircraft across the south Atlantic. Ensign Harry Carter's story helps, by contrast, to understand the importance of flight over the northern routes to Europe.

Ensign Harry Carter USNR (now, Capt. Harry Carter USNR Ret.) tells the story of a flight of a Navy PB4Y-1 (an Army Air Corps *Liberator* converted to Navy use) that originated from the Naval Air Station Norfolk, Virginia on November 11, 1944. In World War II, this transit was repeated many times. The following passages in quotations are taken from Harry Carter's journal of his transatlantic flight across the southern route to England. The ultimate objective was to get the plane and its crew to the Azores to join a Navy squadron performing Anti-Submarine Warfare missions against German U-boats transiting the Bay of Biscay in World War II.

"Our crew gave #90649 a test flight and then flew her to the Army Air Corps base at West Palm Beach, Florida, in the first increment of our journey from the U.S. to the United Kingdom (U.K.) via South America and Africa. There were quicker ways to get there; Newfoundland/Azores or Bermuda/Azores are examples, but the Army in its wisdom decided to give their green crews a longer but safer route to deliver their airplanes, not to mention valuable flight time."

"Fortunately for us, I do not believe our crew could be classified as green. All of us had just completed four months of operational PB4Y-1 training at Chincoteague, Virginia. Our Patrol Plane Commander had over a thousand hours of multi-engine flight time. The copilot was a mature and solid pilot in his own right and even I, a young 20 year old, had completed a couple of hundred hours of operational training in the monstrous Lockheed Vega *Ventura* (Navy PV-1). The plane captain was an experienced mechanic who did a marvelous job keeping us in the air and out of the ocean in the many months that followed."

"At the Army Base at West Palm Beach we went through four days of pre-departure briefings. As third pilot and navigator, I went off to the navigation and weather briefings. I was the only Navy pilot in attendance (at these briefings). In fact, I was the only pilot because the Army had separated the pilot and navigator programs. I found out later that the need for navigators in the Army Air Corps program was greater than the need for pilots."

"The first leg of our journey outside the U.S. was a six-hour flight to Borinquen Field on the western tip of Puerto Rico. The next leg, a seven-hour flight to Atkinson Field in British Guinea was uneventful. The flight over the bright green waters of the Caribbean was spectacular. British Guinea was my first experience with the tropics and with sleeping in a bunk surrounded by mosquito netting. The hot, humid, night air was full of all sorts of flying insects and strange disturbing sounds from the jungle. The next day was November 25th. It was memorable because it was my 21st birthday, and made even more memorable by the fabulous sight of the mouths of the Amazon passing below as we made our way to Belem, Brazil. The six-hour flight from Belem to Natal, Brazil brought us to our last stop before transiting the Atlantic."

"At Natal we had a two-day layover to rest and to visit the town. Our nine-hour flight to Ascension continued into darkness and for the first time I was able to use that diabolical instrument called the bubble octant to determine our position from star sights. The sextant used by my seafaring cousins on the surface of the sea was a civilized two dimensional instrument that behaved rather well. The bubble octant, on the other hand, was a three dimensional machine that wanted to do everything backwards. Keeping the bubble in the center while pulling down the star of your choice into the same position, and hanging onto a lurching airplane and punching your stop watch at the appropriate split second were feats that should have been reserved for an octopus. Regardless, we intrepid navigators learned to do it, and with a little bit of help from the Plane Commander, we landed safely at Ascension Island."

"Ascension Island is a rock. No vegetation. No water. All the drinking water had to be shipped in. It is a small speck in the middle of the Atlantic a little over half way between South America and Central Africa; a place that anybody in his right mind would leave as soon as possible, which is what we did. We had arrived after dark and departed the next morning at dawn for a six-hour flight to Roberts Field in Liberia. This was followed the next day with a short flight to Dakar, Senegal. From Dakar we were given the option of flying straight on to Marrakech, capitol of French Morocco, or to fly up the coast to Agadir, Morocco. We took the second option and on December 1, 1944, after a pleasant eight-hour flight to Agadir, spent an interesting night in a beachfront hotel overlooking the Atlantic. After a short, one-hour flight to Marrakech, our shoving off base for the U.K., we settled in for our second night in Morocco."

"Briefings for the last leg of our journey to Dunkeswell Air Base near the southwestern coast of England included a weather briefing which indicated no problems. We plodded along the coast of neutral Portugal at about five thousand feet enjoying the beautiful weather and, for me as navigator, a perfect day. However, as we approached our destination, the clouds began to thicken. We dropped to four thousand feet to stay under the clouds, then three, then two and finally we were skimming along the wave tops. Unbeknown to us, all other aircraft had been called back to Marrakech due to bad weather all over the U.K. Our radio operator had neglected to monitor a certain required radio frequency after take off. For me, all hopes of celestial navigation had long ago vanished and I had been dead reckoning for the past two hours. At only a hundred feet or less the white cliffs of the British mainland loomed directly ahead and our pilot, 'Shug,' lifted 90469 up into the soup. Thus began one of the most interesting and frightening episodes of our entire deployment."

"During the war, the Brits had devised two very simple and effective ways to bring in a lost airplane in conditions such as we were facing. These two devices would keep us from bailing out of our fuel deficient aircraft while only minutes from our destination. In our navigation briefings back in Marrakech I had been given a map of the U.K. laid out in ten-mile squares. The Brits had provided a household, usually a farmer, somewhere in the center of each grid, with a weak transmitter capable of transmitting only about ten miles. Thus, a lost aircraft such ours could navigate about the U.K. by merely calling out on a certain radio frequency and receiving an answer giving the grid coordinates which would place the aircraft within a few miles of its actual position. It worked like magic! We were given the coded name of an airport to fly to that was open, but unfortunately, Marrakech briefing had failed to give us the decoded name for the airport. (It turned out to be Orly Field in Paris that had just been taken over by Allied troops. Had we known the code we would have spent the night in Paris!) As we flew along in the soup, we were vectored to the Valley Air Base in Wales where we were brought in by radar. The field was still socked in, but, again, due to the ingenuity of the Brits, we arrived near the end of the runway with the overcast cut back up to at least 500 feet like a gigantic rectangular piece of pie etched out of the heavy fog! It was spectacular. Giant Bunsen burners ringed the airfield and the approach. The heat generated by these torches literally burned the overcast away."

(Author's note: When asked if this capability had been known as FIDO, pilot/navigator Carter confirmed that acronym. Even an environmentally sensitive airline pilot of the 21st century might occasionally wish that FIDO, an acronym for Fog, Intensive Dispersal Of, might on occasion be available to make it more certain to break contact on a difficult instrument approach.)

"We landed without further incident and as we taxied toward the flight line, one of our starboard engines ran out of fuel. This ended the last leg of the exciting journey of 90469. We had arrived in the U.K. Mission accomplished. We flew on to Dunkeswell for a few days of briefings."

"Then we flew on to the Azores to join our squadron, VPB-114, on the tenth of December 1944 in an uneventful flight. We landed at Lages airfield on the Island of Terciera, touching down on a landing mat consisting of interlocking pieces of steel to support the 60,000-pound planes."

The "interlocking pieces of steel" that Ensign Carter noted in Lages was known as Marsden matting. The remainder of Carter's deployment story covered ASW patrols from the Azores, the end of the war in Europe, and his return to Boca Chica, Florida to join a hurricane reconnaissance squadron.

There are two key points to be drawn from Ensign Carter's flight journal. First, over 40 hours of flying and even more time on the ground had been consumed in the month it took to get the aircraft from the United States to Britain. That was useful for crew training but unacceptable for the war task the U.S. undertook to support Britain before and during World War II.

Second, finding that alternate field to Dunkeswell for their first landing in British Isles, and a successful landing there, illustrated what the northern route pilots who had the British Isles as destination might face in almost any attempted landing along the route. British ingenuity contributed original solutions to instrument flying. Low frequency, low power highly localized radio transmitters and FIDO were confidence-builders for thousands of Allied pilots.

The next illustration shows the challenges that planners faced when evaluating their options for flying the northern route to the British Isles in World War II. There were two main challenges. Fuel, and weather. Did the aircraft have "legs" for the trip? Was there enough gas to get to a destination field and have enough fuel left to go to an alternate landing field if the destination field was below landing minimums. Was the aircraft equipped for instrument flying and were instrument-qualified pilots available to fly it?

(Author's note: A proofreader might disagree with the word "minimums," as did mine. The Latin student would prefer "minima." In my experience, pilot-talk always used "minimums." American Heritage supports both.)

For a comparison with the southern route that Navigator Harry Carter took in his PB4Y-1 to Dunkeswell, England, we turn to "The Yankee Flyer," a Journal of the Massachusetts Aviation Historical Society, Issues 25 and 26, from 1999. The author is Paul S. Larcom. Captain Carter's extensive trip to the U.K across the southern route will be put into perspective using Larcom's story of Operation *Bolero.*, an effort to air ferry combat aircraft to the British Isles in World War II.

Bolero began in 1941. Illustration 16 is a chart of the North Atlantic as *Bolero* planners envisioned it for their airbase planning in 1941.

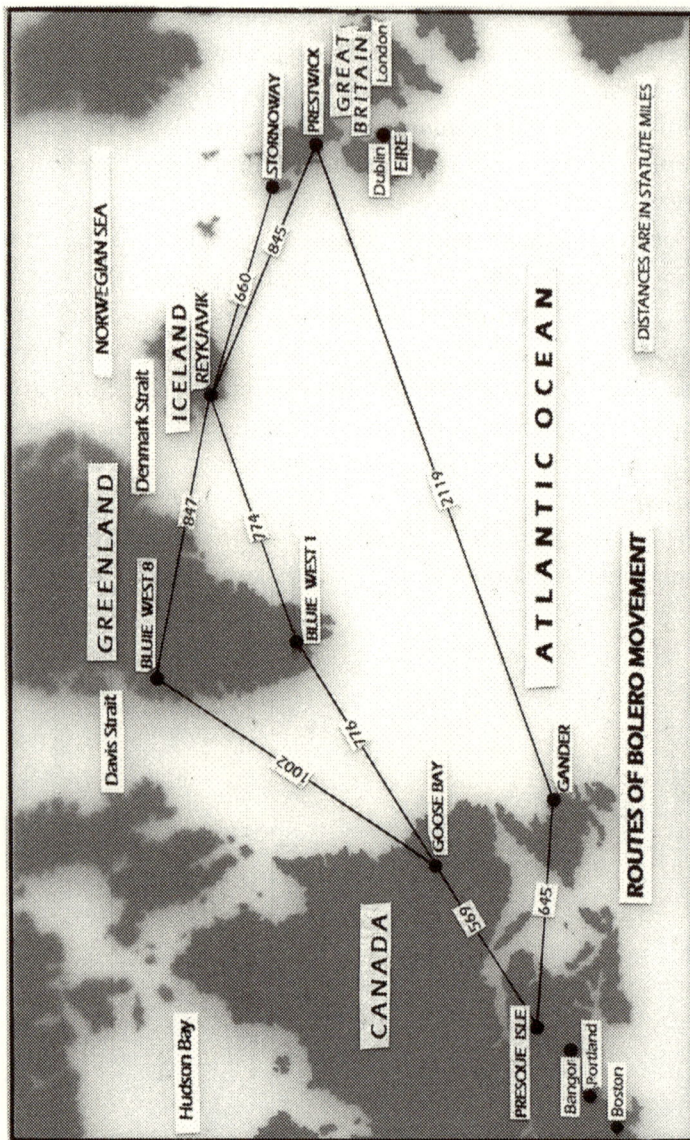

Illustration 16 - North Atlantic by air, 1941

Atlantic Air Transits: War in Europe

The northern route across the Atlantic frequently had poor, and even deadlier for pilots, poorly forecast, weather. The obstacles in the region to aircraft navigation and piloting did not yield easily. For these reasons, the southern route across the Atlantic never completely lost its relevance. It is quite apparent, though, that the savings in distance meant that elapsed-time and flight-time savings on the northern route were persuasive. An all out effort began to learn how aircraft could safely transit that route.

In a series of revisions in World War II planning, *Sledgehammer*, the name for the earliest planned invasion of mainland Europe from Britain in 1942, gave way to *Roundup*, the second such plan set for 1943, which in turn gave way to *Overlord*, the actual invasion at Normandy in June, 1944.

All invasion plans to assault continent Europe called for movement of large numbers of U.S. military aircraft to the British Isles. The effort commenced in late 1940. The United States was not yet at war. Great Britain and Canada set up The Atlantic Ferry Organization (ATFERO) at the Dorval Airport in Montreal. In November 1940, the first Lockheed *Hudson* (this plane would become a twin-engine, land-based workhorse for Britain's Coastal Command) was air ferried to Ireland through Gander, Newfoundland. Flights of B-17Ds *(Flying Fortresses)* and B-24s *(Liberators)* commenced flying from Gander, Newfoundland, to Prestwick, Scotland in March 1941. These aircraft types had long cruising ranges and were instrument equipped for flying in bad weather.

During 1941 and 1942, twin-engine P-38s, A-20s and B-25s were being lashed to the main decks of ocean going freighters for conveyance to England from U.S. east coast ports. P-38s were used first as fighters and then as fighter-bombers. The A-20 and B-26 aircraft were the short-range bombers. In order for the fighter aircraft and short-range bombers with their more restricted cruising ranges to make it to England, a northern flight route consisting of a series of legs needed to be planned and implemented.

The Triumph of Instrument Flight

A large portion of U.S. aircraft production was concentrated along the southern California coast. A Polar Route to the British Isles would have been the most direct. A potential set of landing stations was actually examined for flight along such a route. Germany's failure to invade Britain bought a little more time for U.S. military planners so the flight risks of the Polar route were set aside, and the planners fell back on the north Atlantic rim alternative. Finally, the Lend-Lease Act of March 1941 opened up base options that had earlier seemed too provocative to the U.S. during the period before formal U.S. entry into the war.

The RAF Ferry Command took over from ATFERO in July 1941 and the U.S. Army Air Corps Ferrying Command (ACFC) set about provisioning a northern aircraft ferry route complete with weather reporting facilities. Presque Isle, Maine became headquarters of the North Atlantic sector of the Air Corps Ferrying Command in January 1942. The Ferry Command's responsibility began at their headquarters and extended to Prestwick, Scotland.

U.S. Navy PBYs were operational at Argentia, Newfoundland, by July 11, 1941 and on July 15, NAS Argentia was established. On August 6, 1941, the U.S. carrier Wasp delivered Army Air Corps P-40 *Warhawks*, and PT-13s (trainer planes that could be used for aerial observation) to Iceland, by flying them off the carrier to airstrips ashore.

The U.S. relieved Britain of garrison duties on Iceland in July 1941. The U.S. Navy's PBY Catalina aircraft from squadron VP-72, based on the seaplane tender, USS Goldsborough, were in place in Iceland by July 4, 1941. These planes were to give air cover to an incoming seaborne Task Group bringing the first U.S. Marine garrison troops from the United States. Shortly after the Marines' arrival, the airstrips at Reykjavik, Iceland, were beefed up for busier traffic. Iceland was about to play a crucial role in world events.

Carl Schoenacker enlisted in the U.S. Army Air Corps on Monday, March 17, 1941 at Rochester, New York, and shortly became Serial No. 120023769. He thought that if the U.S. went to war, it would be over in 3 years. He could not get a permanent job because of the probability of being drafted. Because he had read of the trench warfare of World War I, he wanted no part of the infantry. He was assigned to the 58th Pursuit Squadron, 33rd Group, and was sent immediately to Mitchell Field near Hempstead, Long Island. He missed most of basic training with scarlet fever. Carl was walking his post, June 21, 1941, when he heard the radio announcement that Hitler had invaded Russia. Here is a portion of Carl Schoenacker's account of those days.

"We were not at war but our President was very pro-British. Iceland was vital for weather forecasting and also because we did not want the Nazis to use it as submarine base. The British had soldiers there. In July, our 5th Infantry Battalion was sent there to relieve some of the British. About the time that the isolationists learned that we had soldiers there, and were screaming to get our boys home, our War Department decided to send an air force squadron to protect them. I was transferred into that squadron."

"The 33rd squadron of the 8th Pursuit Group was selected. It was given 32 new P-40C planes. Pilots, other key officers and non-commissioned officers (noncoms) selected their sergeants and corporals, then other squadrons were cannibalized to fill the T.O. (Table of Organization) Radiomen came from the 58th so I went to Iceland without schooling less than 20 weeks after enlisting. I was overseas on $21 a month in an outfit with a full T.O."

"We shipped out of New York Harbor on the steamship, SS *American Legion*. I think it was the last Sunday in July, '41. We headed south, which confused us. We picked up our convoy off Newport News, Virginia."

"Our new planes had been hoisted onto the aircraft carrier USS *Wasp*. Our pilots, but not the crew chiefs, were with them. With very little training, they were to fly them off when we reached our destination. This had never been done before, but it was believed that with a small amount of fuel it was possible. I was later told that if the first three did not make it, the rest would be brought back to the States. They all made it (to Iceland) but with some difficulty."

139

"We were stationed at Reykjavik. I think the trip took nine days, so we landed in early August. The days were still very long and the weather good for a while."

"I was there two winters, which were not cold, but dark, damp, wet, windy with mud under the ice, often with just enough snow to hide the ice and mud. The Gulf Stream moderates the climate of Reykjavik. Winter temperature ranged generally from 20°F to 40°F, seldom really cold. Rarely did we see the sun. It rose in mid morning and set in early afternoon, never getting far above the horizon, and there were always clouds on the horizon"

"Summers were pleasant. It was never dark. The sun would set before midnight and rise shortly after midnight. It rained easily. There were many rainbows."

"I found a mentor and dear friend in Harry Lippert from Easton, Pa. Harry was in the same position as I. He did not get to radio school either, but he did not have to because he was a radioman and ham in civilian life and an excellent one. He had a fine mind and knew more than the non-commissioned officers, which sometimes caused problems. He knew he was good, but did not volunteer. He just waited until there was a problem no one else could solve. Slowly he advanced from being a 'know-it-all' to being a respected, knowledgeable airman. Harry and I jointly owned a short wave radio and worked together whenever possible. Harry was my teacher, my radio school. As air traffic increased, radio problems on transient aircraft also increased. Because he lacked seniority and because he was reliable, Harry was usually called and I went along. All planes are different and just finding the radios, then finding the messed up radio could take hours. One summer night as I sat in the cockpit of a transient plane with a radio problem, flicking switches for Harry, I watched the sun set and a short time later rise again, without getting out of the pilot's chair."

"Keflavik base was built and we were to expand. During all of this I took radios out of planes, checked them and put them back. Each morning every plane on line had to be checked. We had a few problems, mostly from worn cords or broken connections, or from pilots who forgot how to use the equipment."

"One of our pilots, a friend, crashed while taking off in the fog. Normally, officers had little contact with NCOs (another term for non-coms). One morning, Lieutenant Kassos was assigned to fly to the mouth of the fjord to see if it was fog free. Our fog would be gone by the time he returned, but he had to take off in it. He was scared. We talked, then as he got into the plane he talked with Lieutenant Meyers. He took off, became disoriented and flew into the hill. The field was named for him. Kassos Field was there, don't know if it still is."

"In the spring of 1943, Lippert and I, among others, came back to the states. Our ship landed in Boston.

I was assigned to the 332nd Fighter Control Sqdn. at Bradley Field, (Hartford) Connecticut. I was a misfit. The 322nd had new UHF (ultra high frequency) equipment. My knowledge was obsolete; Lippert had not taught me UHF. Picture a person excellent on an IBM Selectric, suddenly transferred into a modern computerized office, and you have my situation."

Thus concludes a segment of Carl Schoenacker's early war recollections of the variety of aviation support services and other duties he was called upon to provide in Iceland during the creation of a northern air route to the British Isles in World War II.

The flight that Carl Schoenacker related in which Lt. Kassos was lost is particularly poignant. Kassos was not instrument qualified, yet was sent aloft in fog to perform a mission. There was a near-zero chance that he could succeed. These losses were not combat losses. These were called "operational losses." The family was probably informed in a letter that Lt. Kassos was doing his duty and he was. An e-mail on these matters told of the flight of a *Liberator* crew en route to the China-Burma-India theatre making a stop for refueling at a field in the Middle East. The pilot would see that field just one time in his life. Someone inadvertently turned off the runway lights just as the pilot was approaching his flare out to land. The plane hit a tree. Only one crewman survived. It would have been tabulated as an operational loss. In a future chapter, this story will encounter extensive loss of life in military air training commands. The characterization of a human death as a loss defined as "combat," "operational," or "training" serves the statistician. But history should record that all such deaths occurred in the service of the nation and all advanced its objectives.

Without the generations of crewmembers and support mechanics and radio/radar technicians, military and civilian, all of whom had helped overcome very challenging obstacles to aviation's advances in all weather flight operations, U.S. military aviation's rapid response to World War II would not have been possible. One byproduct of this military buildup effort was the beginning of a worldwide air route structure.

Imagine the thoughts of the Army Air Forces pilots assigned to fly the fighters off a Navy carrier's flight deck. It was general knowledge that they would launch the first three planes, and if none of the three made it off the carrier deck successfully, they would terminate the use of this method of aircraft delivery. No mention was made of rescue attempts for failed launches, but there at least, U.S. Navy carrier operations had long anticipated the potential for a ditching by a Navy pilot. The Navy stationed plane guard destroyers astern of its aircraft carriers for such outcomes. What one does come away with from these stories is the reminder that loss numbers were a part of military operations. The human content of losses was on everyone's mind. The objective could be pursued with more spirit when loss of human life was known to be a potential tradeoff to gaining a military objective. People were keenly aware of these human challenges and would work hard to figure out ways to minimize loss of life.

Military life with a nation at war is life in a hurry. With the nation at war in Iraq, The Springfield (Massachusetts) Republican newspaper of Sunday, May 25, 2003, headlined an Associated Press article by Darlene Superville with, "Rumsfeld orders reduction in rate of military accidents." It is good that the Defense Secretary noticed the high aircraft accident rate in Iraq operations. The repeated loss of *Blackhawk* helicopters was particularly noticeable in news stories from Iraq; a number of these were not combat losses. If Rumsfeld's order was as conveyed in that headline, it was a disservice to remediation. Stepped up safety surveillance, better procedures and careful conduct of loss investigations have demonstrated success in the past. "Orders" to reduce accidents mislead the reader into thinking that outcomes are amenable to orders. No more than orders to a pilot to undertake an instrument flight for which he or she is not qualified.

During a period before the Japanese attack on Pearl Harbor, United States Navy Task Groups departed from U.S. east coast ports and from Bermuda on 4,000 to 5,000 mile "neutrality patrol" cruises. Whenever the USS Wasp was in company on these cruises, a delivery of land based U.S. Army Air Corps planes to West Africa locations or to North Atlantic bases was made. There were several such voyages. One even made it to Malta, the beleaguered island in the Mediterranean.

One of three planned runways at Goose Bay, Labrador, was in operation by December 1941 and three different locations on Greenland were also ready for air traffic in 1941. One of these was located on its southwestern tip, another on its west coast and one was located over on the east coast of Greenland. These bore the war-familiar names Bluie West One, Bluie West Eight and Bluie East Two, respectively. Two more bases on Iceland were completed later. The distance concept of these landing field choices was that a P-38 *Lightning* need not fly more than 850 miles to advance to the next base, leaving the aircraft enough fuel to return all the way to its departure base if the destination base went down for weather. Here is an excerpt from author Paul Larcom's research.

"In January 1942, Air Corps Ferrying Command contracted with Northeast Airlines to establish airway radio range navigation beacons and weather communications facilities along the northern ferry route from the U.S. to Prestwick, Scotland. Northeast used USAAF C-39, C-47 and C-53 aircraft to transport the equipment and personnel to the facilities starting in February 1942. On July 3rd and 4th, the first transatlantic flight was made by a C-47 piloted by Capt. Milton Anderson. Anderson was chief pilot and VP of Northeast Airlines' operations and an early pilot-employee of its predecessor, Boston & Maine Airways. Al Marsh was the copilot and Fred Lord the navigator while Sam Solomon, President of Northeast, served as a 'flight steward.' The purpose of the flight was to deliver radio range equipment to Stornaway, Scotland."

At this point in his Yankee Flyer article, author Larcom details a series of short duration management changes in the Air Corps Ferrying Command. A rapid war buildup was now in progress in the United States and the scope of operations was increasing daily. By June of 1942, command of the effort to pursue the ferrying responsibility passed to the U.S. Army Air Corps' Air Transport Command (ATC). It became its job to arrange for the movement of P-38 fighters, B-17 bombers and C-47 transports to Britain between June and August 1942. Two 165-gallon wing tanks increased the range of the P-38s from 1300 to 2000 miles. Four fighter groups were organized to deploy in stages of 500 to 800 miles. Eventually, because even their new external tanks would not have provided enough extra range, two fighter groups of P-39 Bell *Aircobras* were dropped from the air ferry plan.

Paul Larcom's Yankee Flyer article on *Bolero* is much more detailed than we can quote verbatim. Until otherwise noted, the next few paragraphs are my summary of what Larcom has detailed. The P-38s now formed the core of the fighter group movement overseas. Pilots would fly their own planes. The C-47s would carry ground crews and equipment to support the fighters when they became part of the Eighth Air Force in England. The instrument-equipped B-17s would be pathfinders for the fighters. Despite prodigious effort, there remained gaps in the communications, navigation and weather support facilities at some stages of the northern rim base facilities. One interesting method to fill the gaps in weather reporting was to have B-17s fly from the terminal destination next in line for the advancing fighters. The B-17s would fly back along the reverse of the fighter's flight path to let them know if the weather held promise for that terminal objective. U.S. Coast Guard cutters stationed along the path would also help with weather information. Final fitting out of the P-38s at Lockheed plants on the west coast included new oxygen systems and a British radio for voice communication for each P-38. These preparations were all done in the name of Operation *Bolero* for which strict secrecy was observed. On May 17, 1942, 80 P-38s left Long Beach and arrived at Dow Field in Bangor, Maine after a series of flights across southern routes in the United States. The C-47s staged out of Westover Field in Massachusetts.

Then, there came a delay, with a change-of-orders. On June 2nd and 3rd 1942, the fighters, the C-47s and the B-17s were ordered to head back to the west coast. The sea Battle of Midway was being joined and the U.S. Pacific coast had been denuded of air support. It was day by day for the United States in that summer of 1942. The success of the U.S. fleet at Midway caused an abrupt reversal of these orders, which had only been partially carried out. By June 11, the P-38s were back at Bangor, Maine.

Goose Bay, Labrador, and Greenland were now pronounced as ready as they were going to be for this operation. On June 18, 1942, 49 B-17s, 85 P-38s and 52 C-47s moved to Presque Isle, Maine. The C-47s with Northeast or American Airlines' pilots would head for England on their own, using the new base structure along the way as dictated by fuel and weather. Each 24 plane P-38 squadron was divided into three 8-plane sections. Four P-38s would accompany each B-17, two off each wing.

On June 23, seven P-38s in the company of two B-17s left for Goose Bay, a 571-mile leg. 18 B-17s and 20 C-47s also made that same leg on that day. Ten B-17s departed Goose Bay for Greenland on the 27th of June and did not fare well. They flew into one of the support gaps. There were still no air controllers on duty in Greenland. The weather turned foul 400 miles out. Seven of the B-17 aircraft returned to Labrador. Three pressed on and ran short of gas. One of those made it into Bluie West-8 further up the west coast of Greenland and the other two ditched at sea though the crews were rescued.

There was discussion of abandonment of the project but the fighter groups did not want to give up. Two P-38s with senior pilots tried it by themselves on July 2 and made it into BW-1, a 779-mile flight. 24 P-38s then made it with six B-17s and finally 24 more with B-17s made it that same day. The C-47s and the B-17s not engaged in path finding had gotten into BW-1 earlier that day, each proceeding independently. The 4500-foot runway at BW-1 with its steel mat was a compromise between terrain on the approach, the slope of the terrain under the mat itself, and prevailing wind, and often favored none of the above. One group got out the next day and made it to Reykjavik, Iceland.

The last 16 P-38 fighters with their four B-17s left Goose Bay on July 6. Four fighters and their B-17 made it to BW-8 but foul weather caused the rest to head back to Goose Bay, and all had a hair-raising time just getting back in. By July 10, all had made it to BW-1 though there was considerable shuttling up to BW-8 because of aircraft overcrowding on the ramped area at BW-1.

Six P-38s in company with two B-17s attempted to make the 845-mile jaunt to Iceland from BW-8 on July 11. A fast moving front played havoc with this flight. The destination, Iceland, proved to be out of the question. Now in icing conditions, they headed back to BW-8 but it had closed in so they tried for BW-1, which was in the clear. Short by 200 miles, one by one all but one bellied onto the ice cap, with one B-17 able to send an SOS before landing. The first P-38 tried to make it down with his landing gear extended and flipped over but the pilot was not severely injured. The others elected wheels-up landings. Miraculously, all personnel survived. A sea rescue party reached a point 15 miles from the downed group on July 17. Now with dog sled, the rescue party obtained guidance from a Navy PBY to the location of the downed aviators. All were returned to BW-1. (In 2003, a team from the United States reported successful excavation of one of those P-38s which it had previously located, submerged in several hundred feet of ice. The aircraft was returned to the states and photos of it, completely restored, have appeared in media.)

The first seven fighters along with their B-17s had reached England on July 9 although one B-17 operating independently had gotten in on July 1. The last aircraft of this first main aircraft movement involved in the *Bolero* operation left Presque Isle, Maine on July 18 and except for some aircraft intentionally left at Reykjavik, all had arrived in England or Scotland by July 26. The Iceland group came on to the UK on August 28. A second *Bolero* movement with much the same complement and planning followed almost immediately. Their losses were one P-38 and one B-17. More experienced Air Transport Command pilots took over the duty of flying the lead aircraft in this group. The United States 8th Air Force in Britain was now in business.

Weather reporting gaps, radio communication gaps and decision gaps were gradually filled. Author Larcom's *Bolero* article notes in summary that by January 1943, 179 P-38s, 366 heavy bombers, 150 medium bombers and 180 transport planes had made it over. For his *Bolero* story and his authorization to summarize from it, I am indebted to author and aviation archivist, Paul Larcom.

Success rates over the North Atlantic route improved dramatically with flight experience and facility improvements. Ten thousand aircraft were finally delivered over the North Atlantic route. The southern route via South America and Morocco accounted for 2000 aircraft during this time. Even with the steadily improving success rate for the northern rim, in the winter when weather locked in some stages for weeks at a time, the southern route was a necessary alternative.

Multi-engine transport aircraft were finally able to make the transatlantic passage almost routinely across the northern route.

Bolero, flawed by equipment and experience gaps in its early days, made aviation history, almost by a brute force conquest of the elements. In the end, flying man took his knowledge and rendered unto the Caesars, the elements, what was theirs, but learned to finesse those elements and get through by judicious selection of times and places where man and his machine could win. Most of the time, with the proper resources, the flight could go through. Man still had to exercise restraint in the fewer and fewer instances where that call had to be, "wait."

Joe Januszewski became Flight Engineer of a B-17 that made the North Atlantic transit to join a squadron assigned by Colonel Jimmy Doolittle to explore night bombing of German targets. Januszewski's daughter, Ann Richards, forwarded a memorandum written by Pilot F. E. MacSpadden in 2003 on his B-17 crew's experience. The excerpts that follow give a picture of training, transit and mission of B-17 crews.

MacSpadden had been transferred to Blythe, California for combat flight training in B-17s after completing his pilot training, February 1, 1943. The paragraphs in quotes were written by pilot MacSpadden. (parentheses in following quoted paragraphs are by this author)

"After 34 hours of copilot training, the powers that be decided to make me a first pilot. This required that I be assigned a crew of my own. We trained at Blythe until April of 1943. We then picked up 2nd Lt Jack S. Noce as our new copilot (the original copilot was given his own crew). We were transferred to Walla Walla, Washington for 2nd and 3rd phase training. While at Walla Walla I trained everyone in the crew to land the aircraft. During one of our cross-country training exercises, while in flight formation, the leader took the entire group into the clouds which required that we each go on instruments and work our way out of the clouds. After that experience, the Flight Engineer decided he did not want to fly any more and SSgt Joseph Januszewski was advanced to Flight Engineer."

"Upon transfer to Grand Island, Nebraska, we were told that we would be assigned to the 305th Bomb Group, 422nd Squadron, Station 105, upon arrival in England. We were assigned a brand new B-17F. On June 26, 1943, we were transferred to England. Our first stop was Bangor, Maine. Our next leg was to Gander Lake, Newfoundland. We ran into some bad weather and were grounded there until July 2, 1943. We were cleared (that day) to fly to Prestwick, Scotland. This was an overnight flight and took 13.5 hours. Just after leaving, the bombardier spotted a German submarine on the surface, probably recharging his batteries. The sighting was radioed into the coastal patrol. We ran into a large storm which had not been forecast; this required us to be on instruments for most of the flight. Copilot was sick and the auto-pilot did not work properly, so I was required to fly the entire flight without relief and your Dad (Joe Januszewski) stood by. We needed to verify our position so I climbed in an attempt to get a star shot. I was unable to get above the clouds, so we then descended to beneath the clouds to get a drift (wind drift) shot off of the water. Just before reaching Ireland we broke out of the clouds. We had to pick up a radio beacon in Ireland to get our course to Prestwick. We were successful and landed in Prestwick, Scotland on July 3, 1943. We later learned that we were the first combat crew to fly its own aircraft across the North Atlantic. I have been told there is a plaque with our names on it, at the International Airport in Prestwick, Scotland, commemorating our flight."

(In light of author Larcom's researched report, a comment is necessary: The term, "first combat crew," requires definition. Many aircraft were flown over by ferry crews. The words, "across the North Atlantic," are important. B-17s with Air Corps flight crews had been making it across in stages as noted earlier. My assumption is that it was a first, for a combat crew flying its own aircraft, to make the long jump from Gander to Prestwick, nonstop.)

"On September 6, 1943, we were requested to fly for the 366th as a replacement crew, using one of their aircraft, 'Madam Betterfly.' Our assignment was as 'tail end charlie'-last in the formation. This is one of the hardest positions to fly because of constant repositioning of the formation. You use more fuel. It is like being the tip of a dog's tail when it is wagging. It moves the farthest. Our target was the Braun Bovari Magneto plant in Stuttgart, Germany. We used additional fuel on the inbound flight as the leader got lost on his way into the target...Being the last over the target, the anti-aircraft guns had pretty much determined our altitude of 26,000 feet and were getting pretty accurate with their anti-aircraft fire. The English fire bombs did not release and hung up in the bomb bay, making it impossible to close the bomb bay doors. As we left the target our fuel gauges showed less than 100 gallons of fuel per engine, which was not enough to get us back to the coast of France."

This flight landed in Switzerland. The crew was interned and later repatriated to the United States.

Just as it had to the Viking's sea-borne vessels, the North Atlantic yielded to the aircraft. What had at first been heroic became routine through the sacrifices of aviators, their flight crews, ground support efforts of the U.S. Army Air Corps, U.S. Army, and air and sea support from U.S. Navy personnel. Career airline pilots and support employees borrowed from airlines like Northeast Airlines and American Airlines played a major part.

Chapter 8 - Territory Alaska: Early Airbases

T he demanding conditions of Alaska's weather for any form of human movement have provided many challenges to flight over its spectacular but often forbidding land and sea masses. Flying the Aleutian chain of islands as an every day duty is a testing challenge even for experienced, instrument-qualified pilots. Building that experience took many lives. In World War II, combat forced the military services to introduce inexperienced pilots and ill-equipped aircraft into a region that lacked even the most fundamental radio aids to navigation and communication.

Based on 1938 war plans, by 1941 the U.S. Navy had established three Alaskan bases. Nearest to the continental U.S. was a seaplane patrol plane base at Sitka, Alaska. That base was on the northeast coast of the Gulf of Alaska and does not show on the next illustration.

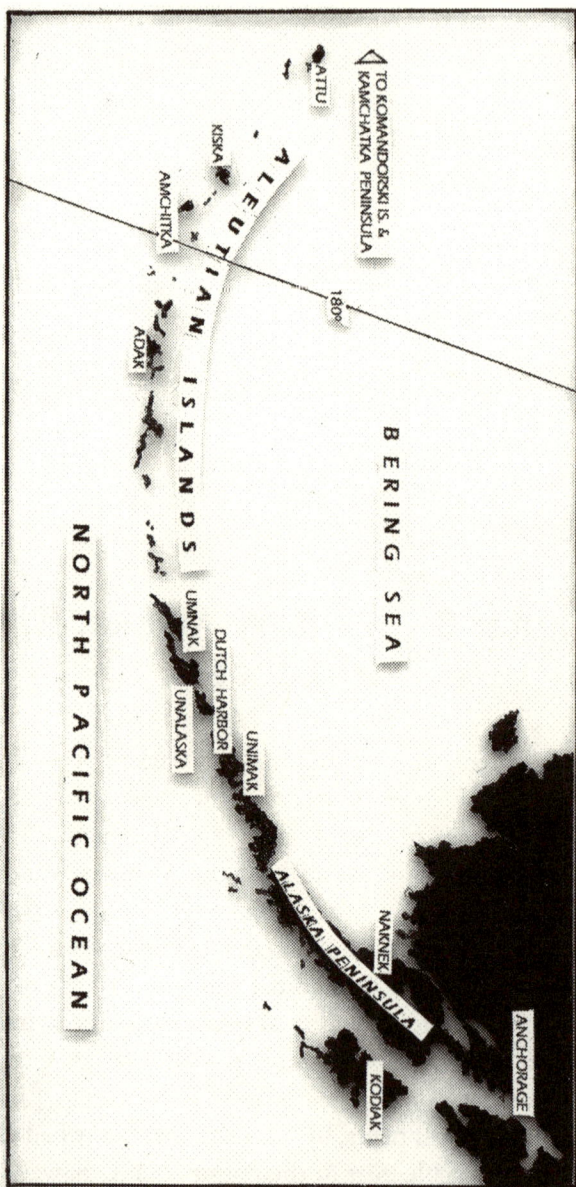

Illustration 17 - The North Pacific

Territory Alaska: Early Airbases

West and south of the base at Sitka, across the Gulf of Alaska, an airbase, NAS Kodiak, Alaska, went into commission on June 15, 1941 along with a submarine anchorage right next door. Kodiak is the large island off the south side of the Alaska Peninsula.

Further west, the U.S. Navy put a seaplane base in operation at Dutch Harbor on Unalaska Island north and west of the end of the Alaska Peninsula. This base also accommodated submarines. Before 1940, Dutch Harbor was the nation's only active naval base in the Aleutian chain of islands.

Retired naval officer Lee B. Di Napoli provides an intimate glimpse into the establishment of the U.S. Navy's early Alaskan bases. He, along with his friend Roy A. Evans, reported to seaplane squadron VP-16 from the USS Langley in November, 1938 (Langley was the U.S. Navy's first aircraft carrier). At the time, both men held the Seaman Second Class (2/c) rating. VP-16 and a number of other seaplane patrol squadrons, then based at the Naval Air Station (NAS) Sand Point, in Seattle, Washington were shortly re-designated numerically into the VP-40 series. VP-16, one of the five patrol squadrons at Sand Point, became VP-41, flying PBY-3 aircraft. Two of the patrol squadrons flew PBY-3s, and the other three flew the predecessor aircraft, P2Y-2s.

Two ships that were berthed at Sand Point served as squadron seaplane tenders. One was the USS Williamson, a converted World War I four-stack destroyer, and the other was the USS *Teal*, a seagoing tug. A seaplane tender fills many of the functions for seaplanes that an airbase does for land-based planes.

The squadrons deployed to Sitka, Alaska, on a rotating basis, for three-month tours. From Sitka, during its three-month tour, each squadron would deploy at least one time to Kodiak, Alaska, and to Dutch Harbor, Alaska. One of the Sand Point seaplane tenders would have been sent forward so that it would be in place at each of those stations when the aircraft squadron deployed.

Squadron flight personnel would be housed aboard the tender while the aircraft were at Kodiak or Dutch Harbor. The aircraft would moor to buoys. The buoys had been placed at Kodiak and at

Dutch Harbor in the mid-thirties. No ramps were available to beach the aircraft. There were no Navy land plane airfields in Alaska until the early war years. All pre-war Navy aircraft activity was sea-based. The aircraft in the next illustration were the 1930s predecessors to the famed PBYs.

Illustration 18 - A formation of Navy P2Y-2s

On paper, each aircraft squadron had twelve planes. Due to budget constraints, only six aircraft were assigned to each squadron. Each squadron usually had eight commissioned officer pilots assigned. Six enlisted pilots and a dozen aviation cadets filled out the pilot complement. Since the seaplane tenders were usually below their prescribed enlisted complement, junior radiomen in the aircraft squadron would be assigned temporary additional duty (called TDY) to supplement the tender personnel in manning the duty radio circuits. Lee Di Napoli, who had become a radioman striker, made trips to all three squadron deployment stations in Alaska on both the

Williamson and the Teal. Selections from his memories of those days are condensed in the following four paragraphs.

The pace of activity quickened in the spring of 1939. Materials for six prefab buildings were loaded aboard the Williamson at Sand Point destined for Kodiak. Di Napoli, now a radioman third class (RM 3/c - a rated petty officer) made that trip to Kodiak on the Williamson. He helped assemble the 20-foot by 20-foot buildings along the beach of Women's Bay at Kodiak. These buildings were intended to house crews that would come later to begin constructing NAS Kodiak's support buildings and later, a landing field. The advance construction force from the Williamson found many prospector claims in old tobacco tins nailed to posts along the beach. Navy personnel simply pulled the posts from the ground and threw them into the bay.

A four-man crew left Sand Point, Washington, in the summer of 1940 in a cabin cruiser proceeding to Sitka, Alaska, via the Inland Passage. Now a RM 2/c, Lee Di Napoli was part of that crew. The boat was put into service in Sitka's harbor to send radio signals to seaplanes trying to get back into Sitka during bad weather. Many times Lee Di Napoli went out in the boat to put his now practiced radio finger on the transmitter key to send radio signals for a returning PBY-3 or a P2Y-2. The aircraft would take radio direction finder (RDF) bearings on Di Napoli's radio signals, make a let down through the overcast and land in the ocean offshore, then taxi into the harbor. There were no fixed radio installations at sea. Landing in a sea area where you had visual contact with the water, and then taxiing in to a fogged-in harbor base, was a recognized operating procedure. The designated water landing area closest to the base might have a very low ceiling, too low to attempt a landing, but usually would have enough forward visibility to taxi safely on the surface under the low ceiling.

By the spring of 1941, Di Napoli, who had moved up to RM 1/c, became the first radioman of aircraft number 41P2, piloted by Lt. Paul Ramsey, who would later become Commander in Chief

155

Pacific (CINCPAC). The crew chief was Ed Froelich, an Aviation Chief Machinist Mate (ACMM). Copilots rotated from crew to crew. On one deployment to Sitka, this aircraft then made stops at Kodiak and Dutch Harbor.

Construction was now well advanced at Kodiak, with a dock in place for the seaplane tenders and a ramp for the seaplane (the seaplanes could be joined to special beaching wheel-sets, then pulled up the ramp for maintenance on dry land). During that deployment, the aircraft crew could see that activity had also become more intense at Dutch Harbor. Though seaplanes still moored to buoys there, it was clear that the Navy planned for increased activity. These trips, Sitka, to Kodiak, to Dutch Harbor, back to Kodiak and then back to Sitka took about two weeks.

From a pilot's point of view, the north Atlantic route and the north Pacific route presented similar weather and geography challenges. The pilot would want radio aids for navigation in place along with air traffic control and voice communications capability that would enable him to safely conduct mission flights from a departure point to an assigned destination.

War visited the North Atlantic sea region before it came to Alaska. Airbases along the north Atlantic rim, along with some weather and air traffic control facilities, were in place before December 7, 1941.

Seaborne materiel shipments to Britain needed air surveillance patrols from the North Atlantic rim of bases. Even during the U.S. "Neutrality Patrol" period, air support, though spotty, was sometimes available. The ships moved millions of tons of cargo. Later, passage of convoys was subject to U-boat attacks. Sea schedules had to accommodate slippage in arrival times. Aircraft could make several trips while the ship made one. Aircraft could carry critical parts and supplies, specifically pre-ordered, ready for use soon after arrival. This frequency and coordination of ship and aircraft activity did not exist in the North Pacific. There was no

"Battle of Britain" and no *Overlord* counterpart responsibility in the North Pacific.

Canada and Britain were allies in the North Atlantic. Denmark had been overrun by the Blitzkrieg and Danes were eager to cooperate in Greenland. The British had prepared a war footing in Iceland and our ground forces relieved theirs. U.S. deployed forces found some surface support facilities already in place. They had been given an advanced starting point upon which to bring in their own troops and materiel. The United States did not have to wage war or even skirmish to establish airbases.

While the weather was similar, many other challenges in Alaska were different. It had been a territory of the United States since the previous century. Our citizens lived there and felt somewhat neglected. These citizens never let their non-statehood existence interfere with their commitment to the effort to make Alaska ready for its critical role in readying for war, and for war's prosecution when it came. Alaska's role was never the logistic support role that was primary across the North Atlantic. Britain was an ally. Japan was an enemy.

Well before Pearl Harbor, active war came close to the land and islands along the North Atlantic rim. Fierce U-boat wolfpack attacks sank merchant ships and some warships. As noted, our bases along the rim provided some air cover to convoys within reach. Some flotsam and human remains that did not go to the bottom washed upon the shores. But the land stations were spared from the fighting.

Active war, land, sea and air combat, did come to the outermost tip of the Alaska Peninsula and to the Aleutian Chain of islands. Three important war engagements had a direct impact on our ability to ready Alaska and the Aleutian chain for full aviation operations. In the North Pacific, readiness was much more of an issue. The area, and a timetable not of our choosing, collaborated in a crash course in instrument flying, with the word, "crash," a disturbingly repeated reminder of too many outcomes.

While the U.S. and the USSR gazed at each other across the Bering Strait, and each speculated how it matched up against the other, Japan, actively antagonistic to both countries, made the first overt move.

The Aleutian/Alaskan area, along with Panama and Hawaii, were part of the western defensive region in the 1939 war plans of the United States. With the exceptions of Sitka, Kodiak and Dutch Harbor, the U.S. Navy, though professing its assigned role over defense of the Aleutian Chain of islands, could hardly claim that it had demonstrated a high priority in implementing its avowed responsibilities. It took a United States Army officer and his superior on the West Coast of the "lower forty eight" to give the U.S. military presence in Alaska's mainland and then the Aleutian Chain a major pre-war shot-in-the-arm.

The Department of the Army and its U.S. Army Air Corps, in the main, were no more enamored of Alaska than the Navy. Fortunately, Lieutenant General DeWitt, USA, in charge of the U.S. Western Defense Command, picked Colonel Simon Buckner, USA, to go to Alaska to implement a plan for the strategic military development of the area.

Colonel Buckner arrived in Anchorage, Alaska in July 1940. The U.S. can be thankful that Buckner had a vision for the strategic military position that the United States possessed in its almost orphan territory. Buckner could see that the challenges in creating a base support structure were going to be monumental. The U.S. Navy had made progress with its own effort, but that effort had been centered on the ability of its seaplanes to land on the water and be supported by sparingly built land-based installations and some seaplane tenders.

Simon Buckner soon realized one of the many paradoxes of his new command responsibilities. Alaska loved the airplane. Its bush pilots, another distinct breed of pilots like the barnstormers, made things happen in Alaska and their work was appreciated. They moved supplies to outposts that were not reachable any other way. Often these were life saving medical serums and life giving birth supports for newborn babies struggling to live. Those pilots adapted to the region, using skis and pontoons on their aircraft when required. One famous Alaskan bush pilot, Bob Reeve, actually formed Reeve Aleutian Airways after World War II to fly from Anchorage to the Aleutian chain of islands. But prewar, the bush pilot paradox was that their canny adaptive skills meant that facilities like paved airfields were not built. Too hard to build and too costly. There were other ways to do it, particularly where budgets were limited.

Buckner, who might have turned out to be a regiments and battalions and divisions kind of Army officer, saw the wisdom of the airplane. He appreciated and used the skill of the bush pilots and at the same time began an effort to build airfields and air support facilities. This ground-trained officer was evenhanded in his relationships with the Army Air Corps and the U.S. Navy. Where interests coincided, and the other parties were dedicated to the objective, he worked with Navy and Army Air Corps personnel to get a job done that he saw needed to be done. He was not addicted to personal fame. He moved to get his airfields built.

Buckner found believers like an Army Air Corps pilot, one Colonel Eareckson, and a Navy Captain named Ralph Parker. Buckner's passion, animated by his accurate evaluation of Japanese military intentions, was contagious to his small contingent of strong men. Buckner was no purist. He occasionally was moved to diverting funds from other worthy purposes to direct use in enhancing the region's military preparedness. His vision was disciplined. He studied the territory and conducted a survey of sites along the Aleutian chain which would be suitable for airfields.

Buckner's effort to develop a defense scheme for the U.S. position in the North Pacific rim resulted in the following airbase developments:

Elmendorf Field at Anchorage;

Ladd Field at Fairbanks;

Dutch Harbor-improved defenses of the seaplane base;

Fort Randall at Cold Bay, Alaska-an airfield;

Fort Glenn on Umnak Island-an airfield.

The Triumph of Instrument Flight

For all of the geography education a U.S. schoolchild acquires, including the oft told tale of the purchase of Alaska from Russia, most U.S. citizens know little about Alaska itself.

A word challenge is introduced by the names given to two of Alaska's important geographic features. The Alaska Peninsula, reaching southwest from Alaska, is dominated by the *Aleutian* Range of mountains. This range extends right into the heart of Alaska itself. The *Aleutian* Chain of islands, however, does not actually begin until Unimak Island, the first major island off the western tip of the Alaska Peninsula.

The North Pacific region's great challenge to flying was its weather and the terrain it enveloped. It was a challenge to pilots and to their aircraft. The U.S. had some widely separated weather reporting stations in the Aleutians. A major difficulty came when weather, as it so often did, changed suddenly, with no advance indications. There was almost no long term weather forecasting capability in meteorology in those days and what did exist needed to be regarded with caution.

Don Fortune, in later civilian life a San Francisco newspaper editor and author, learned about weather in the Gulf of Alaska first hand while serving as an ordinary seaman on board a 1362-ton ship delivering supplies to Cold Bay near the end of the Alaska Peninsula in 1942. A "coaster," in seagoing terms, the SS Taku had become the USAT (U.S. Army Transport) Taku by the time ordinary seaman Don Fortune made his way aboard for duty during several supply trips between Seattle, Washington and Cold Bay near the westernmost tip of the Peninsula on its south side.

In following paragraphs, Don Fortune provides some details about one sea trip between Cold Bay and Seattle in those storm-driven Alaskan waters. The names Cold Bay and Ft. Randall are used interchangeably.

"I got the impression that almost everything was underground. I was also told (in 1942) that the Japanese did not know of Fort Randall's existence there. On one trip, a storm hit the ship that

160

almost sank the vessel and resulted in my being carried off in a canvas wrapping. The crew quarters were aft and above deck. The black gang's ("black gang" -sea lingo for the men assigned to the engineering spaces of a ship; stems from the time when the propulsion fuel was coal) quarters were on the portside, deckhands on the starboard. Their cabins were abandoned and I was told later that the doors were torn off their hinges. The storm was so powerful that lifeboats were stove in and useless. Superstructure was hammered. The ship could not make headway. I was carried midship to the Second Mate's cabin, and left soaked and badly bruised for what I was told was almost 36 hours. Finally, the skipper pulled into Juneau, Alaska, possibly against orders. I was wrapped in canvas and carried topdeck. The men carrying me had to twist and turn through the officer's mess and other narrow spaces. It hurt. I was lowered to a launch and taken to the hospital. The Taku spent some time in drydock after it arrived back in Seattle."

Don Fortune's lines about the rigors of passage across the Gulf of Alaska introduce the reader to the storm factor that influenced so many aircraft missions before, during and after World War II. With the advent of the passenger jet age in the 1950s, the aircraft could fly above the weather that had been so controlling for the World War II era pilots, and especially for those flying the Aleutian Chain. The jet age also brought aircraft that could fly to Japan, at first from the U.S. to Anchorage Alaska as an intermediate fuel stop, and eventually could fly all the way from the U.S. mainland to Tokyo with no stop in Alaska at all.

Storms are regularly generated where the Japanese current meets the frozen northern tundra and its adjacent waters. Fog banks can suddenly move to shroud a landing site. Fog can suddenly materialize out of clear air. For aviators, an added factor south of the chain is that at least until 1948 there were almost no radio aids to air navigation in that airspace. An aircraft had to be self-sufficient electronically.

Some exciting, some bizarre, and some tragic events of war occurred between a Japanese fleet's first attack on Dutch Harbor on June 2, 1942 and Japan's occupation of Attu and Kiska, which began just five confusing days later on June 7 in the summer of 1942.

It was as part of the northern prong of its attack on Midway Island, that the Japanese, on 7 June 1942, occupied Kiska and Attu, out at the end of the Aleutian chain of islands. These occupations were preceded by Japanese aircraft carrier raids on the U.S. Navy installations at Dutch Harbor, located on Unalaska Island.

In the context of the six years of active hostilities in World War II, Japan's stay in the Aleutians turned out to be relatively brief. On June 7, 1942, the Japanese commenced landing on Attu and Kiska and quickly captured or killed the occupants there, some of whom were in the weather crew. Just a year later, by the end of May 1943, after a bloody three weeks on both sides, with the killing of most of the Japanese defenders and the capture of but a handful, the Japanese were eliminated from Attu.

A Japanese objective in the Aleutian phase of its attack on Midway included bombing attacks on Dutch Harbor, primarily to make the U.S. Navy believe that its Dutch Harbor seaplane base installations were an occupation target. From code breaking, Admiral Nimitz at Pearl Harbor knew that after their attempt to divert U.S. Midway Island forces to the Aleutians, Japan's Aleutian intention was to make occupation force landings on Adak, Kiska and Attu. Overlooked by the Japanese until its forces had undergone air surveillance and resistance from islands not believed by them to be militarized, was a U.S. Army Air Corps air base on Umnak Island and another at Cold Bay. These had been constructed by the U.S. Corps of Engineers and were part of Buckner's handiwork. P-40 *Warhawks*, B-26 *Marauders* and B-17 *Flying Fortresses*, using steel matting runways, were operational there when the Japanese struck Dutch Harbor.

The disturbing discovery that there were gaps in its intelligence about U.S. airfields in the Aleutians very likely led the Japanese high command to its decision to abandon the Adak landing objective and concentrate on Attu and Kiska. This change left the door open to a major opportunity for the United States. That opportunity was Adak, and Adak ultimately became the pivot of the U.S. Navy's air and sea operations in the Aleutians.

The U.S. Navy base at Dutch Harbor on Unalaska Island west of Unimak Island supported PBY *Catalina* patrol seaplanes, and their seaplane tenders. There were fuel storage facilities, some radio communications towers, and a detachment of U.S. Marines. It was defended by anti-aircraft gunnery installations. These were well dug in, but of insufficient range and without modern fire control. Four-stack U.S. destroyers dating from World War I were also based there but their gun systems were also outmoded.

As noted, Nimitz knew what the Japanese were up to with their thrust in the north. He was certain that their main effort would be directed against Midway. Nimitz sent a small cruiser-destroyer force north under Rear Admiral Theobold as his response to the intelligence information.

For their part, the Japanese had good communications, experienced ship handlers and skilled pilots. Their Admiral astutely used the adverse weather to the best advantage that could be achieved in atrociously bad weather conditions. His celestial navigation information was outdated by the time his task force arrived off Aleutian Island shores. His location, therefore, with respect to his preliminary Dutch Harbor bombing objective was not as good as he would have hoped. What he did possess was nearly precise knowledge of the location of the leading edge of the weather front he was able to hide in. This was accurate enough for him to control the time he would be able to poke his force out ahead of the front and launch aircraft. A Navy PBY on a long duration patrol mission did spot the Japanese force through a break in the overcast. The Japanese task force was able to mount two air attacks on Dutch Harbor during which the Japanese pilots encountered almost no aircraft resistance over their target and only futile AA fire.

Realization by the Japanese that U.S. aircraft sorties from Umnak Island might be able to interfere with recovery of Japanese aircraft aboard their carriers was perhaps the deciding factor in their abandonment of Adak as an occupation objective.

Key airbase events in the year it took the United States to dislodge the Japanese occupying forces on Attu and Kiska were the Navy's occupation of Adak on August 30, 1942 and Amchitka on January 12, 1943. At Adak, an aircraft runway was operating in an incredible twelve days after groundbreaking and on Amchitka it took about five weeks to begin flight operations.

In March 1943, there occurred a stirring sea battle that marked the end of any Japanese hopes to retain a foothold on U.S. soil. Then in May 1943, with the U.S. landings on Attu, the beginning of the end for the Japanese was in sight.

The Battle of the Komandorski Islands is an event that marked a change in the fortunes of war in the North Pacific. It is what did not happen during that battle that is of interest here. Here is just a sample of the scope of the battle and where it took places.

Lack of air navigation capability under instrument conditions, primitive air traffic control facilities and great gaps in weather forecasting facilities hamstrung effective use of the U.S. aircraft. A dreadfully inadequate communications infrastructure in the entire Alaska-Aleutian region compounded all problems.

The Komandorskis' sea battle took place roughly along Latitude 53 degrees, 20 minutes North, about midway between Attu and Siberia's Kamchatka Peninsula, in a sea space just south of the Komandorski Islands. The U.S. sea force under Admiral McMorris consisted of two cruisers and four destroyers. The Japanese under Vice Admiral Hosagaya had two heavy cruisers, two light cruisers, and five destroyers. These were escorting two fast, armed, merchant cruisers and one slower transport. These latter three carried the supplies and reinforcements for Attu and Kiska. They never made it to their goal and returned to Paramashiro.

In his Volume VII, *Aleutians, Gilberts and Marshalls*, of the History of United States Naval Operations in World War II, historian Samuel Eliot Morison sets the picture that unfolded.

"At 0730 March 26 (1943), an hour before sunrise, this (the McMorris) task group lay 180 miles west of Attu and 100 miles south of the nearest Komandorski island. The ships were strung out in scouting line six miles long, steering N. by E. Destroyer USS Coghlan was in the van, flagship, cruiser USS Richmond next, followed by destroyer USS Bailey flying Captain Rigg's (Rigg was Commodore of the destroyer Bailey's squadron) pennant, then destroyer USS Dale. Cruiser USS Salt Lake City steamed next to last in the column, with destroyer USS Monaghan in the rear. They were making 15 knots and zigzagging. Temperature was just above the freezing point."

Captain Stanley Hogshead USN (Ret), who was in charge of the U.S. destroyer Bailey's plotting room during the battle, described it as the longest day battle of major sea forces of the United States and Japan in World War II. Even though destroyer Bailey and U.S. cruiser Salt Lake City took major damage, it was the Japanese who broke off the battle and headed for Paramashiro.

Admiral McMorris had sent word immediately to U.S. shore installations that the battle was about to commence. He included the coordinates where it would take place. U.S. aircraft were actually launched from Adak and Amchitka. They never arrived in the battle area despite the rare good visibility at sea. The relatively good weather at the sea battle location did not mean that Adak or Amchitka weather was good or that the airspace between those bases and the battle area did not pose some challenging instrument flight weather.

Even with our acknowledged weakness in the air at the time, it is still incredible that U.S. aircraft never managed to find a major sea battle that covered an entire day, involved 18 ships that were in sight of each other, covered hundreds of square miles of seaspace, and took place in good surface visibility.

The inability to get all land, sea and air units working together became the trademark of the U.S. Aleutian effort in 1942 and 1943. Had Admiral Hosagaya persisted at the battle site, the results might have been entirely different. But he too was influenced by lack of information, and took as his reason for turning away just when his force had achieved a decided advantage, that U.S. aircraft had ample time to reach the scene and would soon become a deciding factor.

General Buckner's airbase legacy, originating in 1940 for the future support of U.S. military operations, particularly air operations, was huge. Reflect for a moment on a comparison with Buckner's Alaska airfield building program. In the year 2003, in the friendly confines of the United States, it takes ten years to plan and build a major commercial aviation facility. If any would doubt the Buckner contribution, certainly the passengers and crew of a Delta MD-11 in March 2001 would not. En route to Japan, the aircraft made a cautionary landing at Cold Bay, Alaska, due to smoke in the cockpit.

To maintain a consistent aeronautical presence, air operations need to be coordinated over reliable radio communication channels. Light beacons were not enough. There were only two light beacons for night navigation in mainland Alaska in 1942. After the debacle in air to ground communications displayed by U.S. forces in the defense against the second Japanese air attack on Dutch Harbor, the U.S. Signal Corps was ordered in. They were told to start from basics and provide Alaska a desperately needed communications capability. It was also time, past time, to consider the introduction of low frequency radio range transmitters for radio beam generation, both for point to point aircraft transit and for aircraft let down to safe landings in instrument conditions. No region in the world is shrouded in instrument conditions as much of the time as the Aleutians.

The lesson for the military and indeed for Alaska was the need for the reliable air navigation and communication installations. Until those needs were met, the military could not begin to address command and control.

As noted, the Signal Corps was ordered to remedy the situation. Almost three years later, in 1946, the remedial process was still in progress. Radio range stations, and voice communication systems for air and ground control, required planning first, and then time to install. The Aleutian experience in air traffic control implementation involved one added factor when contrasted with the earlier progress in the North Atlantic rim. Aleutian-based folks could say, "There was a war going on here!"

A major change in U.S. strategic posture came with the construction of the Naval Base at Adak. Accommodations for land and water based aircraft plus ship and submarine berthing were erected in record time. From the summer of 1942 to the summer of 1943, Adak went from practically unoccupied to a city of over 50,000. It jumped alongside Kodiak in major importance for naval operations. The military pressure vector that had pointed so ominously west to east after Pearl Harbor, turned around and became east to west after Midway. This occurred despite Japan's face-saving occupation of Attu and Kiska. Conditions for the full turnaround would not exist until the Japanese were eliminated from their Aleutian foothold.

History has a way of making early decisions into barely recalled events. The critically important locations in WW II moved rapidly westward. Sitka was left much too far to the east to be a base of importance in the main effort against the Japanese in World War II. Sitka fulfilled its early role as the staging base for Kodiak and Dutch Harbor. Dutch Harbor was primarily a seaplane base. The seaplane had a role early in World War II but the landplane displaced it for military use.

It is an irony that aviation's progress can be marked by the abandonment of airbases, sometimes because their location has been over-flown and sometimes because their facilities are no longer relevant. Not so different has been the abandonment of many early civilian airfields in the United States.

The U.S. took maximum advantage of the Japanese decision not to occupy Adak and established its own important base there. With the addition of wheel-sets as an integral part of the PBY Catalina, to upgrade it to amphibian status, resulting in the PBY-5A model, Adak could handle all *Catalina* configurations. This diminished the importance of Dutch Harbor, which base then receded into history. For the Navy, then, in World War II and on into the early years of the Cold War, Kodiak and Adak became the principal bases in this theatre.

Every aircraft introduced into the Alaskan theatre in the 1940s had to undergo climatic modifications. Some made the transition by little more than the introduction of new procedures. The Navy's PBY fared better than most. Although it could carry armament, it was designed primarily as a patrol plane. When it became an amphibian, capable of setting down on land or water, its landing options were increased. With very few early landplane fields, extra landing options could make an amphibian aircraft especially endearing in Alaska. Even without wheels for landing, the early PBY pilot was probably envied because he could land in more places, and that meant more places that might provide a ceiling and visibility welcome.

The B-17 *Flying Fortresses* had to undergo configuration changes to make them suitable for flight in the Alaska region. For the fighter aircraft, the P-40s and later the P-38s, combat life could be demanding and the attrition was high. By May 1943, with a landing strip on Amchitka in use to support the U.S. effort to retake Attu, some of the Army Air Corps fighter inventory was moved out to Amchitka.

By this time, the Navy PV-1, known as the Vega *Ventura*, had also been introduced to the Aleutians. This aircraft had a lot of negatives. Its positive impact was its airborne radar. In addition to the military surveillance use in finding enemy ships, airborne radar on more than one occasion proved to be the means for a crew to get a plane back safely on the ground when all other alternatives had been foreclosed. Good airborne radar was especially appreciated in Aleutian regions devoid of land based radio aids to air navigation.

The *Ventura* stemmed from the Lockheed family of aircraft which had included the early *Electras* and *Lodestars*, the *Hudsons* and later the PV-2 *Harpoon* and much later the P2V *Neptune*. Unfortunately, the *Ventura* member of the family had some drawbacks.

Captain Harry Carter, USN (Ret), had the rare opportunity as a civilian to manufacture a plane he would later learn to fly as a member of the military. He was a civilian employee on the Lockheed assembly line at Burbank, California and worked on the PV-1 assembly line, beginning with the engine nacelle units and progressing until he was selected to indoctrinate women, "Rosie, the riveter" apprentices, teaching them how to drive and buck rivets.

Later, now a naval aviator, Harry Carter was sent to Lake City, Florida for training in the PV-1. He reports that the aircraft was treated with deference. Engine-out simulation in the PV-1 at altitude required all the muscle a pilot's leg could put into holding rudder on the good engine side of the aircraft. Training instructors simply ducked the issue and "engine out" training at Lake City was conducted in the good old twin Beech. Fatalities were too often the result when an engine quit on takeoff. And it nearly as marginal when single-engine landings had to be made. Carter reports gas fumes were often present in the cockpit. Fortunately for Ensign Carter, he got through the training without severe emergency scares, and through a quirk in orders, he and another pilot never even went to an operational PV-1 squadron. The two ended up in PB4Y-2 *Privateer* training at Chincoteague, Virginia, for which Carter reports he was ever grateful.

A good prognosis for instrument flying under instrument conditions is to be flying in an aircraft that is steady and forgiving. Instrument flight requires concentration. Distractions of the kind Carter reported from his training command duty at Lake City work against the confidence that young pilots must acquire during instrument training.

The PV-1 had been the first land based patrol aircraft that the Navy introduced into the Aleutians for full operational missions. It was not a good choice, even with its valued short wavelength radar.

3Immediately following World War II, with a new mission at hand, the key bases for aircraft patrolling the Aleutian Chain, became NAS Kodiak, NAS Adak, and the U.S. Army and Army Air Corps Base, Fort Glenn. The fourth important air base was the Army base at Cold Bay. This is the airfield that we knew in 1946 as Fort Randall. By 1946, the airfield at Cold Bay had become the home of the U.S. Army Air Force's 10th Rescue Squadron, flying OA-10 aircraft. The OA-10 was a PBY-5A *Catalina* pressed into Army use.

By 1946, Shemya was no longer a military operations base. It became one again later. Unencumbered by mountains, this atoll just east of Attu, had an excellent approach right down on the water, and was used as an emergency alternate airport when NAS Adak, Ft. Glenn or NAS Attu were socked in.

The PV-1 *Venturas* and the later PV-2 *Harpoons* were gone from the Aleutians by 1946. Even with progress in electronic ground installations, and the sophisticated electronics carried aboard later aircraft, flights that departed from an Alaskan or Aleutian airfields continued to disappear.

Objectively, for Alaskan flying in the late 1930s and early 1940s, the disappearance of aircraft without a trace was not confined to the PV-1. All U.S. aircraft types fared poorly when combat came to Alaska and the Aleutians.

Postwar air travelers between the United States and Japan first became accustomed to landing at Anchorage, Alaska, for refueling and changing of flight crews. Subsequently, when the trip became non-stop with the Boeing 747, on a good day, the air traveler could see, on the window side toward the north, that impressive rim formed by the Gulf of Alaska and the Aleutian Islands. That was an experience I shared with passengers on one non-stop as a civilian traveling from Dallas to Tokyo. It was exciting to see from an aircraft window what I had formerly only been able to see on maps and charts, the entire expanse of the North Pacific.

Chapter 9 - Wartime Pilot Training

The early pilots, like the Wright brothers, were self taught. Later came instructor pilots who introduced methodology to pilot training with at least a 'safe to solo' flight check. The earliest instrument pilots were also self taught, and self qualified. Later, as had occurred with pilot training, instrument flight instructors added more structure to instrument flight training, and the custom of an instrument flight written exam followed by an independent (of the instructor) instrument flight check was introduced. This more detailed discussion of flight training will begin with military flight training programs in World War II

Two decades of civil aviation pilot training and nearly a decade of airline instrument flight training were available as models for military flight training for World War II.

Experienced civil aviation pilots furnished the instructor backbone for a program of pilot training in the United States known as Civilian Pilot Training, C.P.T.

C.P.T began at Fayetteville, Arkansas in 1939 and was the most ambitious program ever undertaken in any nation to prepare its citizens for the aviation era. The government had an ulterior motive. War clouds were gathering.

Many of the primary stage flight instructors at military aviation training stations after 1939 had their own introduction to aviation in C.P.T. Some of their students also had C.P.T. training. Together, instructors and students were forming the backbone of a third pilot generation in the U.S. The intensification of effort that war brings found the military taking the best from general aviation, from the C.P.T. program, and from the still young air transport industry. The military added structure to its flight training programs.

Naval aviator Captain Harry Carter's first experience in flying came in C.P.T. He was 18. At Bakersfield Junior College in California he recalls being issued silver wings and khaki uniforms as his class departed for Lone Pine, California for flight training. Bakersfield handled the ground school and Pembertan Flying School the hands-on air training. He still has his C.P.T. Rating Book that served as his flight log. He flew the *Luscomb 8A* while others flew *Porterfields* and *Cubs*.

Once war began in December 1941, the pool of available student pilots like Harry Carter in the Aviation Cadet programs being conducted on some college campuses was greatly augmented from college and even high school sources. In addition, enlisted and officer personnel returning from shipboard duty, who desired to fly, were ordered into flight training programs. The author was one of those flight students who came from sea duty.

Consider the flying preparation of Dick Sullivan who became a Navy instructor pilot at Naval Air Station (NAS) Ottumwa, Iowa in 1944. He had applied for the Navy's V5 aviation program in early 1942. He was accepted in mid-August not long after his 20th birthday. After being sworn in, the Navy instructed him to proceed to Northwestern University, Evanston, Illinois for C.P.T. training. At Sky Harbor Airport in Northbrook, Illinois, he began flight training with instructor Virginia Banks in the J3 Piper *Cub*. Dick Sullivan remembers that she was a teacher with patience and he needed all of it. She successfully saw him through drift-control practice maneuvers around pylons, S-turns over roads, training that he found challenging and which sent him on to Navy pre-flight school at the University of Iowa in Iowa City. Thirteen weeks of class room and physical fitness training there moved Sullivan to Primary Flight training at NAS Minneapolis. At the completion of Primary, he then went successively to Saufley Field, Whiting Field and then to Corry Field, all satellite fields of NAS Pensacola, Florida. At Saufley he took formation flight training in SNVs (BT-13s in the Army Air Corps), affectionately known by all as the Vultee Vibrator. Naval Auxiliary Air Station (NAAS) Whiting Field, near Milton, Florida, was next, with concentration on instrument training in SNJs (Army Air Corps AT6). He had received some Link training in Primary but it was at Whiting where Link sessions were scheduled in earnest. Dick Sullivan's final student stage training came in the Navy PBY *Catalina*, flying out of Bronson Field at Pensacola. His graduation took place Christmas Eve, 1943.

The first stage of hands-on flight instruction prepared the student pilot for solo flight. Good flying technique learned in that first stage provided the foundation for later transition to instrument flying.

By 1944, military flight training programs in the United States had settled into three stages: (1) primary training which included clearance for the student pilot to solo; (2) basic training, using higher performance aircraft and providing an introduction to instrument training with some actual experience; (3) operational training, in which the new pilot would be flying the aircraft type that he would take into combat. For the multi-engine pilots, this third stage would include as much exposure to actual instrument flying as U.S. skies would offer during the period that the new pilot was completing his flight training. There was no "wait" period for actual weather to hone the instrument flight skill. A student pilot either flew actual instruments or an equivalent amount of time "under the hood."

The aviator aspirants in the primary flight training class to which I was assigned were very young men. The few fleet transfers, both officer and enlisted, were all at least five years older than the aviation cadets (AVCADs). The fleet people were in the minority. The only good reason for the Navy to bring them back from overseas for flight training was investment for the future. As far as winning the World War II in progress, for the most part, the fleet transfer contingent, the "seniors," were not going to be required.

These seniors had already crossed paths with plenty of aviators, British, American, German and Japanese. Those aviators flew single engine fighters and fighter-bombers, twin engine bombers and night fighters, and two and four engine patrol planes. The surface fleet combatants had seen those flying machines. Each had a mental image of Supermarine *Spitfires* or North American *Mustangs* or Lockheed *Lightnings* and marveled at the ease with which those aircraft had moved rapidly through the air. The Dornier 217s and the Ju-88s could carry ship-killing ordnance. Pacific warriors had seen the *Zeros* and *Bettys* among the Japanese aircraft.

Before leaving those days of observing air traffic in contested waters, what would the information revealed by their air activities have told me about the state of their flying art?

Pilots of all of those craft arrived in combat areas by applying their knowledge of terrain and sea. They used ground references like railroad tracks, bridges and population centers, lakes and rivers, and of course the sea and its coastlines. Later, in the great mid-west heartland of the United States, the student pilots in our group were introduced to section lines. Those carefully tended farm demarcation lines provided additional excellent aids to navigation.

German planes that harassed a Mediterranean destroyer at night with their flares and bombs, and the friendly Allied night fighters that attempted to interfere with those unfriendly forays, arrived in combat areas by adding skills to the day flyer's terrain-based knowledge. These flyers demonstrated the advanced skill of night flying. Among those night flyers, there were some that had achieved an even more advanced skill known as instrument flying. Their aircraft arrived in our vicinity in spite of the weather.

Weather along the route was not a hindrance to the Luftwaffe while flying to, from, and over the Mediterranean in 1942. Destination weather might hinder the effectiveness of their attack, but did not interfere with getting there or getting back to base.

Of course, allied shipboard personnel did not speculate then about German aircraft and the state of readiness of German pilots. There was no time to project thoughts into those cockpits or even appreciate the apprehensions that might exist there. The immediate sea-bound combat concern, very personal and completely self-centered, was whether a shipboard observer could get a peek at an enemy night air marauder sufficient to lay a gun on him and then shoot at him without giving away too much. One needed a clear sense of advantage before firing, because, if you missed, the enemy pilot was left with an enhanced knowledge of his opportunity. Luftwaffe pilots still had to apply their flying abilities to a successful return to base but the welcome there would be much sweeter if some serious damage had been left behind.

Weather subtleties had great influence on results. A clear horizon often meant a successful dusk attack. Haze changed everything and haze at night imposed conditions different from daytime haze.

The Battle of Midway in the Pacific occurred in generally good weather. A chance sighting of key elements of the Japanese fleet through broken clouds was the margin of success for the United States in this pivotal action of World War II.

At night, friendly night fighter aircraft were generally not available to defend surface ships. Night air-to-air combat flying was rare. Even for day operations, the concept of airborne fighter control was new. "Control" was the operative word. Combat Air Patrol, CAP, in a fully coordinated and controlled sense, was in its infancy in the Navy in 1942. Air traffic control on civil airways in the continental U.S. was just a few years old. And there, everyone was expected to behave.

Air defense, with friendly night fighters, of important land based installations against enemy air raids was "a work in progress." When three land based searchlights could triangulate on one high level enemy bomber, they could hold him and track him and get a fire control solution, and often shoot him down. Friendly fighters had to stay away from the enemy in those situations or they too would be subject to air-bursts from ground based AA guns.

A ZI, for Zone of the Interior, was defined around each important land based defensive perimeter. Any plane, visible or invisible, friend or foe, was going to be shot at in that zone. Any attempt by an Allied plane to assist in the defense of a convoy at night, especially a convoy with surface escorts capable of anti-aircraft fire, was fraught with danger for the well-intentioned aircraft. At sea, there was no inter-service protocol, not even something like the ZIs that were defined over land installations. The ships at sea could not see and identify who the marauders were. The electronic system, IFF-Identification Friend or Foe, was just being born. For these reasons, a convoy's defending air cover, if there was one, withdrew at sunset. Some very courageous *Beaufighters* of the British RAF would occasionally hang around after dusk.

Storm-tossed Allied C-47s coming in with airborne paratroopers for landings along the Sicilian coast in 1943 were shot down by friendly fire. The planes had been blown off course in a rapidly evolving storm and there had been no way to get that information to the smaller landing craft approaching their night assault beaches on that July 11, 1943, night. The flight crews had done a magnificent job instrument flying and pretty much maintaining their formations. In Volume IX of his official narrative of U.S. Navy operations in World War II, Samuel Eliot Morison wrote that for lack of inter-service communication to the smaller seaborne elements of the landing forces, for an airdrop instituted by the air branch of the Army at a late hour, 23 of the 144 troop transport planes did not return.

Flight training in the military required a flight physical exam. Mine was obtained from an Army Air Corps flight surgeon of the 15th Air Force in Naples, Italy in the summer of 1944. As soon as the flight surgeon discovered that this prospective Navy pilot was not likely to dilute the capability of his Army Air Corps, he became quite lenient, almost cooperative, in his more relaxed pursuit of any physical factors that would compromise my ability to fly.

Transportation back to the States in October 1944 was a C-54 (Douglas DC-4 in the civil aviation world; the Navy called this aircraft the R5D). Pilots under contract from American Airlines flew the plane. Its route was from Port Lyautey, Morocco, to Lajes on Terceira Island in the Azores, thence to Goose Bay, Labrador, and finally to the port of entry to the U.S. at Naval Air Station (NAS), Patuxent River, Maryland. That trip was an introduction to North Atlantic rim flying.

The first stop, Lajes in the Azores, was dark and cold with heavy rain. The approach and landing took quite a bit of time. Next day, the North Atlantic dawned gray and somber underneath the overcast, lighter between stratus cloud layers. Snow was on the ground in Labrador. Thunder and lightning and early darkness put the pilots to due diligence in a long final approach over the Chesapeake Bay to the Patuxent River Naval Air Station. After landing, there was much confusion about baggage, customs, and transfer to a C-47 (a DC-3 "Gooney Bird" operated by the Army Air Corps; the Navy designation was R4D) for a flight to the Norfolk Naval Air Station.

Those Army Air Corps pilots did not go up into the boiling storms with any of the circumspection of the American Airlines overseas contract pilots. The DC-3 was obviously overloaded, standing room only, and all the passengers were hanging onto overhead straps like the standees in a New York subway train. The aircraft lurched down to Norfolk using VFR (visual contact with the ground below) flight rules, tracking the western shore of the Chesapeake Bay, occasionally visible in the lightning flashes. The landing was rough.

For primary stage flight training, my assignment was governed by the Naval Air Primary Flight Training Command. The aircraft in which I was to learn to fly was the Stearman. This biplane, designated an N2S by the Navy, was often improperly called a *Yellow Peril*. Stearmans were painted yellow. The term *Yellow Peril* had already been pinned on the Navy-designed N3N, a plane quite similar in outward appearance to the Stearman. Unless you knew aircraft, you would not see the fine distinctions.

The first air station assignment was NAS Ottumwa, Iowa The primary flight training stage began in mid-October 1944. Twenty months later, at Pensacola, Florida, a much smaller contingent of officer and enlisted pilots was deemed ready for fleet air flying status. That operational assignment began for me on 1 July, 1946. Subtracting short leaves, in-transit travel and unaccountable delays, the aviation training consumed about 16 months, and consisted of a series of relatively short temporary duty assignments at several U. S Navy air training bases.

The amount of flight time needed, before solo, in the less formal civil aviation instruction programs of the 1930s and 1940s varied. Some civil aviators had no more than five hours of dual flight instruction before soloing. Some had perhaps fifteen. My logbook shows 17.1 hours of dual training before my first 1.5-hour solo flight, all in the Navy's N2S Stearman biplane.

Pilot training efforts for World War II, from the outset, were influenced by the training of pilots before the war, because between-the-war pilots became the bulk of the instructor contingent, and brought with them what they had learned.

NAVAER 80-R-19 of July 1946 furnishes relevant historical information. For the Navy, the Aviation Cadet Act of 1935, provided for the eligibility of college graduates between 20 and 28 years of age, to receive appointments as aviation cadets in the Naval Reserve. Thirty eight weeks, with flying time in four major types of naval aircraft, and ground school for half of each day, gave the Navy an experience base that suddenly became important the day Germany invaded Poland. The program then went to six days a week, landplane training came first instead of second, and a course in instrument flying was instituted. The college degree requirement was lowered to a high school diploma and the age to 18.

The Civilian Pilot Training program became a key component of the accelerated aviation training effort to get pilots trained for war duty. From 1939 to 1942, selected colleges arranged for training, and transportation to Civil Aeronautics Administration (CAA) approved flying schools. No military affiliation was required. Between June and December 1942 the military entered the picture, furnishing quarters and subsistence through reimbursement to the colleges, and requiring the student to be signed up with the Army or the Navy. CAA still acted as the disbursement intermediary. From December 1942 to October 1944, enrollees in what had now become the CAA War Training Service Program, found military officers in charge of the 40 hours of flight instruction and 200 hours of flight ground school. The CAA still handled the contracts with the colleges. In the fall of 1944, the military services programs became fully staffed and the relationship to the civil branches ended.

A segment of WW II instructor pilots came from the military's in-house training programs. The other major segment came from general aviation. The Army Air Corps' pilot training programs and the Navy's were quite similar, often using the same type of aircraft.

A unique contribution to U.S. aviation existed in a program at Embry-Riddle Aeronautical University. The school is now located in Daytona Beach, Florida. Founded in 1925 in Cincinnati, Ohio, its basic mission was to train pilots. This university became an important center for setting training standards in civil aviation. Embry's program evolved to a core aviation education and training program, including engineering studies, meteorology, navigation, power plants, airframes and electronics.

Physical skills at or above a defined norm, an even temperament, a desire to learn, and an alert intellect were deemed basics in the formal training programs.

The student pilots at Naval Air Station, Ottumwa, Iowa, plunged into a demanding and concentrated program. Those students were too busy to speculate on the origins or maturity of their flight training program. The programs were highly organized and appeared to have been in progress for a long time. It was only years later, after puzzling out the sequencing, that it became apparent that elements of those military flight training programs were in many ways being devised or revised sometimes just weeks ahead of the arrival of a class of student pilots.

Ground school for one half-day and flight school for the other half-day. October in Iowa. The weather was rapidly turning cold. Open cockpits with no heaters. The Red Cross ladies knitted woolen headpieces with eye, nose and mouth slits. These fit over the head and under the helmet, making the pilot look like a member of the KKK. Those headpieces saved nose and ears from certain frostbite.

Students were told to read *Stick and Rudder*, a well-known and well-written book by author Wolfgang Langweische. The ground school and flight activities filled all available hours and a student pilot was hard pressed to keep up. I did not read as much *of Stick and Rudder* as I should have. I did read selected parts after a new-to-me flight event occurred. On those occasions, I regretted that I had not read the book first.

The very first activity that took place in the student pilot ready room, just a half-hour or so before a student's first training flight was to begin, seemed incongruous. A photographer came in to shoot pictures of student pilots in their flight suits. The suits, government issued, consisted of a tan, full-length, flight suit with pockets in the legs just below the knees. A fleece-lined leather jacket and helmet, goggles, white scarf and calfskin gloves completed the outfit. That scarf was the feature of the photo, with the leather jacket and its sheepskin collar forming the frame. A face, with goggles on its forehead, became a centerpiece of the photographs. All that remains in my possession is that picture and the leather flight jacket. The jacket's leather is cracked and worn because a couple of sons appropriated it after I had come down out of the sky for good.

It had struck me as odd that the first main event on the flight line was picture taking. I had thought that would have been part of a graduation schedule. In the next few weeks, the class lost several young men in flight accidents that occurred during early solo flights. The wisdom of the photo session came home. All that a family or wife might have had from the young man's aviation experience was that picture.

The Stearman in Iowa meant open cockpit, single-engine sky. The sheepskin lined leather jacket was a lifesaver in late fall and winter. Sometimes, for days on end, the weather was bad and we did not fly.

Student pilots were divided into two wings, North and South. The North Wing used the North mat for flight origin and destination. The South Wing used the South mat. A mat was a few acres of flat asphalt on the ground in a kind of rounded square. The two mats were close to each other. Depending on the wind direction, one mat would use right turns to a landing while the other used left turns to a landing. Usually only one mat would be in heavy use at a time. For station utility aircraft, there was also a runway to use. Station pilots had a twin-engine Cessna known as the "bamboo bomber" for utility flights.

Some weeks, students flew in the morning and went to ground school in the afternoon, and other weeks it was the reverse. The wings alternated the use of the ground training facilities and ground school instructor personnel.

Pilot training involves an introduction to the cockpit and to the instrument panel. The Stearman had a simple instrument panel. There were no radios to contend with. Gas was gravity-fed to the Stearman engine. The all-important gas gauge was the simple sight gauge inherited from the automobile.

I remembered thinking back to a rear car window in the 1920s when my Dad pulled into Coapman's Gas Station on Main Street, next to the New York Central Railroad tracks, in the western New York State village of Brockport. There was a line of five tall metal stands, each with a glass cylinder surrounded by a wire enclosure on top. There was a window in the mesh of that wire enclosure. The transparent sides of the glass cylinder revealed its contents, gasoline, in various shades of light yellow or light red, depending on the gasoline company whose pump was ready to deliver gas to a customer. The glass cylinder had numbered horizontal lines. Those lines marked the gallon levels in the cylinder. The attendant responded to Dad's wish and lowered the level in the glass by the called-for number of gallons as he let the gas flow by gravity into our car's gas tank.

Early airplane gas gauges were like that, just smaller in scale. The Stearman gas tank gauge was not a remote electronic indicator on the instrument panel but was directly connected, liquid-wise, with the tank. And considering the many engineering years in between, it was a surprise to find liquid gas in the sight gauges in the first operational plane I was to fly, the PB4Y-2 *Privateer*. But at least that later aircraft had "modern" fuel flow meters and fuel pressure gauges.

I was assigned to the North Wing at NAS Ottumwa for primary flight instruction. Verschoyle is the name on the first page of my first aviator logbook is. He was my first flight instructor pilot. He came from Dallas, Texas. He had over 10,000 hours of flight time, unusually high in any aviator group in 1944. Together, we began my A-stage flight training.

W. Rowe Verschoyle began flying in 1927 at age fifteen at Love Field in Dallas. That year marked the historic transoceanic flight of Charles Lindbergh, and it represented the passage of a half generation of U.S. life after World War I. With his extensive flying experience, Verschoyle received a direct Navy commission as a Lieutenant (junior grade) at the outset of World War II. To get his Navy wings, he was still required to complete the Navy's Primary Flight Training program at NAS New Orleans. He was then ordered to NAS Ottumwa as a primary flight instructor.

By the time Rowe Verschoyle (his first name was Walter but his family knew him as "Rowe") instructed student pilots at NAS Ottumwa Iowa in 1943-44, he was then a generation older than his students. He carried the aviation torch between the two war generations. Had there been no wars, he would still have had a major impact on aviation. But, there were two wars. The second of these two war-generated surges of U.S. aviation activity benefited enormously from civilian pilots like Verschoyle who provided a bridge from the World War I cadre of aviators to the World War II generation of aviators.

Verschoyle was an excellent instructor and I made good early progress. He could make the Stearman bi-plane do things that I never mastered. He later became a Senior Check Pilot in the Naval Air Training Command.

During the latter stages of our flight class' training days at Ottumwa, a three-man Standardization Board came to the Air Station. Those boards consisted of Senior Check Pilots. They gave standardization flight checks, not to the student pilots, but to their flight instructors. A number of flight instructors disappeared from our flight schedules during these Board visits because they did not pass those check flights. Although the Verschoyles of military flight training were important to their students, their greatest influence came from the standards of piloting and pilot instructing they set for the thousands of flight instructors hurried into the flight training commands. Here now, 60 years later, as pilot turned author, a belated thank you to the Navy's instructor-pilot standardization effort in World War II.

My student pilot good luck streak in the fall of 1944 soon ran out. Instructor Verschoyle was transferred to another command. And the Flight Standardization Board that might have made my life easier had not yet arrived at Ottumwa.

Verschoyle's replacement as my flight instructor was one of those men who had taken up the wrong employment. He, like Verschoyle, had come from civil aviation. He interpreted his Navy Officer's commission to mean that he not only had skill seniority but also rank seniority over his students. He had not counted on having a fleet officer as a student. I was already a Lieutenant USN. This man seemed unprepared to teach flying to a man almost his age, especially a man who had no special aptitude for flying.

In the Stearman aircraft, "gosports" were used for pilot-to-pilot communication. The gosport consisted of a plastic voice tube connected to an instructor's mouthpiece and connected at a student-pilot's end to earpieces on the flight helmet. Instructor mouth to student ear. One way! The instructor sat in the front seat and student in the rear seat of the Stearman aircraft.

A few of the Navy Stearmans had cockpit enclosures for cross-country flight but the early student stage N2S trainers all had open cockpits. Some had metal propellers and some had wooden propellers. The more skilled pilots could tell the difference in flight. Lycoming or Continental built the 220-hp radial engines. The propellers came from Hamilton Standard.

This new instructor was known in the flight training trade as a Screaming Eagle. He yelled constantly into that voice tube which led directly into my ear. There were sufficient reasons for his nervousness when our aircraft was one of perhaps fifteen Stearman trainers in various stages of takeoff from the north mat of NAS Ottumwa. With me partly in control (I could feel his hand on the stick and his feet on the rudder pedals at all times) our wings would wobble and the plane would bob up and down and the airspeed needle was never steady. Later, during the same flight, at a comfortable altitude and with few planes in our vicinity, he still yelled. All the early progress made with instructor Verschoyle began to melt away. Confidence waned. I fell behind my class and had to ask for an extra flight period. The onset of severe Iowa winter weather exacerbated the Mediterranean cough I had brought back to the States. In desperation, I went to Sick Bay for a few days. "Cat fever" was the immediate diagnosis.

That was a standard diagnosis at Navy medical facilities, no matter what the patient had. I learned later with some relief that "Cat" was an abbreviation for Catarrhal. (And much much later I learned through my discharge X-ray at Chelsea Naval Hospital in Massachusetts that I had a blotch of TB in one lung from those Mediterranean days. Fortunately, it is encased in calcium and dormant, but I cannot pass a TB patch test.)

A sick bay stay would entitle a student to an extra flight training period. That would not be enough to salvage my effort for Navy wings. I got up my courage and asked for a new instructor. My request was quickly granted, which surprised me.

The third instructor was a brand new 2nd Lt. Marine officer. He had just obtained his aviator's wings along with a few extra flight hours in the same Navy flight-training program that I was undergoing. His name was Johnson and his first objective was to land the Stearman going backwards. He almost made it happen one windy day at an outlying grass field with the wind gusting to 45 knots. Thankfully, his second objective was to get me qualified.

While not typical of the student resource pool best suited for military flying, I was able to take advantage of a war-forced change that affected all primary flight students in the Navy programs in late 1944. U.S. Navy combat ships in the Pacific war abruptly found themselves recoiling from the fatalistic vigor of young Japanese Kamikaze pilots. "Picket" destroyers were being sunk every day.

The students in a military flight-training program have a way of knowing when local check flight success/failure rates are undergoing change. It was clear to the mid-stage student pilots in the summer of 1944 that a program had been in progress in the Navy's primary flight training program to thin out the student ranks. The war had been going favorably and the over production that military programs always generate was producing more pilots than needed. Student pilot "washouts" were the order of the day.

That attrition program was suddenly canceled. The pace of training picked up and many of us who had been mired in A-stage training quickly progressed beyond our solo check flight and were allowed to solo. B-stage training, for recovery from spins and stalls and learning how to avoid them, was accomplished in short order. The Kamikaze pilots took a severe toll on U.S. Navy personnel in the Pacific and saved many stateside naval aviation careers. The Armed Forces have never found a way to go back and redress inequities. So, those already washed out of flight training rarely got back in.

As student-pilot experience increased, wing tip scrapes on the mat became less frequent. At Ottumwa, many of the yellow

Stearmans were fitted with curved wooden struts. Made out of plywood, these struts extended below each lower wing tip to protect the wing fabric when the student would land and swerve into a ground loop or otherwise cause a wing to go down and scrape the ground. Interestingly, snow was welcome because then the wing would scrape snow and no damage would result.

Even with the unannounced lowering of student attrition rates, the dreaded C-stage almost proved a downfall. Flying "figure-eights" around two pylons on the ground with a strong wind aloft was difficult for good pilots. Again, the pressure of those Kamikaze pilots was transmitted to our instructors to mean that we were permitted to continue in the program even though our figure-eight might be a little bulbous or elongated. Throughout my flying days, though, discomfort always existed when the flight requirement called for a very tight turn. The feeling is much like an Interstate Highway trip at 65 mph or more. Sometimes the curves are not engineered for that speed and those in the car can "feel" it if the driver does not slow down.

For the "seat-of-the-pants" aspect of flying, the lesson from Primary Flight Training that was most useful in later flying was the instructor demonstration, followed by student practice, of "slips" to a landing and "crabbing" to a landing. Conscious use of one or the other of these techniques in a visual approach is designed to keep you flying down the imaginary downwind extension of the runway centerline as you approach the runway in a crosswind. Slipping involves dipping the wing into the crosswind and holding a little top rudder. It gives a higher sink rate, sometimes useful but can be harmful if not checked at the end, and it increases the speed at which a plane will stall. Crabbing keeps the wings level and the plane's heading cocked into the wind. Both techniques keep the plane down the centerline. At the point of touchdown, to avoid wiping out the landing gear, the crab maneuver heading is swung back to runway heading and a sort of combo effect is the result, with the upwind wheel touching a bit before the other.

It is getting ahead of our story but remember, "crabbing." On an instrument approach, the aircraft is crabbed into a crosswind in order to stay on the line of approach to a runway. When the pilot "breaks contact" and looks straight ahead from the nose of the plane, he or she is not looking down the runway line if the crosswind is strong and the "crab" is several degrees to the right or left. That is momentarily disconcerting until the pilot looks at where the airplane is actually going and begins to see familiar reference points.

Primary flight training in the Navy was done in five stages, A, B, C, D, and E. All stages and all later flying benefited from good execution of slips and crabs. No matter the mission, an aircraft ultimately has to land someplace.

At the end of A-stage, the student pilot was permitted to fly solo on practice flights and not constrained too much on what he might do. He was given an area in which to fly and a minimum and maximum flight altitude but otherwise informed to just check his wristwatch and come back by the end of the period.

B-stage was for spins and stalls and progressive stalls. The "falling leaf" was a maneuver in which the plane was successively stalled, first to the right, then to the left. One student at Ottumwa got so intrigued with this sequence that he neglected to check the approaching ground underneath, and met his death as a result.

Instructors thought it humorous to take a student up high and invert the Stearman and then tell the student to adjust his seat height. Of course, the seat fell to its upper stops for upright flight, and the student-pilot felt he was on his way out of the plane, while the instructor was laughing up a storm. Those instructors sure trusted the mechanical stop latches of that seat adjustment. Or perhaps they were trusting the student's ability to use the parachute in the seat pack on which he was sitting and to which he was harnessed at all times when airborne.

C-stage was for aerobatics. Maneuvers like snap rolls and Immelmann turns and loops and wingovers and even chandelles were handled without difficulty, but as noted, the figure-eights on the pylons almost put me out.

D-stage was for a flight check on everything to date.

The flight class was now in the dead of an Iowa winter and for E-stage cross-country flights, those still in the program were given a Stearman equipped with a canopy. The object was to plan and execute a solo flight away from home base. Charts were provided for Visual Flight Rule flights to a choice of several optional towns or cities. The first cross-country for this pilot was a round robin flight with no stopover, to Mt. Pleasant, Iowa thence to Iowa City and back to Ottumwa. The final check flight was a stopover flight to Moberly, Missouri and return.

Moberly had a nice field and I drew a fine day for the flight. As a born conservative flyer, I chose the Moberly option because the city was on the same North-South section line as Ottumwa. Section lines occur in the regularly spaced mid-west farmlands where one farmer's north-south fence meets the next farmer's land and fence. All the check points from the knee-pad chart, railroad tracks, rivers and road intersections were spotted during the flight but the section lines were an extra security blanket. The flight to Moberly, landing, servicing, and return to Ottumwa took three hours. This pilot's log shows that my flight time in the Primary Flight Training program involved 100.2 hours flight time of which 58.6 hours were recorded as "solo." No other person in the world that day in early 1945 knew that a Navy Lieutenant had landed at Moberly, Missouri but the Lieutenant was quite pleased with his accomplishment.

So, a combination of forces entirely remote from Ottumwa, Iowa, plus good instructor pilots had seen me through. With good fortune on the weather on the days my wing was scheduled to fly, there were no accidents or even incidents to mar the flight record.

W.T. "Barney" Rapp, a fellow student and fine pilot, was involved in an "incident." It occurred during night qualification in the Stearman biplane. Our wing had qualified for day solo flights by that time. An instructor acting as check pilot went along while each of us made one night landing. That landing was made by the student from the rear seat, with check pilot in the front seat. The area for touchdown was defined by a square of four flare pots. Except for the rotating beacon at NAS Ottumwa's tower, there was no other light. The night was overcast, no moon, no stars, very black.

Night flying is an accomplishment. Night takeoff and landing qualification, a step up the ladder in flying, was being handled in this program in one adventuresome night.

With obvious relief, those check pilots exited the front seat as fast as possible after the student had made that first night landing. The student secured the harness in the rear seat and climbed into the front seat. The student was then alone. Even from the front seat, the forward visibility from the Stearman cockpit was not good, certainly not for taxiing (fishtailing was advisable) and not much better when flared out for landing.

After the final landing, all student pilots were required to taxi back to the parking apron. It was still pitch dark with no horizon, no stars, just overcast. A station crew had left a truck parked in the taxiway and Lt. Rapp's wingtip nipped the truck in the dark before he spotted it. Students are always at fault. As his penalty, Rapp had to go out and re-qualify again the next night with four more perfect landings.

There were two sections of Stearman aircraft in the night flying qualification at Ottumwa. The upper section of six aircraft circled while the lower section of six made four landings each into the square of flares; then, the sections traded positions.

My aircraft was assigned to the upper section for the first half of the evening. The planes were supposed to fly loose formation, port wing toward plane just ahead, while the whole section circled the base in a lazy left circle. The base airport was next to the city of Ottumwa. The city had a hotel at its center. The hotel had a red warning light on its roof.

I "flew wing" on that roof light for a few minutes before I realized that the geometry was not working out and the other planes were circling over the landing flare pots at NAS Ottumwa. Hastily I joined them, chagrined at my error, and hoping that no one had noticed.

Then, our section descended to the lower landing pattern altitude for our four tries at the flare pots. It was left turns to a landing. At the 180-degree point (abreast the beginning of an imaginary landing runway, but on the reverse heading, going downwind), just before turning in to the flared square, we were supposed to "cut gun." This meant retarding the throttle. We were to show how we had learned to trade altitude for air speed and land just like a carrier pilot. I plopped my Stearman into the flare-square the required four times. One time, I was off heading, got it into the square of flare pots OK, poured on the throttle to climb out and as the nose went down I could see that I was heading directly for the fire truck whose occupants were leaping off in all directions. I lurched into the air and over the truck wondering if I'd botched it. I had to assume later that those in charge, in deference to the fire truck crew, decided it was best to give me an "up" after that first night. No sense testing fate again for those in the fire detail.

"Barney" Rapp became a Vice Admiral in the U.S. Navy. He is gone now after an illustrious career. He was a fine father, husband and family man. He was a natural born pilot from beginning to end. Barney's career included command of patrol squadrons in the North Atlantic. These were home based at NAS Brunswick, Maine and deployed on operational patrol tours to a U.S. Navy airbase in Iceland during the Cold War. Several tours along that North Atlantic rim, added to his outstanding aptitude, confirmed him to be more than your average instrument pilot.

Two pleasurable events relieved the intense ground school and flight school routine at NAS Ottumwa. Tour groups were booked in for an evening's entertainment. One evening I was able to take my wife Peggy to a dance. The bandleader was Frankie Carle. (His obituary at age 93 appeared in the Springfield (MA) *Union-News* in early March 2001) His band was quite well known in the 1940s and its stature was enhanced by Mr. Carle's ability to play the piano. The other event was a visit by the Harlem Globetrotters. A man named Reese "Goose" Tatum was a headliner of that group. Those events helped relieve tension and I appreciate to this day all those who contributed to those troop entertainment tours.

At the completion of Primary Flight Training at Ottumwa, many in that primary flight training class were ordered to advanced flight training at Naval Auxiliary Air Station (NAAS), North Whiting Field, in Milton, Florida. The first leg of my train trip was on the Missouri Pacific railroad. From its loud speakers, rail passengers learned of the death of President Franklin D. Roosevelt at Warm Springs, Georgia, in April, 1945.

One of the first duties at Pensacola was to become qualified in the water to improve survival chances in case of a ditching at sea. There were a number of tests for swimmers to pass in the NAS Pensacola's Olympic size pool. The tests of concern were: swimming a mile, and a trip down the Dilbert Dunker. The mile swim was made easy because student pilots could use any stroke and take as much time as needed.

The Dilbert Dunker was another matter. The device consisted of perhaps six or seven feet of the pilot's section of a single engine aircraft's fuselage. With the pilot in full gear, strapped in, and canopy closed, the contraption was sent down a steep rail into the water. Once in the water, it immediately rotated to the upside down position. The occupant had to get the canopy to slide back, and with water rushing in, had to get out of the seat straps and then out of the parachute and its harness. The trick was to mentally remind oneself that the initial posture was upside down. The student was to go down first to clear the sinking plane, then to the side, and then up to the surface. For those with Red Cross lifesaving experience, it was not too difficult. Some men, who had passed all the checks of primary flight training, failed this test and were "washed out." Figuratively, and literally.

The class of student pilots that preceded our class in the next phase of Navy flight training, known as basic training, had trained in the SNV aircraft. The V was for Vultee. Our oncoming class was lucky to be assigned to the more advanced SNJ for training. The Army Air Forces called it the AT-6, the *Texan*. The SNJ was a single engine, two seat low wing monoplane built by North American Aviation. It was an all metal plane and had retractable wheels. There are some SNJs flying in our new 21st century. Recall that most students had just come from the Stearman, a fixed landing gear trainer. A number of the SNJ instructor pilots had also just come from instructing in Stearmans. (Gussied up Stearmans are also flying today.)

One night, while waiting for a night flying turn at North Whiting Field at Milton, Florida, we saw an SNJ come in for a night landing, flare out for touchdown, and land in a shower of sparks, like a sparkler on the Fourth of July. An instructor with student aboard had landed with the landing gear up. All waiting students were of course sorry for the student-pilot but inconsiderately though understandably had less sympathy for the instructor, who really needed it. His Navy flight career was probably ended.

One of North Whiting's outlying fields used for practice landings and takeoffs was a grass field called Pace Field. It seemed risky for the training command to expose the brand new silvery SNJs in the hands of student pilots to touch-and-go landing practice in a cow pasture. In this stage of training, students were also introduced to formation flying and briefly saw themselves as fighter pilots. At North Whiting, student pilots who were headed for multi-engine training began intensive sessions in the Link Trainer.

Under the heading, "Instrument Training," NAVAER publication 80R-19 published in January 1946, stated that the Navy recognized "the combat necessity for instrument flight training" by establishing two schools at NAS Atlanta, Georgia, in 1943. One was the Link Instructor School, where enlisted Waves were trained for 10 weeks in and on the Link Trainer, covering attitude (flight attitude), instruments, code, radio range and direction finding so that they could move on to other training stations and teach Naval Aviator candidates instrument flying in the Link. At the same station, the Navy established its first Instrument Flight Instruction School (IFIS), turning out 100 instructors every six weeks after a program of one hour of Link training and three hours of actual flight per day.

Like the Link instructors, these instrument flight instructors were also sent to appropriate air stations to spread the word.

Let me take a few lines here to refresh the time line. That Navy Instrument Flight Instruction School was formed in 1943. The "Northeast Airlines Reference Manual for Instrument Flight," was *revised* in July 1943 after Northeast moved its instrument flight ground school and flight school and its whole Training Division to Burlington, Vermont. A formal instrument training effort had been underway at Northeast since the late 1930s. Northeast was training pilots, and already had trained instrument pilots. Robert Mudge, the Northeast pilot and author whose book was referred to in an earlier chapter, is listed as the Meteorology Editor of the Northeast reference manual, a copy of which he loaned this author for help on this book. The airlines had formalized instrument flight training a few years before the Navy instrument instructor program was instituted in Atlanta.

The Preface of the Northeast Airlines Reference Manual states: "Therefore, this Manual will deal with instrument flight as the basis of all flying, not merely as a means of flight when the natural horizon is obscured. The operation of power plant and the use of radio and other accessories will be covered from the viewpoint of their use by the pilot, and the theoretical and mechanical details will be discussed only to the amount necessary for a pilot to understand proper use of the controls, and proper interpretation of the instrument indication."

For the Navy's aviation training program in 1944-45, students who were programmed to go on to multi-engine flying received their first multi-engine instrument training in SNB Beechcrafts at NAS Corry Field in Pensacola. The Beech, a D18 in civilian life, had two radial engines, a low frequency radio range receiver and a radio direction finder (RDF) to home in on low frequency radio transmitters. There was also a navigator's station with a basic plotter and drafting board. Some of these planes even had a little astrodome. Putting that astrodome to use, students could learn to use the bubble octant instead of the sextant used for celestial navigation on board surface ships.

The Triumph of Instrument Flight

At NAS Corry Field, ground school continued to include long sessions in the Link Trainer. The device simulated flight on instruments even to the point of "crashing" if the pilot failed to grasp the technique of flight through instruments. In actual flight, instrument training involved a hood that was placed on the student's head. The hood denies the student pilot windshield vision and restricts sight to just the instrument panel. Hooded flights, even if the pilot under the hood has mastered the art of instrument flying, are dangerous because half of the visibility arc in the cockpit is lost. The practice of "see and be seen" finds part of that duty compromised.

Our first student pilot "twin Beech" cross-country flight was a round trip from Pensacola to Houston, Texas. As part of learning, the aircraft landed, was gassed, the two pilots filed a return flight plan and came back feeling pretty good about their accomplishment. An instructor pilot named Swinney, likely a graduate of that Navy instrument instructor school at Atlanta, gave Barney Rapp and me our first in flight instrument instruction. He also gave us tremendous confidence by cutting one engine in all sorts of situations and making us learn to get back to a field and land on one engine. Turn into the good engine was the right answer. When the left engine was cut, the student pilot ended up making a right-handed landing approach for which his position in the right hand seat was ideal. Those were sweat jobs, not only because of the "engine out" challenge, but because Pensacola was a hot and sweaty place in the summer of 1945.

Pilots returning to Corry Field each morning from their homes or apartments or barracks were flying in the same wet flight suit in which they left the day or evening before. The fabric would not dry overnight in humid Pensacola.

The Beech became a lifelong friend. She was a sturdy little plane and in it, I survived some violent storms. Years later, one such flight found me flying with Ed Hogan. He had been one of my Alaska flight tour Commanding Officers and was a fine pilot. Ed had flown the 4-engine PB2Y *Coronado* seaplane and had had a full tour as Commanding Officer of a Gulf of Mexico hurricane squadron. The two of us almost met our fate together in a violent storm flying a JRB out of NAS Brunswick, Georgia, on an instrument clearance to NAS Anacostia in the District of Columbia. The JRB was one of the many Navy variations of the twin Beech.

Two older pilots joined our NAS Corry Field student pilot group during the latter phase of the twin Beech instrument training. These men had crash-landed their PV-1 (Lockheed) Vega *Ventura* on the Kamchatka Peninsula in Siberia sometime in late 1943. They had been on a bombing mission to Paramashiro, Japan. According to their briefing, since their gas load and the current weather meant that there was no chance for them to get back into Adak, Alaska, they were to head for a Russian crash landing or a ditching at sea once their bombs had been dropped. They did as instructed and were interned by the Soviets in marginal conditions and were confronted each day by hostile interrogators. Russia was not then a participant in the war against Japan. The Russians finally released them to the United States. The Navy flight training command was trying to move them on a fast track back to flight duty. The men were civil to us in all respects but extremely withdrawn. They could fly just fine but they reminded me of soldiers I had seen in the rest camps in North Africa, men who were physically fit but would never fight again. Combat had taken too much from them.

With about 50 others, I received Navy flier's wings on the tarmac at NAS Corry Field on October 16, 1945. A resplendent Commodore Lester Hundt USN, in full white service, pinned on the wings.

Except for the training commands, I never had warm weather duty. That graduation was perhaps one of the two or three times I ever wore an office"s white service uniform.

Two October 1945 dates remain forever in my mind. My wife, Peggy, gave birth to our first child, a boy, just two days before I received my wings.

Illustration 19 - A Navy pilot, with wings

The next duty was a short stint in a Bachelor Officer's Quarters (BOQ) at Cocoa Beach in Florida where a large group of new Navy pilots were quartered while assigned to flight duty at NAS Banana River, Florida requiring PBY-5A *Catalina* flying boats. This short assignment occurred in the Air Bomber Training Unit (ABTU). We did not fly the aircraft. We were in the back, next to the gun blisters. Our objective was to learn to use the APQ-5 bombsight.

We had one series of flights in the *Catalinas* where we used binoculars instead of twiddling the bombsight's cathode ray tube dials. Most of our ABTU class participated in the search for a flight of five Navy TBM (single engine, General Motors' manufactured, torpedo planes) aircraft that had left NAS Fort Lauderdale and never returned. (A helpful reference for finding more on this episode is the Navy's designation of the flight as "Flight 19.")A Naval Academy classmate of mine, a new pilot just as was I, was lost in that mysterious flight disappearance.

"George William Stivers, Captain USMC, already a World War II combat veteran of the 2nd Marine Division, while attached to NAS Miami and on a routine training flight on the afternoon of December 5, 1945, was lost in the vicinity of Fort Lauderdale, Florida."

That quote is the official announcement. Subsequently, it could not be ascertained whether the flight ever made it back to the Florida peninsula. Our *Catalina* (PBM *Mariners* also participated in the search, and one never returned) search flights covered a broad stretch of the Atlantic. Other searches covered the Gulf of Mexico. Lack of coherent voice radio contact, for the later period in which they should have been able to stay aloft, clouded efforts at assessment. Fuel starvation would finally have forced those young pilots down at sea one by one.

From NAS Banana River, most of our flight group received orders to NAS Hutchinson, Kansas. This new duty assignment was designed to advance a multi-engine student's flight abilities to include the heavier combat aircraft that he would be flying once assigned to the fleet. The organization that conducted this training was the Navy's operational training command. It involved flying the Navy PB4Y-2 *Privateer*, the student's first experience flying a 4-engine aircraft. This plane was the Navy's re-design of the Army Air Corps' *Liberator*.

This training foretold the type of sea duty most of the group was likely to get after completion of flight training. The path of training had actually begun to change when flight students entered the multi-engine instrument phase at Corry Field in Pensacola in twin engine SNB Beechcrafts. In that phase, we had begun our training not solely for the objective of getting an aircraft out and back safely. The twin Beech training at NAS Pensacola's Corry Field had been the beginning of our training for future operational missions in all-weather conditions. That path was now being extended one more step at NAS Hutchinson, Kansas, to an aircraft that was being assigned to fleet operational squadrons.

There were just two pilots on Hutchinson training flights. I was assigned as copilot for a young, aspiring, Patrol Plane Commander (PPC). Although our Hutchinson *Privateer* aircraft had a navigator's plotting board and an astrodome for viewing the sun and stars, there were no navigators in those Hutchinson flight crews. We flew with minimum officer and enlisted man flight crews. Flights were scheduled to develop the pilot's aircraft handling proficiency through an intensive series of touch and go landings and takeoffs, plus five or six hour round robin airways flights. We were not sent off in severe instrument weather. As in all earlier flight training, the objective was to master the aircraft first under favorable conditions before tackling weather.

For later operational flights, this 65,000 pound four-engine aircraft required eight to ten man crews. Later reflection brought home the fact that minimum crews meant minimum loss of life in training accidents. Training accidents in the flight training programs occurred too frequently.

On one Hutchinson takeoff, the recap on our 56-inch starboard tire came off and drove big holes in the starboard flap. Through the yoke, we could feel the nose wheel shimmying uncontrollably. A glance out of my copilot's right side window resulted in a yell to the novice pilot in the left seat that the right side-mount tire was shredded. ("Side-mount" was jargon for the landing strut with wheel attached.) The pilot aborted the takeoff and we came to rest at the very end of Hutchinson's 8000-foot south runway.

After the pilot explained to the tower what had occurred, that young patrol plane commander-candidate was ordered to taxi the plane back to the ramp. I took another look at that side-mount and the damaged flaps and we deliberated. He then called the tower and told them he was not going to taxi that plane but needed a mule (a little tractor-like vehicle capable of mounting a tow bar, and towing aircraft by attaching the bar to the nose wheel) to come out and tow the plane in. The tower finally gave in and sent out a tow crew. I was not professionally qualified to do so, but I would have given that young pilot an "up" for using his head in opposing a mindless order from a tower operator. I note now that my logbook for that episode shows one-tenth hour of flight time though our wheels never quite left the ground.

We then flew a few night round-robin "cross-country" flights to Texas and New Mexico to build up flight experience.

At Hutchinson one day, I was assigned to be a fill-in copilot for a flight to Wichita, Kansas to pick up repair parts. The plane assigned was a *Liberator*, the twin tailed predecessor to the *Privateer*. The *Liberator* was being phased out of Navy service. I can say to those who so bravely flew that aircraft out of the British Isles in World War II that I have flown the plane, too. The flight to Wichita took less than an hour. We did not keep our own flight logs. That flight was never entered in my logbook. Still, on 4/8/46 my logbook shows that I had been designated as qualified by the Training Officer of VB4 OTU #1 at NAS Hutchinson, Kansas as a copilot in both versions of the PB4Y, the 1s and 2s.

It seems laughable now, but apprehension about flying the *Privateer*, the first four-engine experience, was that my hand was not big enough to control four throttle levers.

For our group, it was then back to Pensacola for a second time. We were sent once again to North Whiting Field in Milton, Florida, for our final operational training in the *Privateer*, this phase to be with full flight crews. Before we would receive orders to operational *Privateer* squadrons, we needed Navy flight training experience that prepared crews for all critical aspects of the Navy's operational flight responsibilities. First and foremost, this involved navigating over long stretches of open water. For us, this meant *Privateer* flights with full crews from Florida to the lower Yucatan Peninsula of Mexico and return.

In those Gulf of Mexico training flights to Yucatan, pairs of pilots who had recently received their Navy wings were assigned to alternate as copilot and navigator. The Patrol Plane Commander (PPC) was also a student pilot but he had the advantage of many more flight hours than those of us who had gone directly from Primary to Basic to Operational training. In this training crew, I rejoined my Naval Academy classmate, William T. "Barney" Rapp. He and I were the alternate navigator/copilots for one of the three crews in our assigned "flight" at North Whiting field.

One of those Yucatan trips was at night and turned out to be especially memorable. The weather was 100% instruments and quite violent. We searched for an altitude that would smooth things out but the *Privateer* (no turbo superchargers on the engines, just a two-stage blower, therefore no altitude capability above 14,000 feet) was no match for Gulf of Mexico thunderstorm buildups. We finally elected to go down to 500 feet above the wind-streaked water and try to stay under the worst of the turbulence and take the brunt of the torrential rain. Those Gulf rainstorms were so heavy that the pilot's greenhouse would leak, sometimes generating a wet green wall much as one would experience if underwater.

The copilot rotating into the navigato's station was expected to take responsibility for the fuel flow valves that were on the bulkhead right behind the navigator's plotting table. There was a crew chief (plane captain) but in training, the enlisted crew might change from day to day. There was an array of four red valve handles with flow lines in red. Red lighting was used to keep our eyes dark-adapted while plotting the course at the navigator's table. Not much of the fuel system array was very visible under those red lights that we were using to see the charts. In fact, red lines on the charts could not be seen either. We had made our radar landfall on Yucatan and the aircraft was now headed back north, still about three hours from Pensacola. The #4 engine quit cold. A frantic search with a white flashlight showed a valve connection that seemed to agree with the empty level in a fuel sight gauge across the aisle. I rotated the valve handle to the position I figured would supply gas to #4 engine, and after some sputtering, it came back on.

Another flight during our second tour at Naval Auxiliary Air Station (NAAS) North Whiting Field, Florida, was memorable for its tragedy. Lt. John Bolthouse as Patrol Plane Commander (PPC), and "Barney" Rapp and myself as copilot/navigators were the assigned pilots in one aircraft crew of a designated flight of three aircraft. PPC designees Lt. Joseph Kohout, and Lt. Roland Edstrom, respectively, piloted the other two planes in our three-aircraft flight. Those two men had begun their Navy careers as primary flight instructors and had known each other before arrival at Whiting Field. One morning when our own aircraft was down for maintenance, the other two planes went off on a formation training flight that normally would have been a three aircraft flight.

I have no good answer to this day to the question of why the Navy would have put formation flight training into a program for Navy *Privateers* that would just about always search the ocean waters on single-plane patrol assignments. I can surmise that formation flying would have occupied much of the attention of the pilots of the two four-engine aircraft. Near Munson, Florida, the two planes locked wings and both crashed. There were 27 deaths, no survivors, and 20 widows in Milton, Florida that evening. An Associated Press article carried a Beedland, Florida, farmer's story that he saw a smaller plane strike one of the larger planes "in the tail" and that the larger plane then rolled over into its formation companion aircraft. From another report, it is clear that the "smaller plane" returned to its base successfully. The Pensacola morning paper of May 11, 1946, stated that the two PB4Y-2s were on a fighter familiarization training flight engaging in defensive maneuvers while an F6F *Hellcat* fighter simulated attacks on the formation. In the course of one dive by the F6F, the PB4Y-2 flying in wing position formation on the lead bomber rolled into the lead plane. The subsequent damage to the two PB4Y-2s led to uncontrolled crashes by both. The F6F returned to its base.

Many of us had struck up a friendship with Lt. (jg) Wallace "Wally" Jones, Edstrom's copilot, a genial Irishman from Boston. He was also in the copilot/navigator training program and was married. Events in those training days stopped for no man. There was not even an opportunity for us to express our sorrow to Wally's widow.

Through all this period of primary flight training, basic training and operational training, ground school classes were being held during the half-day that students did not fly. Meteorology, called "aerology" in Navy aviation ground training classes, was the most helpful subject and navigation the next most helpful. Not much was provided in ground school on power plants except for cockpit engine instrumentation, and even less was given on the innards of radio equipment. Some sessions on instruments such as the turn indicator, the gyro horizon, and the autopilot were helpful. A Pitot/static tube (this tube houses the external sensor for the airspeed indicator) lecture, especially dealing with instruments whose external sensors could ice up and give deceptive readings, was covered. Of course, getting the cover off the Pitot tube in the pre-flight check was emphasized. And to that training I can credit the observation I made to a stewardess to tell the pilot on a civilian passenger flight many years later that I could see that the aileron battens were still on when we taxied out.

I can still read more into the weather maps shown on the TV than the weather presenter seems able to understand. I must admit I cannot now recall the subtle meanings of the terms "wet and dry adiabatic lapse rates," except that they were measured in "degrees per thousand feet." "Occluded" weather fronts seem to have disappeared as terminology in modern meteorology. In navigation, those of us who came from shipboard navigation discovered that HO (for the Navy's Hydrographic Office) 218 tables for aviators were simpler to use than HO 214 tables for surface mariners. We could see why the bubble octant for aircraft celestial navigation replaced the sextant used aboard ship. The *Privateer* was equipped with Loran and we made use of the few Loran stations that were still maintained after World War II. Ground school introduced us to Loran. To get lines of bearing for navigation purposes, two Loran ground stations, each with a "master" and a "slave," needed to be operating. There was almost nothing offered in ground school on low frequency radio range station equipment and performance. We were informed that there were subtle differences between Loop and Adcock antennas sending out the "Ns" and the "As" of the radio range stations but not informed what those differences were. Some operating instructions for the Automatic Direction Finder (ADF) equipment were provided. Nothing was ever mentioned concerning how the accuracy of the bearings might be affected by the particular metal fuselage and wing structure of the type of aircraft on which the loop was mounted.

Information content can be in the form of intelligible voice, or numbers or letters in Morse Code dot and dash sounds. Important information content was the call letters identifying a navigation or communication station that was broadcasting. The information content on the 500 kilocycle (kc) distress frequency is the familiar Morse Code sound for SOS, dit-dit-dit (pause) dah-dah-dah (pause) dit-dit-dit, for the "S" and the "O" and the "S," respectively.

There were, as has been stated, differences between the civilian pilot's training and the military pilot's training. Those differences carried over into the respective instrument training programs. The differences had economic roots. General aviation pilot aspirants were pay-as-you-go investors and flight training took not just resolve, but money. The military trainee was not paying, but in fact was being paid.

Sharper in degree were the differences that became evident from examination of the instrument training program of a military pilot trained on the eve of or early in World War II and one trained during the war itself. Vital content had been included from the beginning. But, as time progressed, the major training change was to spend more time on each step. This occurred in the face of increased demands for military aviators up to about a year before war's end.

These comments emphasize the period of focus of this examination. We barely touch on the impact of sophisticated flight simulators that became so important in flight training and certainly in instrument flight training in the latter years of the 20ᵗʰ century.

For me, and I assume for most pilots, the aviator training program made some lasting impressions. I will offer a few.

One event in the early training program has remained etched in my mind. It was a movie on in-flight icing, a kind of hands-off simulation. Whenever local weather precluded flight-training operations, this film would be shown in the ready room. The aircraft depicted looked like a Lockheed *Lodestar* and was obviously a model. It was configured with "boots," rubberized material in the leading edge of the wings, and on the leading edges of the vertical and horizontal stabilizers. Pneumatic actuators would cause these boots to expand and contract.

When that *Lodestar* was flying through icing weather, and in the film the model jerked back and forth like a plane on a string which it probably was, the narration introduced the subjects of rime ice and clear ice. "Rime ice" should be left to build up on the leading edge of the flight surfaces (not too much of course) before actuating the "boot" to break it off mechanically. "Clear" ice was portrayed as so much of a hazard that the pilot had better think about landing somewhere as his first thought.

Propeller ice was not discussed because alcohol deicing and propeller blade heaters had not been developed at the time the film had been made. Failure to invoke the practices the film narrator advocated sent the model plane into a stall, a spin, and a crash, with accompanying disaster music. The action was depicted using rudimentary movie technology even for the 30s and 40s; the aircraft was cast in a dark and gray atmosphere, and the sound track spelled impending disaster. Unrealistic as it was, I occasionally still have a nightmare which I attribute to so many showings of that training film, most of which took place in the North mat ready room at NAS Ottumwa, Iowa in the winter of 1944-45. That rather crude film (my recollection is that it was a Jam Handy film) taught me to respect ice.

It served a useful purpose for the flying that I was going to experience.

One lesson of that film's memorable teaching came back to me many years after the events that make up the core of this story. In 1957, I was a "weekend warrior" (Naval Air Reserve pilot) commanding a squadron of twin engine P2V-6M (Lockheed *Neptune* aircraft equipped for *Petrel* missile launch) aircraft at NAS Niagara Falls, New York. *Neptunes* had the Wright R-3350 engines.

On this particular late winter weekend, the schedule called for me to renew my instrument card. The Navy had three categories of instrument flight qualification. The lowest was an entry level aviator's "restricted card." Until I received my wings, mine had been pink. After demonstrating higher proficiency, a Navy pilot was issued a "standard card," often referred to as a "white card" since these were all printed on white card stock. To those pilots demonstrating peak proficiency after many instrument flight hours, the Navy often issued a "green card."

At Navy air stations, a "green card" would let a Navy pilot take off when the destination weather was forecast to be at absolute ceiling and visibility minimums. For example, let's use 300 feet ceiling and one quarter mile visibility as the set minimums for a given destination airfield. With a "white card" I could be cleared if the forecast was 500 feet and one half mile, a little above minimums established for that airfield. Another privilege reserved for the "green card" pilot was that he could set his own takeoff minimums. Some very well qualified instrument pilots did not live to rue the day they exercised that privilege. The reason that takeoff, in near zero visibility conditions, is most often *not* elected by experienced pilots, is the potential loss of an engine on takeoff and the subsequent inability to reach any airport.

Weekend warrior (in my case, Naval Air Reserve) pilots and crews flew one weekend a month. Some years, particularly in the military services' gasoline budget economies of the 1950s and 1960s, we were restricted to just four hours of flying or even less in a given month. Louis Johnson, was an early Secretary of Defense who defined his tenure with the term "budget cuts." One of his cuts resulted in severe gasoline restrictions for all military aircraft. Except for the airline pilots who were also doing reserve duty in our squadron, most of us were happy just to be able to maintain "white card" instrument proficiency in the Naval Air Reserve.

A white card is the card I held when I found myself one forbidding Friday evening as Bud Britton, the instrument flight check officer attached to the Niagara Falls Naval Air Station, prepared with me for take off to NAS Sanford, Florida. Though a Reservist, Bud was on active duty and was getting in a lot of flight hours. He was courageous enough to let me fly as PPC in the left seat and he flew copilot. Not far south of Lake Erie, at about 8,000 feet over western Pennsylvania, we encountered icing. Clouds always persisted along the south rims of the Great Lakes for at least half the year but our forecaster had not put icing down on the briefing. Recalling that old Lodestar movie, I asked for a higher altitude and got 12,000 feet. We were still picking up ice. The wing heaters were not working but the propeller heaters, which were working, told us what our wing lights did not completely reveal about ice on the leading edge of our wings. The propeller deicers were electric and worked "on" and "off" in cycles. Near the end of the "on" period one could hear ice breaking off the props and hitting some part of the wing or fuselage. I was taught in that early film that the moisture that formed ice on a cold aircraft had to come from a higher elevation where it was warmer. The outside air temperature at 12,000 feet was indeed warmer than it had been at 8,000 feet. Since the wing heaters were not working, I needed to go up a bit more to prevent the ice altogether. I was reluctant to ask for a higher altitude because we were not using oxygen. I discovered that if I cheated about 300-400 feet above the 12,000-foot assigned altitude, the ice situation improved dramatically. That is what I did and Bud did not argue with me. We broke out into clear weather over Tennessee and made it down to the beautiful city of Sanford in Florida.

("Cheating" on an assigned instrument flight altitude is definitely wrong. One pilot might be cheating the "down" while another is cheating "up" and the safety margin in altitude separation is used up.)

As part of the instrument check that night out of Niagara Falls, though NAS Sanford was not that night on instrument conditions, I was to make a low frequency radio range let down. I made a beauty. On final approach, I made a jolting discovery. The field I was approaching was on the "wrong" side of the "low cone." I had looked at the letdown chart, and saw in my tired mind a mirror image of it, and executed the procedure accordingly. My check flight instructor had not noticed it. The folks on the ground were not tracking me visually or on radar, and there were no other flights within fifty miles. I had to sheepishly tell Bud Britton what I had done, while receiving landing instructions from the tower. Made a good landing and resolved not to fly at 12,000 feet without oxygen ever again.

I had encountered the oxygen lesson in flight once before in the Pacific northwest in 1947. Because it had happened to the other pilot, I assumed he slumped over into an apparent deep sleep simply because of his own personal anoxia (lack of oxygen) vulnerability. I assumed that it was a weakness that I did not have because on that occasion I had taken the controls and obtained clearance for an immediate letdown over Portland, Oregon under Air Traffic Control procedures. Another time, during my training in the oxygen pressure chamber at Norfolk, Virginia, the lady operator took 15 pilots up to 30,000 feet. Then, one at a time, each pilot took off the mask, and turned over a deck of playing cards, card by card, naming the card as he went. Most of us began to fail to identify cards properly about the 10th or 11th card. At this point, the pilot would be instructed to put the oxygen masks back on and the next pilot would begin the process. My companion that day, Harold Norman, a great friend and great pilot, instead of misnaming cards, began to convulse. The two of us closest to him worked furiously to get his mask back on and the lady in charge "pulled the plug" down to 15,000 feet. Ouch! The ears screamed for equilibrium. She then took us to ground level and Harold had to go to the local Naval Infirmary until he recovered.

The lesson, somewhat beyond the usual lesson, was that some folks undergo a convulsive episode out of the norm. One develops a lot of respect for oxygen.

At the end of the operational training period, it now being June 1946, the officers in our flight crew received individual orders to a command based in San Diego.

The long, long train ride on the Southern Pacific Railroad to San Diego seemed even longer when told that it was necessary to get on the Santa Fe Railroad and head north. The destination was to be one of the three operational squadrons that rotated from NAS Whidbey Island in the state of Washington to NAS Kodiak, Alaska. I was proceeding to VPB 107 at Whidbey and (unknown to me at the time) Barney Rapp had been ordered to VPB 120, also based at Whidbey. Our Patrol Plane Commander-in-training on the Yucatan flights had been John Bolthouse. When orders finally came to join operational squadrons, John went to a warm Pacific base while Barney and I went to Alaska. I never saw John Bolthouse again. He was a very good pilot.

Many Navy men have received orders that sent them on long trips to the wrong place while the high command was probably still trying to decide where the person should really go. It was a feature of Navy life and some thought it a deliberate ruse to confuse the enemy.

Chapter 10- Mission: Fly the Aleutian Chain

In June of 1946, Navy pilots and flight crewmen who had come from England, from the Azores, from the western Pacific, and from flight training bases in the United States joined three Navy patrol squadrons. These squadrons were being reconstituted as part of Fleet Air Wing Four (FAW-4) to pioneer a new mission. The place that they gathered was the Naval Air Station, Whidbey Island, Washington. This island is located in the Puget Sound. The main airfield was Ault Field.

The disparate geographic origins, of the commands from which these pilots and crewmen came to FAW-4, are reminders of dramatic U.S. military personnel shifts occurring in late 1945 and early 1946. By the thousands, World War II enlistees and draftees were leaving the service and returning home. Their accumulated "points" determined who got out first. Some of those who had elected to

209

remain on active duty came to Whidbey Island from Fleet Air Wing Seven based at Dunkeswell in England. A pilot I was to meet at NAS Whidbey in 1946 came from VPB 110 at Dunkesweell and another pilot that I was to meet much later through the process of writing this story came from Fleet Air Wing Seven's VPB 114, based in the Azores.

To bring a handful of remaining commissioned units up to strength required personnel searches for pilots and crewmen throughout the world. The result, not part of any plan for optimization, was to bring men together who had greatly different flight experiences.

Some came from ASW missions against U-boats in the weather-laden north Atlantic, others from missions over hostile but generally sunny waters of the south Pacific, and still others from continental U.S. training commands. These men and their new squadrons in Fleet Air Wing Four became a work-in-process.

Typical of military commands constantly forming and re-forming, the pace of the new events blotted out almost all exchange of information about past events. When one flew with a new pilot or new crewman, the subject of where he had served before and what he had been doing there almost never came up.

From the new squadron's forward base at Kodiak, Alaska, all flights except local practice landing flights would be instrument flights. Upon reaching the home base of Fleet Air Wing Four at Naval Air Station, Whidbey Island, a squadron pilot's focus would be on learning to be an instrument pilot in an operational aircraft while at the same time attaining proficiency in the aircraft itself.

We saw in Illustration 17 a view of the North Pacific Ocean with the Alaska Peninsula and the Aleutian Chain of islands. In the next illustration, we see the same expanse of sea and islands as the pilot of a transport squadron saw it just after the end of World War II. While Navy patrol squadrons often flew over open waters with few radio aids to air navigation, when ordered to institute a patrol from a temporary base, the crew would use a chart like Illustration 20 to make the transit to the new airfield on airways.

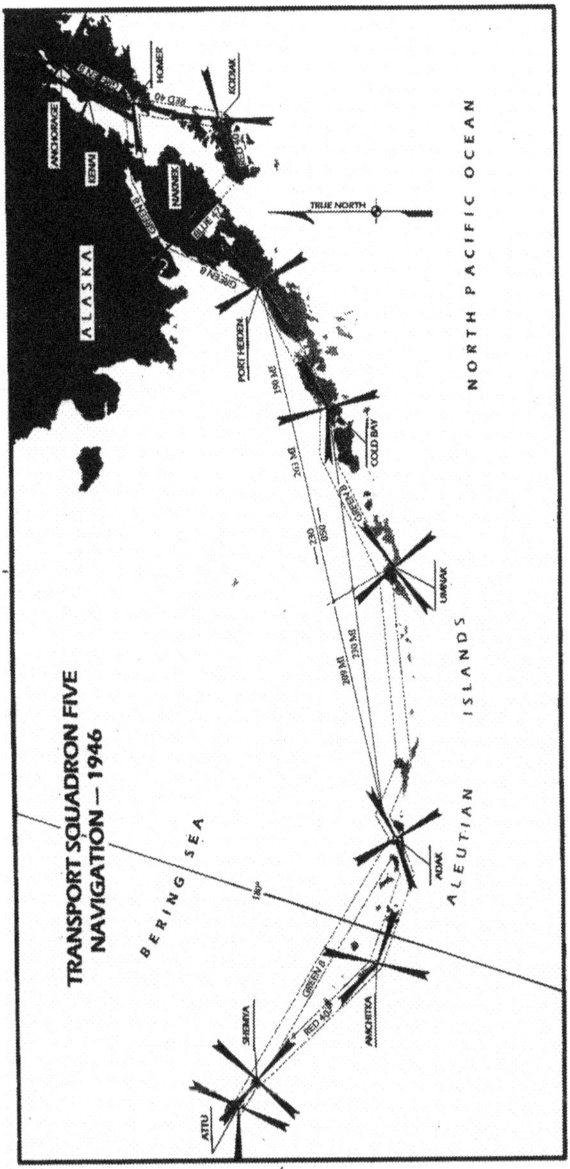

Illustration 20 - Aleutian Chain; Airways View

The airways view in Illustration 20 is based on a chart labeled for use of the navigation department of Air Transport Squadron 5 (VR-5). The squadron was a unit of the Naval Air Transport Service (NATS). The chart is a very early postwar navigation aid and was in use in 1946. The open water to the north (converging meridians) is the Bering Sea and to the south (diverging meridians), the North Pacific Ocean.

In 1946, VR-5 operated northward from Seattle to Kodiak and Adak. Military pilots, military transport pilots, and commercial airline pilots used charts like Illustration 20.

To the junior officers and lower ratings in the Naval Air patrol squadrons, no announcement of a mission still being defined was ever made. It is reasonable to infer from what took place, that whatever mission statement the new squadron commanders were given, it was brief, and not fleshed out in any detail. The "doing" would create the new mission. The operational flights would most often be over-water, off airways.

After an intensive training period of a few months that included over water flights, night and day instrument flights, and half-day "sweat-jobs" devoted entirely to touch-and-go landings, three PB4Y-2 *Privateer* aircraft squadrons were ready to participate in alternating rotation assignments, one squadron at a time, for duty in the Aleutian chain of islands. The forward home base was NAS Kodiak, on the island of that name on the south side of the Alaska Peninsula. Strictly based on its geography, Kodiak was not an Aleutian base, though it would be used primarily for Aleutian Chain patrol flights.

Winston Churchill, British Cabinet officer in WW I, and Prime Minister (PM) with responsibilities for the British Empire in World War II, had been, along with his Conservative Party, peremptorily dismissed at the end of World War II by British voters. Clement Atlee, Britain's first Labor Party PM in many years succeeded him. Churchill came to America, the land of his mother, and gave a remarkable address at Westminster College in Fulton, Missouri.

The date was March 5, 1946. The locale was not a chance choice. Missouri was the home State of Harry Truman, the U.S.

President who had succeeded Franklin Roosevelt. Truman and Churchill had met informally while Truman was serving as Roosevelt's Vice President and had met in Europe as principals at the Potsdam Conference. Westminster is an historic London locale. Churchill's address in Missouri introduced the U.S. public and the world to Churchill's historic characterization, the "Iron Curtain." Behind that curtain lay the Union of Soviet Socialist Republics, the USSR, a colossus that had been the United States' and Britain's recent ally in World War II in Europe, and for just a few days at its end, the war against Japan.

Winston Churchill followed the Missouri speech with a trip to Washington for a series of talks. In *The Forrestal Diaries*, we find Churchill, on 10 March 1946, in James Forrestal's office. James Forrestal was the first U.S. cabinet officer to hold the office, Secretary of Defense. Here are two excerpts from Forrestal's entry of that date:

"1. *Russia:* At three o'clock saw Churchill and was with him for an hour and a quarter. He was very gloomy about coming to any accommodation with Russia unless and until it became clear to the Russians that they would be met with force if they continued their expansion..."

"2. *Task Force in the Mediterranean:* He was very glad of our sending the Missouri (the U.S. battleship Missouri) to the Mediterranean but was very much disappointed when I told him that the plans to have this ship accompanied by a task force of substantial proportions had been abandoned..."

So, while the U.S. Navy's new North Pacific flying mission, on the verge of being implemented in the late spring of 1946, had no precedent, Churchill's vision, expressed in Fulton, Missouri and emphasized in Forrestal's office, was prophetic.

In the absence of any detailed instructions for conduct of the new mission, it is not surprising that what the Fleet Air Wing Four *Privateer* squadrons actually did when first aloft in their Aleutian patrol region was to fly patrols patterned after their World War II experience. Get out safely and get back safely. Conduct some sonobuoy exercises. First used in World War II, the sonobuoy was dropped into the water, usually from an aircraft. Floating there, it could "listen" for submarine noises, and rebroadcast the sounds it heard to the parent aircraft.

Gradually, for periods that lengthened as personnel learned to use airborne electronic countermeasures (ECM) equipment, squadron personnel chipped away at defining a new mission. No one then realized that the beginning of the Cold War would consume almost all of the next 50 years of the twentieth century. World War II patrol flight practices gradually disappeared. The over water flights became electronic countermeasures missions. The party of interest was the USSR.

The electronic countermeasures equipments served as the core tools for these mission flights. The term "snooper" is now used. It was never used in those days. Airborne missions were flown to detect Soviet radar installations, to log their frequencies, modes of use, hours of operation, and obtain bearings on specific locations. With bearings from a succession of plotted positions of our own aircraft, a "fix" could be triangulated for the Soviet's Siberian radars with moderate accuracy. Our aircraft had a radar frequency detection receiver with four crystals, each covering one of four frequency bands. The operator had to insert and remove these crystals one at a time. We had an electronic box called a panoramic adapter to more precisely determine their frequency once located in a band, and we had equipment to determine the bearing of the Soviet radar from our aircraft. We also carried an early jamming device but did not use it during my tour of duty. We were to remain "silent" with respect to our active jamming gear but surely the Soviets were "listening" to our own search radar transmissions.

Flight time and flight experience had marked some of the pilots for selection as Patrol Plane Commanders (PPCs). The rest of the flying officers would share duty as copilots and navigators. These duty-sharing flight officers would also deal with the increasingly technical orientation of the new mission requirements.

The radiomen, radarmen and junior officers who had to deal with the ECM equipment had almost no training on troubleshooting our ECM hardware and no training at all on its use for the mission. The experience they were about to gain would form the basis for training future men and women who would become the specialists not even envisioned in 1946. In the beginning, no one even realized that new talents were needed. While new military billet definitions were undoubtedly being examined in Washington military bureaucracies, even there the picture of what would become a protracted conflict had not taken shape.

For the more recent graduates of the pilot training commands, operational flight experience was being accumulated in 1946-48 in the Aleutians while the individual was still learning to fly. To them, the ECM mission was almost secondary.

My flight logbook showed 404.6 flying hours when I arrived at NAS Whidbey Island in June 1946. That flight time had been accumulated in single engine, twin-engine and four-engine planes at six U.S. Navy continental air stations, all in training.

Here are just a few more details on the PB4Y-2 aircraft in which the operational training had been conducted and for which new flight crews had been assembled for operational duty. The *Privateer* with a single tail (technically, a single vertical stabilizer which supports the plane's rudder) had evolved from Consolidated Aircraft's famed *Liberator* with its four engines and twin tails. The "Y" in PB4Y-2 was the Navy's alphabet designation for planes manufactured by Consolidated (which later became Consolidated Vultee Aircraft, short named, Convair), and the "P" indicated a patrol plane.

The *Liberator*, as originally configured for the U.S. Army Air Corps was, in Navy shorthand, a PB4Y-1. Both the 4Y-1 and the 4Y-2 were heavily defended with dual .50 cal. guns in nose and tail turrets, plus fore and aft crown turrets. The *Liberator* engines had superchargers to take her to altitude. Significant changes were made to convert the *Liberator* to the *Privateer*. The Navy's 1944 intention had been to optimize the makeover to the *Privateer* as the best land-based, long-range, Anti-Submarine Warfare (ASW) patrol aircraft that airframe, engine and electronics technology could create.

The Navy design, in addition to the change to a single tail from the *Liberator's* twin tails, added twin .50 cal. turrets in the waists to replace the *Liberator's* single gun waist blisters. The extra guns were mainly a consequence of anticipated further flight operations in the North Atlantic waters off Europe. Flight crews on this new postwar Aleutian duty rarely, if ever, fired those guns

Although both the *Liberator* and the *Privateer* were equipped with four Pratt & Whitney R-1830 engines, design engineers for the *Privateer* engines had eliminated the superchargers. These were replaced with two stage blowers so that sustaining anything above a 14,000-foot Air Traffic Control (ATC) assigned altitude clearance in a PB4Y-2 was impractical. The weight saved in eliminating the superchargers had been quickly used up in other changes to the Navy patrol version of the aircraft.

Based on World War II experience in the Aleutians, and the shortcomings revealed in earlier-assigned Navy aircraft employed in the campaign to dislodge the Japanese, a number of refinements made the *Privateer* a good choice for its new mission. Redundancy, or "back-up," was a consideration in aviation from its earliest days. The most obvious one is two engines instead of one. The *Privateer* had four. But for instrument flying in northern climes, the "hot wing" was the *Privateer's* great anti-icing attraction for its crewmembers.

Some less obvious redundancies for instrument flying were standard in the PB4Y-2. Here is a passage from "The Pilot's Guide" for the *Privateer*. "The pilot's gyro horizon receives its indications from a freely mounted gyroscope, which remains at all times in a constant plane relative to the earth. The gyroscope within the instrument is turned by atmospheric pressure rushing into its sealed base. The case is partially evacuated by a suction of 4-4.5 inches Hg (Mercury), drawn from the plane's vacuum system. The copilot's gyro is electrically operated."

The aircraft had two gyro horizons, and these had different power sources. There was also a third gyro horizon, the one associated with the Sperry Mark 3 auto-pilot. The indicator was on a pedestal between the pilots.

At NAS Whidbey, the three reconstituted *Privateer* squadrons inherited some of the North African based PB4Y-2 aircraft that had made their World War II debut late in the European conflict. These had their engine cowl flaps opened up so that the inside of the nacelles would stay cooler in the local heat. There were also screens in the engine intakes to keep sand out of desert-based aircraft. For Alaskan deployments, a retrofit was issued to redesign those desert cowl flaps so that they would snug down to the nacelle and keep heat in for cold weather flying. The desert sand screens were removed. The *Privateer* could not climb above much weather. It was a fully instrumented aircraft. Its limited altitude capability consigned the *Privateer* to flying in the Aleutian "soup."

As noted, the feature that endeared the *Privateer* to its crews in Alaska was its hot wing anti-icing system. For this hot wing, the *Privateer* paid a weight price in the form of a heat exchanger. For Aleutian flying it was a godsend. The result was an all weather aircraft, equipped with the best in flight instruments, radio and radio-altimeter, x-band radar, and a Sperry autopilot.

The sight gauges for the main wing fuel tanks were on the forward side of the bulkhead that separated the bomb bay from the forward main cabin. They were on the front side of the hatch, to the port side as one proceeded from the bomb bay to the cockpit. These were not electronic indicators or repeaters but old fashioned vertical glass tubes containing real aviation gasoline, the level of which told the crew the amount of fuel remaining.

Most flight crews were careful about gas fumes. Still, *Privateers* taking off the main runway at NAS Whidbey were occasionally noticed by onlookers because of the flash of a cigarette lighter in the cockpit while the wheels were coming up. The more careful pilots practiced being at cruise altitude in level flight and then requiring a "smell" test throughout the plane before the "smoking lamp" was lighted. Most command pilots would add an oral precaution to be especially careful while smoking. Thankfully, the *Privateer* was pretty good in that it was a rarity for gas "fumes" to be detected.

The *Privateer* could carry four self-sealing fuel tanks in the bomb bay, adding an extra 1,600 gallons of aviation gasoline (avgas). With the wing tanks holding nearly 2,400 gallons, the plane could top out just under 4000 gallons. For Aleutian flying, that gas capacity was the second best feature (to the "hot wing") of the PB4Y-2s. Its Pratt & Whitney R-1830 engines used 100/130-octane aviation gasoline. The squadron aircraft always carried the four bomb bay tanks and except for local familiarization ("fam") flights, these were always topped off before departing any base.

ECM (electronic countermeasure) equipment was originally installed in the PB4Y-2 as an adjunct to its ASW mission. This ECM equipment, an "extra" in ASW warfare, turned out to be the key to the new missions being flown in the North Pacific Ocean and Bering Sea.

"First" flights were the subject of the opening lines of this book. What follows is a short summary of one new flight crew's first flight from the U.S. base at NAS Whidbey Island, Washington to the advanced base at NAS Kodiak, Alaska.

The aircraft was heavy at takeoff and climbed sluggishly up over Vancouver Island. This came home to me with emphasis, after reaching cruising altitude, when I was told to grab the yoke and fly the plane. Hugh Burris, the PPC, informed me that he was going aft to look at our #4 engine outboard on the right wing to see if it would have to be feathered. In the process of "feathering," an engine is turned off and its propeller blades are rotated straight fore and aft to produce the least drag. This engine had been giving hesitation indications accompanied by puffs of white smoke.

Using a direct Canadian airspace clearance, our aircraft had managed to reach a cruise altitude to clear Vancouver Island's rugged mountain range by 2000 feet. Just to maintain level flight, the aircraft had to remain in its takeoff configuration of half-flaps throughout the first hours of the flight from NAS Whidbey Island, Washington. The flight was on instruments.

The plane's allowed peak gross weight for takeoff was 65,000 pounds and we had taken off with about 67,000 pounds. As Material Officer for the squadron, I had personally allowed the over weight condition because a Naval Air Station based R4D (Navy designation for the Douglas DC-3) that was assigned to carry some of our squadron gear to Kodiak was down for maintenance. I did the "Weight and Balance" calculations and our aircraft "balance" was in limits, but overweight.

What struck home with force in those few brief moments was that Lt. Burris trusted me to fly the plane while he went back to look at the engine. As we learned later, the master cylinder's piston rod of our #4 engine had failed. Burris made the decision to turn back to Whidbey Island, though he did not feather the engine because we retained some useful power on #4 until just over the end of the runway on our landing flare-out at NAS Whidbey. At that point, the engine quit completely accompanied by a big puff of black smoke, as fire engines raced down the runway behind us. Whidbey ceiling was 700 feet, visibility 1 ½ miles.

Pilot Burris, out of a World War II *Liberator* squadron at Dunkeswell, England, was a cool pilot. The crew already felt fortunate to be flying with him. The Navigator was Ensign Orville Hollenbeck, USNR, a very intelligent, serious and well-liked man. This crew also had an experienced plane captain (crew captain) in Aviation Chief Machinist Mate (ACMM) Sellers. If any of the other crewmembers felt fear in that first, testing, emergency for our newly assembled crew, it was not evident.

Ours had been the last plane in the squadron to leave for Kodiak. Navy 59645 was our number. Our hangar spaces at Whidbey had been vacated and another squadron had moved in. I strode back into our family's tiny living quarters, a half Quonset Hut, in Oak Harbor, Washington, in flight suit and harness, holding my chest pack parachute under one arm. I was not expected home. After all, I had departed very early that morning on three months deployment. My wife Peggy looked at me and nearly fainted. She had never seen all that gear before. She assumed that I had parachuted from the plane.

There was a QEC (Quick Engine Change) for the R-1830 on an A-frame at NAS Whidbey and in a couple of days we would be on our way again. We took a different route. Again, we did not make it to Kodiak.

Pilot Burris, copilot Dailey, navigator Hollenbeck and plane captain Sellers joined in readying the plane for the second attempt to catch up with the eight planes and crews of VPB-107 which had already arrived at NAS Kodiak, Alaska. The distress at finding our plane overloaded, needing half flaps, in a bit of difficulty over the mountains of Vancouver Island, Canada, with an engine spitting smoke, changed our flight planning for the second attempt.

We were still overloaded. But we would now exit NAS Whidbey Island as the patrol plane we were designed to be, by flying low out through the Strait of San Juan de Fuca to the great Pacific Ocean. We had decent weather, about 1,500 feet overcast. We passed Victoria B.C. on our starboard, with Port Angeles, Washington to port. We flew over the ferryboats that made regular trips between those two cities, as two were passing each other. After clearing the Strait, the aircraft turned northward just off the coast over the water. Vancouver Island was on the starboard side. The flight then proceeded northward, staying offshore of the Queen Charlotte Islands, to a position off Annette Island. There, we began the transit across the Gulf of Alaska direct to Kodiak.

For most of the way, the ceilings and visibility for this flight were much better than the ceiling and visibility we had for the first attempt. And the weather got better as the flight proceeded northward. The Pacific shore of Canada presents one spectacular land view after another. Abreast of Annette Island, we picked up an airways path to Kodiak. "Annette Airways, this is Navy 59645, turning for Kodiak." Burris climbed the plane to our assigned westbound altitude of 8,000 feet. In a rare Gulf of Alaska atmosphere of Ceiling and Visibility Unlimited (CAVU) condition, we could see some of the Alaskan coastline to the north as it arched out the entire Gulf of Alaska. The *Privateer* was not a speedy plane, cruising about 160 knots, so crossing the Gulf to Kodiak was scheduled to take about four hours if the prevailing westerlies were not too strong. And they were not strong on that day.

Just about on schedule, as we were getting our letdown instructions to Kodiak from Air Traffic Control (ATC), the Alaska Peninsula at the head end of the long chain of islands that would be our patrol region came into view. In that first sighting, on the near side of the Peninsula, we could see not just Kodiak Island, but the Naval Air Station Kodiak and its airfield. And its runways, a short one about North-South, and a longer one burrowed into the steep hills to the west. Clouds shrouded those steep hills, typical clouds that one sees around mountains. Hanging there, part of the decoration.

Then, in moments, like a mirage, fog rolled back over NAS Kodiak and the whole scene simply disappeared. Kodiak had gone "instruments." We made a low frequency radio range approach. At the Puffin Island marker beacon, no runway was visible from the cockpit, so Hugh Burris executed a pull-up to the left and elected to proceed to our alternate at Elmendorf Field, the Army Air Corps Base at Anchorage, Alaska. I copied down the revised clearance to Anchorage.

Navy 59645 and its flight crew were now going to learn first hand why Anchorage, Alaska, was the location of the alternate airport of choice for destinations at the eastern root of the Alaska Peninsula. Many flight hours to the west, the island of Shemya and its long instrument runway would become our preferred weather alternate at the far end of the Aleutian chain.

Proceeding northward, we made our checkpoints, mostly low frequency radio range stations or non-directional beacons. I recall Kenai and Homer, Alaska as two of them. Elmendorf Field weather foretold an instrument approach there.

The attraction of the Anchorage area for pilots, we would soon learn, was that it was rarely below minimums even though it did not boast outstanding weather for its ground inhabitants. During the outbound procedure turn on our instrument approach to Elmendorf, we broke under the overcast at about 2,800 feet. It was raining but the visibility was good. We came on in and Burris made a beautiful landing. The crew had been 10.4 hours on their second attempt to deploy to their new operational base at Kodiak. That island place began to seem elusive, and indeed even when we did get there, it still threw challenges at us.

In the next illustration, the reader can see that the procedure turn is a prescribed maneuver in a low frequency radio range letdown and approach typical of the era. "High cone" denotes the start of the outbound leg away from the airfield and "low cone" denotes passage directly over the radio range station on course toward the airfield. In between high cone and low cone, the aircraft is first outbound and after a "procedure turn" is pointed inbound (the left beam in the illustration). Passage over the low cone sets cockpit eyes straining (the right beam in the illustration) to see evidence of an airfield that should be directly ahead a defined number of miles or fractions thereof. "Miles" translates to minutes and seconds in the cockpit of an aircraft.

In most letdowns for this cockpit crew, the pilot in the left seat would make the instrument approach while the copilot would peer ahead and advise the pilot when he could clearly see the field. Then the pilot would "go contact" and make the landing while the copilot would go back on the gauges (pilots used the jargon, "gauges," to mean instrument indicators) to be prepared if anything went wrong and the plane had to make a pull-up. We already knew from study that for Kodiak instrument approaches, "pull-ups" also known as "go-rounds" had to be in progress long before the aircraft arrived at the edge of the instrument runway.

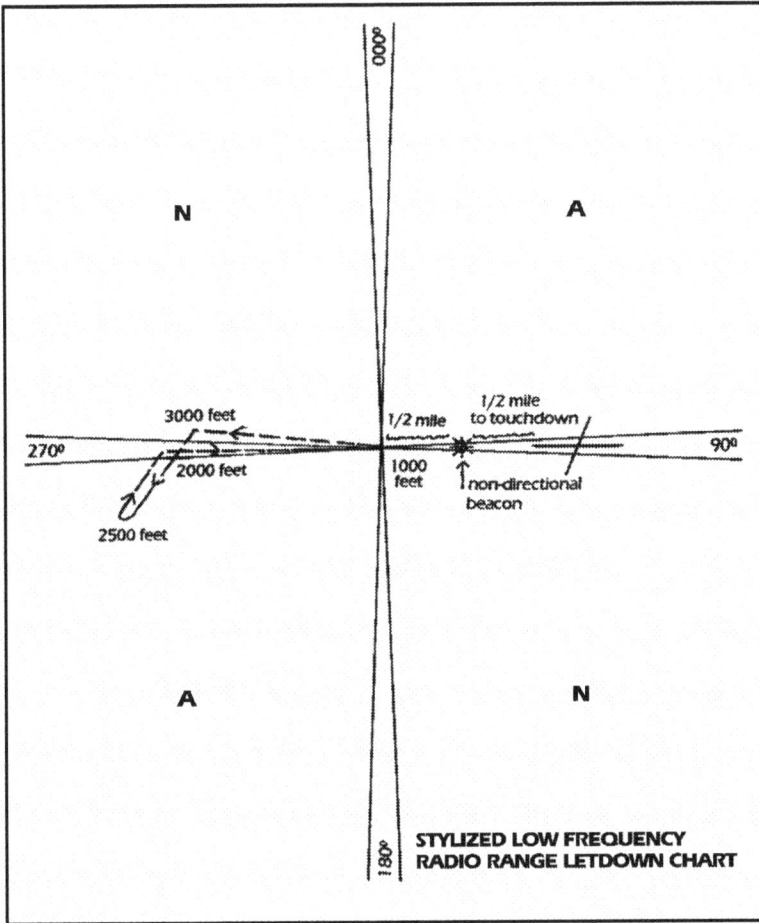

Illustration 21 - Radio Range Letdown Chart

It took another takeoff, and another instrument approach and landing back into Elmendorf, before we were finally aloft on a flight that led to an instrument approach and actual landing at NAS Kodiak, Alaska. On that approach, after flying over Woody Island in the soup, at the Puffin Island marker we broke underneath the

223

clouds and finally saw our new home's instrument runway ahead. PB4Y-2 59645 was in a position to land with wheels and flaps down. We had begun our odyssey on September 1, 1946 at NAS Whidbey Island, Washington and had arrived at our Kodiak, Alaska destination on September 11, 1946.

We were airborne 2.3 hours for the engine-failure flight on 1 September, 3.4 hours on a test flight of our new #4 engine at Whidbey on 5 September, and 10.4 hours on our second attempted flight to Kodiak on 7 September. The 10.4 hours included the run to our alternate at Anchorage, Alaska (Elmendorf AFB). Then, we were airborne 1.8 hours on the first flight out of Anchorage's Elmendorf for Kodiak during which air traffic control (ATC) turned us back to Anchorage, and finally spent 2.8 hours on the flight that actually got us from Elmendorf Field to NAS Kodiak. Total flight time, NAS Whidbey to NAS Kodiak, was 21 hours.

So much for the fast pace of the aviation era! That was not an unusual sequence in Alaska flying in the 1940s.

For the new challenge of flying Alaskan weather, the focus had to be in the cockpit. Things were never going well enough on the flight deck to suit me. Fortunately, other officer and enlisted contemporaries with whom I became associated in Fleet Air Wing Four adapted more quickly and began to work our operational missions while I was still adapting to the instrument flight challenge. The designation, Fleet Air Wing Four, shortened to FAW-4, had evolved from the prewar designation, Patrol Wing Four, shortened in those earlier days to PatWing-4.

Illustration 22 is a photo taken of a *Privateer* in the Aleutian skies with a fringe of "fair weather" Cumulus clouds in the background.

Illustration 22 - Navy PB4Y-2 *Privateer*

The Triumph of Instrument Flight

Although Navy patrol aircraft carried passive electronic countermeasures (ECM) equipment in the latter months of World War II, as an assist in the anti-submarine warfare mission, the use of these aircraft specifically for electronic surveillance had not been part of any long range plan. The *Privateer* was a fortuitous choice for such missions when the cold war began simply because it already had ECM equipment aboard.

It was not possible in real time, that is, while experiencing the pulse of day to day operations, for rank and file personnel to perceive that U.S. Navy aviation patrol missions in 1946 were in a change period. The day to day adjustments occurred in gradually changing flight profiles that evolved into a new kind of mission. No printed header on those flight schedules ever gave a hint of the change taking place.

Each patrol flight was briefed. These briefings were most often based on what the previous patrol had learned. Flight routes and altitudes were part of a "try it, and then see from the results what to do next." The men of these squadrons had little inkling that our Aleutian flights were a part of missions in flux for all U.S. military forces in 1946. These missions used airways only when transit was the assignment but spent much of their time aloft over the water using traditional celestial navigation aids and dead reckoning.

With full crew, Navy 59645 departed for Adak on September 19, taking 7.1 hours elapsed, with 7.0 hours instruments and an instrument letdown and approach. On the 20th the crew flew from NAS Adak to NAS Attu, a 3.1 hour flight of which 2.0 were instruments, including an instrument letdown. On the 21st, there was a 5.2 hour flight to Umnak Island., landing at Fort Glenn, all on instruments, including the letdown. After fueling, it was back to Kodiak, a 4.3 hour flight, of which 3.5 hours were instruments including a letdown. I recall that day particularly because as copilot I was responsible for checks on fuel usage and fuel remaining. I made a repetitive error in my calculations. After checking Kodiak weather and being informed of instrument landing conditions there, I announced to Burris that we would have to land at Fort Glenn on the way back to Kodiak for fuel, a stop that had not originally been scheduled on our eastbound flight plan. After overseeing the refueling operation on the ground at Fort Glenn, I was chagrined when the plane captain told me that the tanks all "dipped" full and we had taken aboard only a portion of the gas I had told Burris we needed. It was my arithmetic error, and it had caused Burris to make an instrument letdown at Fort Glenn to obtain fuel we did not need. I have thought about that mistake many times.

On the 30th of September 1946, with no navigator, Burris and I and a crew of eight made a 2.8-hour flight around Kodiak Island, all on visual flight rules. One highlight was "flathatting" (flying exceptonally low over) an enraged Kodiak bear that reared up on hind legs to challenge the low passage of the aircraft.

Navy aircraft squadrons that deployed northward from Whidbey Island just after the conclusion of World War II also had secondary missions. There was no United States Coast Guard presence in Alaska at the time. The Navy patrol planes were also on call 24 hours a day for search and rescue (S&R) missions.

Two days in November 1946 provided an experience that will always remain vividly in memory. Those were November 4, on which the crew of 59645, assigned temporarily to 59643, flew 5.8 hours to Fort Glenn on Umnak Island. And November 5, on which the crew flew 9.9 hours, all south of the Aleutian chain, ending back at NAS Kodiak. All of the 5.8 hours on the 4th were instrument. Eight of the 9.9 hours on the 5th were instrument, concluding with a night landing at Kodiak.

Both flights were "code Z" The definition in Navy Flight Symbol language, stood for "Flight not falling within any of the above classes, but which are required by the exigencies of the occasion." One of "the above" classes that the keeper of the logbooks passed up was code W, "Emergency or relief work." Using long hand under Remarks, our crew's log keeper had written "Search and Rescue" in my logbook to cover those two days in November 1946.

The Triumph of Instrument Flight

Those two days involved the full crew. Our regular plane was in the hangar for a 60-hour check. We were to be engaged in a search for three men in a self-propelled barge (BSP) that had broken from its moorings in a destructive storm that had moved through Ft. Glenn on Umnak Island. The barge, if still afloat, was presumed to be drifting helplessly and rapidly downwind in the North Pacific Ocean. The storm that had broken over the Aleutian chain was one of the most vicious ever experienced in a region of vicious storms. The barge had broken loose from its moorings with no warning while its occupants were asleep. Although the barge was designated, "self-propelled," its propulsion system never functioned to our knowledge during the entire period of terror those Army men went through.

Four of the flight crewmembers formed the core strength for this flying mission. These were the Pilot, the Navigator, the Radar Operator, and the Plane Captain. Our radar was the APS-15, "centimetric" radar, as the British called it during WW II. It was a close technology cousin to the SG radar aboard many Navy surface ships in the latter years of World War II. Its small antenna required only a small radome. A radome is a faired bulge sometimes on the underside of the fuselage. Ours was never a drag on the *Privateer* aircraft in flight. While not great in range, perhaps 50 to 60 miles reliably, APS-15 was a precision radar that could detect the smallest objects that could reflect electromagnetic energy. Submarine periscopes were susceptible to centimetric radar detection.

Our flight to Ft. Glenn had been hurriedly arranged and the briefing was short. We knew where the barge had departed from but had no idea of its drift rate. Weather would be our major challenge for the entire mission. We took off about noon for Ft. Glenn on Umnak Island in order to use that base as the launch point for our actual search assignment. Burris made a difficult radio range approach to the landing field at Ft. Glenn. We had been advised to keep our barometric altimeter setting frequently updated and to cross check regularly with our radio altimeter. An Army Air Corps Colonel, as local Ft. Glenn lore had it, made the same approach we needed to make at Ft. Glenn. The story was that he had rolled his wheels unexpectedly on a hilltop during the approach and made an emergency pull-up. He then discovered that the altimeter setting was not 29 point something, but 28 point something. Plunging barometric pressures, even below 28 inches, occurred often in the Aleutian weather picture. After the Colonel's near miss, the weather broadcaster's procedure would prefix a 28 point something altimeter setting with the words, "Red, Red."

In the flight to Ft. Glenn westbound out of Kodiak, over the west end of Unimak Island, with early darkness already upon us, the outside air temperatures plunged at our assigned airways flight altitude of 8,000 feet. Cylinder head temperatures plunged in response, despite our snugging down the modified cowl flaps. Number One Engine went below 100 degrees and began to lose power. Burris put down half flaps to slow the plane down and managed to keep cylinder head temperatures on all engines at 100 degrees or above, with the engines "putting out" thrust. Burris made an "at minimums" approach and landing at Ft. Glenn. Weary, we checked in, had a hot meal, and went to our assigned bunks for a short rest.

Up early, well before dawn, we finished our preflight, checked with the weather man, and received an "open" over water clearance with no fixed destination listed. A flight with no destination was a rarity and this is the only one I can recall. It was not a flight plan that would ever be accepted stateside by Air Traffic Control. We took off in the dark and headed southeast out over the North Pacific Ocean. Our flight crew was attuned to this challenging mission and all of our training at Whidbey and at Kodiak would be put into play this day.

NAS Adak had been busy on this search too. Lt. Walter Munk, USN (His full name was Maximilian Walter Munk. Most of his 'class of 1942' classmates at the Naval Academy called him "Max" but I always knew him as "Walter."), flying for a Navy PBY-5A squadron out of Adak, had been airborne the night before while we had been en route to Umnak Island. Adak is east of Umnak. I had known Walter Munk slightly at the Naval Academy, then a bit more at

Whidbey where his PBY-5A squadron had been home-based. Our Oak Harbor Victory Home overlooked the Saratoga Passage on which the waterborne PBY-5s had originally been based. With the advent of wheels for the PBY *Catalinas*, the seaplane base had been abandoned and the newly configured VP squadrons with PBY-5A amphibian aircraft had been moved to Ault Field right next door to our PB4Y-2 hangars. The Munk family lived close to us on that Oak Harbor hill.

Munk and his crew made the first aircraft sighting contact with the barge, the BSP that had drifted rapidly from Umnak to a point south of Adak. The visual contact was made in restricted visibility, under a very low overcast, with a driving wind and driven seas. Those seas can present a haze of water particles in the air. Even in the extremely poor nighttime visibility, Lt. Munk and his crew could see that the men were alive in the barge but that its freeboard was already dangerously low. It was taking water. The PBY-5A could do little for the barge but offer hope. Munk headed back to Adak for fuel.

Walter Munk's crew knew that their Loran fix data on the barge was fundamentally in error because they had determined that their Loran equipment was out of calibration. Wisely, Munk did not attempt to change the calibration when he discovered it out of specified norms, but went back to his base, refueled, and headed back to sea, now in the early hours of the 5th of November. He set out to find the barge again using the Loran coordinates he had recorded earlier with his Loran equipment still out of calibration.

Our barge search mission from Fort Glenn got airborne about the time Munk's PBY-5A, almost miraculously, using its errant Loran data in its errant Loran equipment, and allowing for the rapid surface drift, regained contact with the barge. Munk's crew this time had a raft and a "Gibson Girl" (emergency radio) to throw overboard as close as he could drop them to the barge. They came close, but there was no way the barge occupants, drifting helplessly, could bring aboard either emergency device. The barge would therefore remain out of touch radio-wise, while its freeboard would continue to

230

shrink. Significantly though, for the men on that barge, Munk's second aircraft visual contact had been made with them. Those Army men knew that the Navy was trying hard.

We overheard much of the voice radio traffic that Munk was broadcasting back to his base so we had an updated picture of the situation soon after our takeoff from Ft. Glenn. NAS Adak also sent us the best barge position coordinates they could calculate based on the PBY-5A crew's successive visual sightings of the BSP.

The overcast extended almost from sea level to about 10,000 feet. Our first APS-15 radar "contact" came when we were above the overcast still short of where we felt the barge had to be. We descended anyway, just to make sure we checked every contact. We broke out about 500 feet over mountainous waves with streaks running northwest to southeast. There we discovered an all-white Liberty ship headed for Siberia. The Russians were still taking supplies to Siberia in what had once been a U.S. Lend/Lease "bottom." It was ironic that our basic Alaskan mission was to be looking at them with suspicion. Back to 10,000-feet we went because we needed maximum range to the horizon to help detect radar targets and find that barge.

A descent through several thousand feet of solid overcast to find some visibility "underneath the overcast" is not a trivial instrument flying exercise. Approaching an instrument-equipped, manned, airfield with full tower facilities, pilots are given a succession of barometric altimeter settings for the landing field. When settings are received, both pilot and copilot reset their altimeters. The worldwide convention is that a standard setting of 29.92 inches of Mercury is assigned as the "standard" sea level reading. When it varies from that, and it almost always does, all air stations, knowing the height of their field above sea level, issue new altimeter settings. Presuming the setting is correct, when the plane touches down, its pressure altimeters should read the height of the field above sea level. Our *Privateer* was also equipped with a radio altimeter. These too needed to be kept in calibration and this was done by making sure that their reading matched that of the pressure altimeter when the latter is corrected as just noted.

When an aircraft goes to sea, there is no tower, and no surface weather station to provide pressure altimeter corrections. So, for these letdowns at sea one looks to the radio altimeter and is more confident if that instrument has been recently calibrated. The aircraft begins the letdown from 10,000 feet at perhaps 1,000 feet per minute, the gradually shallows the glide to 500 feet per minute.

Now the situation has developed where the plane has given up most of its altitude. If the radio altimeter reads 500 feet and the plane is still completely on instruments with no visibility and no ceiling detected, and needs to go down further to examine a radar "contact," the pilot shallows his rate of descent and goes down 50 feet at a time and looks hard for a cloud opening. How far down to go before calling it off? It is up to the pilot and the extent of the need. For all these long range over-water missions, patrol planes streamed their trailing wire antenna to get greater reception distance for radio communications equipment. This wire had a "pig" (a cast metal weight) on the end to make sure the wire streamed fully and did not just flap around outside the plane. The pig, and its connecting wire, stream behind the aircraft, and down. If a radioman under these circumstances discovers that he has lost his pig, one conclusion is that it hit the water and was jerked off. The plane is then below safe minimums and should certainly ascend at once. No one would recommend a descent on instruments to such a level but it has happened and the plane involved has pulled itself up from this dangerously low altitude. (This reminds me to add our radioman to the "core group" for this mission.)

Almost too much time seemed to have passed before our radar man reported the second radar contact. Navy 59643 descended again and discovered a surprise, not the barge, but a United States submarine, the USS Bugara, SS 331. She had been diverted from a Seattle destination (as we shortly learned from her by radio), to join the search for the barge. Bugara, a modern fleet submarine of that time, tossed uncomfortably on the roiled surface.

232

Aided by our radioman, our PPC, Hugh Burris, quickly established direct voice contact with the Bugara. With purpose governing his movement, Navigator Orville Hollenbeck came forward to the pilot's compartment. He asked me to estimate the true heading of the Bugara for him. I did. Our thinking navigator, while on top of the overcast at 10,000 feet, had put into service his bubble octant, the sun and moon navigation tables, and the single weak Loran station available. He had kept an accurate position of our aircraft moving forward. He had also used the best estimate from the Adak PBY-5A squadron's information of the BSP position at their last sighting and had advanced that position according to his estimates of the BSP's drift. Munk's calculations, first sighting to second sighting, were Orville's primary input on the drift rate of the BSP.

Orville Hollenbeck quickly informed PPC Burris that the Bugara would be unlikely on her present course to come upon the BSP. Orville suggested to Hugh Burris that he recommend a course change to the Bugara.

In the annals of ships and aircraft, I can tell the reader confidently that ships always felt they had the better of the navigation skill and often they did. A Navy pilot's air navigation training was diluted by pilot training. A shipboard navigator would hold his billet for up to three years doing little else. In addition, Navy ship navigators usually have equally skilled Quartermasters, rated petty officers, on their team. Ships almost always gave heading vectors to aircraft, not the other way around. Still, Burris did not flinch. He immediately contacted the Bugara on voice, and recommended that it change course 19 degrees to port!

The sub had been in the fog for days without any celestial navigation sights. Hollenbeck had been "on top and in the clear" for long enough to get good navigation data. The sub skipper, and I give him great credit, did not hesitate and immediately made the recommended course change. Burris, along with Hollenbeck, then established our present position as a new hub for the search and climbed back to altitude on a course different from the one Orville

Hollenbeck had recommended for Bugara. No need to duplicate search sectors. It was clear to me then that this one aircraft and this one submarine were the only hope, the slimmest hope, for three men on a sinking barge in a raging sea.

An hour or two more passed and we were now moving eastward to a point due south of Kodiak. The weather suddenly cleared and at 10,000 feet, daylight receding to dusk, we could see in all directions. We were about 1 ½ hours south of NAS Kodiak.

We then received electrifying voice messages from the USS Bugara, "We have spotted the barge. (A pause) The water is almost to the top of her gunnels. (Pause) We are closing. The seas are moderating. (Pause) We are taking three exhausted men aboard."

Our PB4Y-2, for that mission #59643, with its own tired crew, approached Kodiak from a rarely flown sector due south of the island, on a northerly heading, and made a routine night landing with local lights visible for miles. Our Ensign pilot/navigator, had kept three navigation tracks going, and had given perfect advice under less than perfect circumstances. Our aircraft equipment, notably the APS-15 radar with its skilled operator, and our radio altimeter, and our voice radio worked flawlessly. One weak Loran station had confirmed the celestial navigation fixes. Two men, the pilot of an aircraft, and the skipper of a submarine, believed the advice given by an Ensign aviator and a radar operator, both of whom had been working under challenging conditions. Pilot Walter Munk and his PBY-5A crew out of Adak made two precision flights. Without Munk and his crew, the whole effort would likely have failed. The Navy at its best!

Although the crew of 59645 already had an ample opportunity to become familiar with Anchorage, with its Elemendorf Air Base and barracks at Ft. Richardson, Alaska, October 1946 must have been set aside for squadron crews to visit some of continental Alaska's airfields.

The logbook shows that as the month began there was a local "fam" (familiarization) flight with Orville Hollenbeck as my copilot and reduced crew in local VFR conditions. I assume we made some practice landings and takeoffs at NAS Kodiak. The main flight schedule for that month took the full crew of 59645, using aircraft serial number 59838, to Anchorage and then to the Army Air Corps' Ladd Field at Fairbanks, Alaska. Both segments were instruments and at Ladd we made a low frequency radio range approach until we were on "final" and then shifted to GCA (the letters stand for Ground Controlled Approach-more details on this precision radar controlled approach later in the story) because of the heavy snow that obscured visibility.

The following day we pre-flighted for a hop directly back to Kodiak. Almost all of the Ladd Airfield support facility is underground, with good reason. It was very cold, the temperature had dropped to about 60 degrees Fahrenheit below zero. When we got back to our aircraft that morning to prepare it for the flight back to Kodiak, we faced an extensive preflight. Our alcohol filled instruments had frozen. The engine oil was so congealed we could not pull the propellers through. Fortunately, the Army Air Corps support folks at Ladd Field had huge gasoline-fueled heaters. These functioned like the Southwind heaters that were standard in some U.S. automobiles for a few years, the only exception being that the ones at Ladd Field were big enough to fill a huge shroud that supplied an entire engine nacelle with heated air. Once mounted over the nacelle, this big heater system could blow the hot air directly into the radial cylinder recesses and warm them and the engine oil. It took about an hour to melt the snow and thaw the fluids and then we could pull the props through and start our R-1830 engines. The flight home was a little dicey because some of our radio equipment was not working and Mt. McKinley at over 20,000 feet was off our starboard wing, obscured in clouds. Thankfully, our Radio Direction Finder was working, and we knew that Kodiak Approach Control could give us vectors followed by a GCA approach when we got close enough. Fairbanks is a continental city not too far from the Arctic Circle. Kodiak is a coastal town south of the Alaska Peninsula. While it could snow hard at Kodiak, the snow usually melted quickly.

Each area has its hazards and the "prevailing weather" can present a variety of situations for pilots.

My last flight as Lieutenant Hugh Burris' copilot occurred on December 5, 1946. PB4Y-2 #59645 and its crew were ordered to return to our U.S. base at NAS Whidbey Island. It was the concluding flight in our first deployment tour in VPB-107. Again, we were the last plane out because I was the Materiel Officer assigned to make sure our spaces at NAS Kodiak had been vacated and cleaned.

It had been a good tour. Only one of our aircraft had become a "hangar queen," to be "pirated" for parts. Two of that aircraft's engine carburetors kept misbehaving in the float test chambers where carburetors were adjusted in maintenance. These finally had to be replaced altogether.

There had been only one damage incident. Our two huge hangar doors were sliding doors that met in the center. These were opened and closed by employing a little tractor (called a "mule") on each door. These mules had small, high torque, internal combustion engines. The mule operators moving the two hangar doors each got carried away one day with their own expertise. A third mule operator on the nose wheel of one of the planes was pulling the plane into the hangar, starting with the two doors wide open. The men on the two mules standing ready to pull the doors closed after the plane was safely in, figured they were by this time exceedingly skillful at timing the entry of the big plane. As the nose wheel of the big aircraft crossed the door threshold, these two, one on one side with one half door, the other on the other side with a half door, were already in motion pulling their respective door sides to the center to close the hangar. They certainly were coordinated, but just a little off on their timing. Each half door nipped a wing tip of the PB4Y-2 and we lost a green starboard wingtip lamp on one side, and a red port wing tip lamp on the other side, and the wingtip panel ends to boot. Once those doors were in motion, all the reversing of the mule's engine was to no avail. It was a slow, silent, graceful, relative motion event. Bystanders' eyes were riveted to the scene. A ghost aircraft stored on the desert near Phoenix, Arizona lost its wingtip panels shortly thereafter.

The final flight back to Whidbey from the first deployment had some drama. Takeoff was scheduled for 4:00 a.m. on an early December morning, Kodiak time. The ready room and the operations room were darkened to keep crew's eyes night adapted. One of the heaviest snows encountered in Alaska at seal level was falling. The wind was from the north. Takeoff would be from the short north runway, about 5,000 feet long. All fuel tanks were full. Pilot Burris was worried about traction, and the drag of the snow on our wheels during takeoff. There was literally no visibility in the snow. Visibility was from one Bartow light to the next Bartow light. In the ready room, there was coffee. I poured a cup for myself and added a liberal amount of sugar. There was no cream or milk. I took a big swallow and almost threw up. Someone had filled the glass sugar bottle with salt.

Burris made a skilled, blind takeoff. The foot of snow did not appreciably hold back our airspeed buildup. With no vision ahead and mountains rising abruptly just after the end of the runway, as soon as we were airborne, and the last Bartow light disappeared, Burris commenced a rapid climbing bank to the right out across the friendly sea. The landing gear came up, and no engine faltered, thank God. The Pratt & Whitney R-1830 engines had performed again. Logged comments in the remarks column read "4 hours night on Inst." The flight, as were most, was otherwise uneventful. The salt taste persisted for the 8.8 hours it took to return to Whidbey Island.

The next two scenes are on the tarmac at NAS Whidbey Island in June of 1948 as the squadron returned from deployment. A mother has outfitted her two sons in their Sunday best. On the left is Michael, age one and one half. On the right, with eyes riveted on the aircraft, is son Franklyn III, age two and one half years. The mother who had prepared the boys for this reunion was and is the author's wife of 60 years, Peggy.

Illustration 23 - Coming Home; two views

It was in the PB4Y-1 *Liberators* flying over the North Atlantic out of England and the Azores that many Alaskan Patrol Plane Commanders (PPCs) attained their early instrument flight experience. This experience proved very valuable for those pilots who would later confront north Pacific rim deployments, particularly flights in Aleutian weather. For Hugh Burris, Aleutian flying had meant a second major tour with long periods of instrument flying. The following paragraphs are Commander Hugh Burris' own summary of his flying life.

"I signed up for naval (aviation) cadet training in June 1941 just prior to graduating from Southeastern Louisiana University. I was very happy to be accepted in the pilot training program. I had been rejected a year and a half earlier due to my being colorblind. The old white-haired Navy doctor said to me on that earlier occasion, 'Son, you passed everything except the color blind test; you go back and finish college for we cannot let you fly in the Navy.' This was good advice. Still, I was young and stubborn and not ready to give up."

"I returned to college and it so happened that an Army Air Corps recruiting team appeared on campus with a full medical trailer and doctors. I went through the same test and the corpsman got the colorblind book and I struggled to read the numbers." (Author's Note: The test book is a book of numbers, formed of different colors in irregular, blotchy, patterns. The colorblind person cannot discern certain numbers because of the intentional confusion of color patterns raggedly outlining the numbers.)

"I struggled to read the numbers but it was mostly a guessing game for me. The corpsman called in the full Colonel doctor and told him I was pretty colorblind. The Colonel said, 'Sign him up. We need as many as we can get.' Well, I knew then that I must try once more to get in naval aviation."

"I hitchhiked down to New Orleans and went to the same Navy recruiting station and told them I had never taken the test before. I had some difficulty reading the color chart pages but I had experience now, so when the corpsman got to the last few pages, the numbers showed up good to me but I said, 'I cannot see any of these numbers.' Those were the numbers I knew now from experience had been made for the colorblind to read. I was accepted and I suppose that proves that good guys win most of the time."

"I completed my flight training at Corpus Christi (Texas) in multi-engine, flying PBYs. In 1943, I was assigned to the Atlantic Fleet. I was then trained and checked out in PB4Y-1 aircraft and assigned to Fleet Air Wing (FAW)-7 with headquarters at Plymouth, England. My squadron was VPB-110 and we operated out of Dunkeswell, England."

"The Dunkeswell aerodrome had only a non-directional low frequency homer (homer: a homing beacon; a ground located transmitter broadcasting a radio frequency signal in all directions) so we had lots of instrument flying and alternate airfield landings. (The alternate airfield is the one designated for the aircraft to proceed to if the primary airfield is below instrument minimums for landing.) Primitive GCA was established at Dunkeswell, England, in late 1944 or early 1945."

(Author's Note: GCA stands for Ground Controlled Approach. At a point on a plane's incoming flight path, a GCA operator in a shack on the landing field near the pre-designated "GCA Runway", would "take control" from the control pilot in the aircraft. That operator would then help the pilot keep on the optimum flight path for landing by telling the pilot to go right or left, and to increase or decrease the plane's rate of descent. GCA operators also included redundant information such as you are a "little to the right of the glidepath" and a "little above the glidepath," plus occasional affirmations that "you are doing just fine" when warranted. We return to Lt. Burris' narrative.)

"My first GCA was at the end of an operational flight at night with dense fog and poor visibility. My confidence in the GCA operator and the equipment was not good but we were able to land safely after two tries. I will say that GCAs have made a great improvement and the same goes for the pilots."

"When Germany surrendered, the Navy personnel were shipped from Dunkeswell, England to Norfolk, Virginia on a seaplane tender, the USS Albemarle Sound. Many of the pilots and crews were transferred to NAS Whidbey Island, Washington, to re-form into squadrons and get checked out in PB4Y-2 aircraft."

"The Japanese called it quits before all the re-forming was accomplished and the personnel began to scatter and return to civilian life. I was ordered to NAS Crow's Landing (near Modesto, California) and was assigned to VPB 107. A goodly number of the pilots and crew were from the squadrons that had been at Dunkeswell, England but some were from squadrons in the Pacific area. VPB-107 was then relocated to NAS Whidbey Island and after a brief period of training, the squadron was deployed to NAS Kodiak, Alaska on Kodiak Island."

"I note in my log that we flew two search and rescue (S&R) flights looking for three men on a disabled barge on November 4 and 5 for a total of 15.7 hours. We found the barge. We flew another S&R flight on November 15, 1946. The members of my crew should be commended and given credit for their perseverance in saving the lives of men on the barge. I was transferred in late December 1946, after the squadron's return to NAS Whidbey Island, to shore duty in the coldest place in the USA, Ottumwa, Iowa."

"When I was in VR-3 (VR-3 was another Naval Air Transport Service squadron) I got into a situation that I was most fortunate to come out of unscathed. In 1952, we had a regular route from our home base, NAS Moffet Field, California, to Adak, Alaska, with stops in between. Due to time taken at these stops to unload and refuel, it was deemed necessary to provide a relief crew at NAS Kodiak. This relief crew would fly from NAS Kodiak to NAS Adak and back to Kodiak with no stops in between. The month was February or March, 1952. As I recall, I was the pilot, and Lt. Hal Kelly my copilot for the relief crew. We were briefed at Kodiak on the weather at 0430 before departure for Adak and told that a landing at Kodiak on our return at approximately 1930 (Navy time-7:30 p.m. civilian time) would be doubtful due to extremely heavy snow and winds. The flight went without trouble until we got back to the Kodiak control area. We were told that weather conditions at Kodiak were below landing minimums. I advised radar control that we wished to make one GCA try and we did. Lt. Hal Kelly was a very competent pilot so I told him to fly the plane and I would be copilot and I would give the command to 'pull up' if necessary."

(Note: There were several terms in use if the pilot reached minimums on a landing approach and could not pick out the landing field. Pilots generally recognize "pull up", "missed approach", and "go around" procedures as equivalent expressions. "Wave-off" is a related term that derived from aircraft carrier landing experience.)

"We commenced our radar approach and the air was quite rough at 1000-foot altitude but not so much as to cause concern. There is a navigation and landing approach marker beacon at Puffin Island; this beacon is approximately one mile from the end of the instrument runway that extends very close to the bluff at wate"s edge. When your plane crosses the marker beacon, if you do not have the runway lights in sight, you should make a pull-up, turning sharply left to avoid the steep terrain ahead and also to your right. As our approach continued and we descended, the turbulence increased and the snow was very heavy. Lt. Kelly was having great difficulty physically controlling the plane. As we crossed the Puffin Island beacon, (The indication that the beacon had been crossed was that the needle on the Radio Direction Finder-RDF indicator in the plane would swing 180 degrees, from directly ahead to directly astern.) I could not see the runway lights but I let Lt. Kelly continue for 30 seconds. Finally, I saw a faint luminous glow of a light source. We had to land now; there was no other choice. We were both now having a real battle with the aircraft, trying in one moment to keep it from pitching into the water and in the next second to keep from going too high on our approach. We finally came over the end of the runway heading about 70 degrees to the right of the runway heading. As we got to the touchdown spot, we cut power and kept the right wing down and used left rudder. I thought surely we would at least wipe out the landing gear but the deep accumulation of snow accommodated us in a 'smooth, smooth' landing. We rolled a very short distance and called for a tow tractor to pull us to the terminal. I got by that time, but my decision was faulty indeed. I learned and retained knowledge from this experience."

Chapter 11- Alaska: Instrument Flight Proving Ground

A t the end of December 1946, just after returning to Whidbey Island, Washington from a first deployment to Kodiak, Alaska, and its Aleutian Chain flying assignments, my logbook showed 526 pilot hours.

Mention has been made of the near obsession that grips younger Navy pilots over concern about building up flight time. I have discovered in my review of my three logbooks that some flights were never entered at all. Most Navy pilots took it for granted that their logbooks, which were never in their possession except when between duty stations, were meticulously updated. Airline pilots, even those who had flown in the service, have told me that flying a commercial transport aircraft and keeping track of the hours flown relates strictly to getting paid. After enough flying hours are accumulated each month for pay purposes, some airline pilots do not even bother to record their flight time.

I recall flying a twin Beech from Lockheed's Burbank field in California to Phoenix, Arizona and back as a favor to Barney Rapp who wanted a copilot along because of night reentry into the Los Angeles basin. I was in the graduate school at UCLA and glad to take an evening off from study. Barney had a shore duty assignment that involved liaison with aircraft manufacturers and needed to go to a Goodyear plant in Phoenix that supplied some avionics equipment. For the most part, it turned out to be a flight in beautiful southwest weather and a nice reunion with Barney. I had become accustomed to the day smog over LA but it was my first experience with the night smog. We took an instrument approach back into Burbank.

The big accomplishment for all copilots in a Navy patrol squadron was to become the PPC, the Patrol Plane Commander, the Navy's nearest equivalent to the Captain of a passenger plane in commercial aviation. A shipboard qualification of comparable significance to becoming a PPC would be a Naval Officer becoming qualified as Officer of the Deck (OOD), Underway, on a Navy warship. I had qualified for the OOD responsibility on a destroyer in record time in 1942 with the help of aggressive Commanding Officers who realized that wartime losses and new construction needs were putting great demands on the availability of qualified personnel. In war, the ship Commanding Officers had to literally scrounge some sleep time, and the OOD found himself with plenty of vital decisions that had to be made before the skipper could be awakened.

Our first Aleutian deployment in VPB-107 had been completed, quite successfully I felt, under Commander Hank Haselton, USN.

By the end of 1946, the squadron was back at NAS Whidbey Island where training began immediately for our second deployment to commence in June of 1947. In Navy operational units like aircraft squadrons or ships, personnel are either "doing it", or "training to do it." It is a never-ending process. My logbook reveals that on

January 3, 1947, I was the pilot for a four hour flight in 59645, with a copilot and crew of nine. The "Character of Flight" was listed as "C" for "training, qualified pilots." We were often training ourselves, much as a primary flight student was given a number of solo flights after being deemed "safe to solo."

They trusted Pilot Dailey to command a plane for a training mission with a full crew, as long as it was not an operational mission. I discovered just before writing these lines, in an entry in my logbook that I had never noticed before, that I had been designated a "First Pilot." That term was almost never used. I was something less than a PPC. I began to wonder if there was something wrong with me. I had over 500 hours. I knew I had a lot to learn but I knew I was gaining in proficiency and confidence.

Hugh Burris, who had taught me so much about instrument flight and plane handling, had been detached from the squadron. I learned later that he had gone to NAS Ottumwa, Iowa to be a Primary Flight Training Instructor. In fact, many of our pilots and flight crewmen had been detached. It was like starting all over again to mold a new squadron with many new names and faces.

A local flight with a pilot named Ed Hogan was added to the flight schedule. He was not in our squadron. I did not realize it at the time, but I was being set up to be Lieutenant Commander Hogan's copilot in a third Aleutian deployment to begin in April 1948.

As it developed, Ed Hogan did later become our squadron's Commanding Officer. I would be assigned as his copilot for a third deployment. Although it was generally known that the Navy Department in Washington planned a couple of years ahead on Commanding Officer assignments, I had no inkling of the fact that pilot assignments in FAW-4 were actually being planned two deployments in advance. I quickly forgot about Ed Hogan as our squadron stepped up the pace of training for its second deployment. We had to deal with the immediate infusion of new pilots and aircrews.

As for hands-on control of the PB4Y-2, I was the only squadron pilot flying left seat to have been sent out at both Kodiak, and later at Adak, to make touch and go landings down the reverse of the instrument runways. This involved taking the aircraft into those mountain valleys, wrapping it up tight, then letting down at greater than normal descent rates, and putting the plane down repeatedly in the first 500 feet of runway. These flights occurred because Pilot Dailey, with a minimum flight crew, was assigned landing practice flight duty on days when strong winds came in from the east. Such winds would have made practice landings on the instrument runways at both Kodiak and Adak unwise downwind exercises. Although Runways 090 and 270 at a given airfield would be the same strip of concrete or asphalt, to controllers and pilots they are distinctly different runways, often with vastly different approaches.

There was tragedy. In August of 1947, flying as copilot for Lt. "Junior" Johnson (there were two pilots named Johnson in our squadron at the time) the flight crew was ordered to Cold Bay.

Our assignment was to search for a PBY-5A that was heading for Dutch Harbor and never arrived. This aircraft was assigned to Naval Air Station, Kodiak. On that day in early August of 1947, it carried two Naval Air Station pilots and the Dutch Harbor baseball team, which included Army personnel. There were 20 aboard. The orders to us in our ready room to get out to Cold Bay came suddenly, at least to me, for I had not heard of the missing plane.

The search crew left Kodiak on August 9, 1947, in PB4Y-2 Serial No. 59701 for Fort Randall at Cold Bay at the far end of the Alaska Peninsula. The log shows 3.9 hours westbound, with a radio range instrument let down attempt at Randall. The station was rimmed with clouds at all levels and the airfield had blowing "scud" right down on the runway. ("Scud" was jargon for wisps and pieces of cloud that seem to break off the main mass of clouds and move rapidly along or across runways.)

Johnson made one low frequency radio range approach and executed a pull up when the aircraft did not break "contact" at the stipulated time after passing the "low cone." Our aircraft went back up to a holding pattern altitude. It was determined that we would probably not see the landing field on radio range approach minimums as long as the weather remained "below minimums." The mission criticality involved the life of those aboard the PBY-5A. We elected to attempt another radio range approach. Our APS-15 radar operator had told us on the first approach that he was getting reliable "radar echoes" that matched the terrain and runway highlights shown on the U.S. Coast and Geodetic Survey chart. We resolved to press a bit below radio range approach minimums the second time, relying on our radar. The pull up procedure while landing to the south at Randall was good, provided the pilot kept the aircraft steady on the approach course heading until getting back to a safe altitude. Guided by our APS-15 radar operator, the aircraft made it the second time to a visual sighting of the north approach end of the long north-south runway at Fort Randall and a smooth landing. The logbook shows the flight out to Randall and the one back to Kodiak as code "U" for the character of flight. That appears to be the code for training flights of that era though my successive logbooks have differing code assignments for that flight characterization.

The next three flights based in an out of Randall looking for the downed aircraft, bear the code designation "W" for "Emergency or relief work." The Flight Department officers in our squadrons changed frequently and there is plenty of inconsistency in coding choices recorded in logbooks. Thankfully, there was pretty good weather for searching on the 9th, the 10th and most of the 11th of August 1947. The log shows that the weather deteriorated in the afternoon of the 11th, and we made an SCS-51 instrument approach (in civil aviation, an ILS approach) to get back into Randall.

While on local flights out of Randall, the search went into valleys and over jagged peaks and got down low over the coastlines. The crew even tried to "see" into the water when waters were clear. Never saw a trace of the missing plane. A logical conclusion is that they went down in the water. Alaskan plane crashes over land are often discovered years later. The aircraft downed at sea rarely reveal their location. We were never given a complete record of the final position report of the Kodiak Naval Air Station PBY and had only an approximate location of the last known position. All we knew for sure was that the team was involved in a baseball tournament for the Alaska military base championship. Our last "local" flight out of Randall was a 3.9 hour flight on August 11, 1947 terminating in the SCS-51 approach at Randall.

SCS-51 was the Navy's designation for ILS-Instrument Landing System, the equipment for which had been installed in May 1947 just before our June deployment. I liked the method and it was a boon at Fort. Randall whose airfield was not equipped with GCA. Randall surely needed a modern precision approach system for aircraft because of its regularly foul weather. Our search mission ended in a return to NAS Kodiak on August 13, 1947 at the end of which Lt. Johnson made a radio range letdown in instrument conditions to NAS Kodiak.

On one occasion, when awaiting a clearance at Randall for one of those three local search flights, the Army Air Corps crew of an OA-10 aircraft attached to the 10th Rescue Squadron, were in the briefing room getting a clearance. They were heading out on a mercy mission with serum for a sick man in the Pribilof Islands. The OA-10 was the Army Air Corps' designation for a Navy PBY-5A *Catalina*. The plane had landing wheels and there was some discussion going on in the ready room at Randall about landing on the one, very short, runway in the Pribilofs. It could be done, I recalled a Navy pilot telling me, as long as there was a very stiff wind aligned with the runway. But then, getting back off again would be a challenge. The pilot of the Army plane ultimately elected to attempt a water landing near a small harbor. The local winds there were not forecast to be too high. Sometimes forgotten is that open seas record a history of previous winds so one might still expect some rough swells even in the lee of land. We had the temerity to suggest some options to the Army pilot but he shrugged his shoulders and said that he was "a veteran of over 20 water landings!" So, he took off and we took off.

After we got back to Randall, we inquired how the OA-10 pilot made out in his attempt at an open sea landing. The operations desk airman on duty showed us a dispatch from the Army pilot. "Plane made normal landing and sank," was the complete text. That remains one of the most succinct military messages in my experience.

The OA-10 from the Army Air Corps squadron at Fort Randall benefited greatly from the one ship a year that put in to the Pribilofs. It picked up the crew of the OA-10. No one was lost. I never found out about the serum.

There were two other situations in which a plane in our squadron made use of the APS-15 radar to make safe instrument landings in tight situations. On a flight from NAS Whidbey to NAS Kodiak, a squadron *Privateer* piloted by Bob Hallman with Spence Ziegler as copilot, was buffeted by terrific headwinds all the way. After cutting across the Gulf of Alaska from Annette Island for his destination, NAS Kodiak, Hallman was informed that Kodiak had closed down. The field was not even taking GCA traffic unless there was no other choice. Hallman started for his alternate, Anchorage, and discovered a rarity in Alaska mainland flying, Elmendorf Field at Anchorage had gone below minimums. With fuel mixtures now leaned out to preserve as much fuel as possible, the plane turned toward Yakutat, Alaska, which had a civilian field with a runway just long enough for a carefully planned early touchdown. The advancing weather front then swallowed Yakutat. But, Hallman and Ziegler were now committed. It had to be Yakutat. Their navigator broke out the Coast and Geodetic Survey charts for the Yakutat area and discovered a river whose path came close the end of the runway. The plane's headings were now turned over to the APS-15 radar operator. Fortunately, the coastal terrain around Yakutat is low and relatively flat and Hallman was able to safely get the PB4Y-2 down to 500 feet. He was prepared to go lower. The radar operator found where the river entered the Gulf and had Hallman fly to a point just west of the mouth of the river. The radarman then vectored Hallman into a lazy turn to the east and indicated the plane could be let down to a minimum safe altitude. Hallman went down to 200 feet and every eye strained for sight of a runway. The tower operator cooperated and turned on every light available. About 500 feet short of the runway, Hallman sighted the field and had enough space to make a slight course correction and land.

Back at Kodiak, the Operations Officer of VPB-107, "Snuffy" Wagoner, gave a sigh of relief and put out the good news on the loudspeaker.

That crew made it into Kodiak the next day. They had adopted a current song hit as their own. The song began, "I'm lookin over, a four leaf clover." We all sang it with them. Under the influence, at the O' club, we sang it many times, probably too many times. Spence Ziegler had been my roommate at the Naval Academy. Some years later I ran into him on the carrier USS Cabot where he qualified a helicopter squadron as its Commanding Officer. I also met up with Bob Hallman later at NAS Pt. Mugu California in 1955. Bob invited me to fly as his copilot for a utility flight in an R5-D aircraft to San Clemente Island and return and I accepted, gratefully I might add. I was on extended additional duty at the Navy's Port Hueneme base and was starved for flight time, needing four hours each month to get flight pay. With six children by that time, we had come to depend on flight pay.

Dick Korn was another PPC in squadron VP-H/L-7 (just a name change from VPB-107) who became the beneficiary of a good APS-15 radar operator while on an instrument flight with his crew. The circumstance began as a simple transit flight from NAS Kodiak to NAS Adak, with some off-airways patrolling along the way. Again Aleutian weather reared its head and as its first challenge provided headwinds much higher than those forecast.

In an aside to the Dick Korn flight to Adak, let me take a paragraph to give the reader a graphic idea of what winds can do to an aircraft in the Aleutian theatre. One day a PBY-5A took off from NAS Kodiak out the east leg of the Kodiak low frequency radio range. The object of this prescribed "climb out" was to go out far enough to reach a certain altitude and then reverse course and come back over the Kodiak range station with sufficient altitude to get over the Aleutian Range heading westward. On this one day, the PBY-5A, a very slow aircraft, made it back over the Kodiak radio range station seven hours later! The plane had reached its assigned altitude of 7,000 feet. The winds had borne the plane so fast on its outbound east course that it had a great distance to fly to just get back to its departure point. Seven hours took a big chunk out of that PBY's cruising range. The pilot just did make it to the other side of the Alaska Range and landed at Naknek, Alaska, way short of the Adak destination.

By the time the Dick Korn and his PB4Y-2 crew got to the vicinity of Adak, the flight had exceeded its planned fuel consumption. Adak had closed in. I happened to be at Adak as a fill-in copilot for our Operations Officer, Lieutenant Commander Wagoner. It was now snowing heavily at NAS Adak. The airfield had gone below GCA minimums. Dick Korn elected to try a GCA approach at Adak as he began to doubt that he had fuel enough to reach his alternate at Shemya. Wagoner went down to Adak's Operations room, right next to the tower. I stayed in our assigned Quonset hut on top of a hill just south of the runway. My next experience was to hear a plane with its engines in full roar making a pull-up to the south and passing so close overhead that the Quonset huts all shook. Then I went down to Operations and found Wagoner in communication with Dick Korn. Wagoner asked Korn to get a fuel report from his plane captain. It took longer than it should have and when Wagoner finally got it, he made some quick calculations and barked out instructions to Dick Korn. "Set your course direct for Shemya, using your radar operator to track you out there. Do not fly via the standard airways route. You do not have enough fuel. Do not try to land here. This field is almost zero-zero." Korn and his crew grasped these instructions quickly and their plane gradually disappeared from the NAS Adak radarscope. Wagoner got into voice communication with Shemya Control and told them the story. He asked that Korn be given a straight-in approach and that the Bartow lights on the runway be set at Strength Five. It was raining slightly at Shemya but they had two miles visibility under a low overcast. The PB4Y-2 radar worked to perfection. Dick Korn and crew made a straight in approach and landed at Shemya. Number one engine quit on final approach and the # 2, 3, and 4 engine tanks when dipped, had twenty, twenty and thirty gallons left, respectively. (The wing tanks held a total of about 2,400 gallons when topped off.) The radar and the radar operator had scored again. Wagoner set another high mark for intelligent and timely decision making. And Dick Korn was smart enough to follow instructions.

In September 1947, Patrol Squadron Seven's second Kodiak deployment was completed, and I returned to Whidbey with Lieutenant Commander Wagoner and his crew, serving as the fill-in navigator for the flight. The logbook shows the flight took off at about just after midnight on September 7. It was 7.7 hours of night flying, 6.0 of which were on instruments. Approaching a mountainous coastline (Canada) on instruments presents the navigator with some interesting challenges. Again, that radar! All the dead reckoning and drift sight corrections found an air navigator wondering if a radar landfall would confirm his work, or would that landfall tell the pilot that he had a poor navigator. On that trip, the visual landfall proved confirming. And this time, NAS Whidbey was going to be VFR.

From October 3 to October 19, 1947, I was assigned TAD (Temporary Additional Duty) training at NAS Coronado, in San Diego California, flying as copilot for pilot Lieutenant Al Lamarre. We conducted night training flights, both ECM, and Anti-Submarine-Warfare (ASW) using sonobuoys. We first operated in the vicinity of beautiful San Diego and then were sent a very short distance up the coast to NAAS Miramar for further ASW training. The flight back to Whidbey from Miramar included an unexpected event.

Pilot Al Lamarre took a "five on top" clearance (500 feet above any undercast) and for the early part of the flight, conditions were excellent. Once into Northern California, however, one could anticipate one of those stationary fronts with cloud tops rising gradually as one proceeded north over Oregon. Al gradually increased altitude to maintain 500 feet on top of the rising cloud tops. Dusk was settling over the area now, and we became more diligent in our airways reporting requirements, carefully tuning in the radio range station ahead and shifting voice frequency to Portland (Oregon) Approach Control.

Our plane began to porpoise gently and our course became erratic. A glance at the pilot in the left seat raised warning signs. Our altitude was 13,500 feet. Beaming a flashlight on him, I could see that Al had passed out. I grabbed the yoke, called Portland, and asked for immediate descent to the lowest safe altitude they could give me. They gave us 7,000 feet. At about 9,000 feet Al stirred and at 8,000 feet he seemed fully conscious. He was informed of the revised clearance we had been given. As the plane leveled out at 7,000 feet, now in the clouds, he said that he was OK and resumed control of the aircraft. I learned the downside of taking a "five on top" clearance and learned the wisdom of the (then) current Navy rules on altitude. At 10,000 feet, pilots should don their oxygen masks. If night flying, and expecting to go to 10,000 feet or above, the flight crew should use oxygen from the ground up.

My logbook reveals that in November 1947, I flew our newest PB4Y-2, serial # 60003, as First Pilot, and practiced night radar approaches for ASW operations, and then made a night radar approach and landing at NAS Whidbey. The radar experience during three very important flights on our previous deployments had convinced me that the APS-15 radar was an additional precious tool for getting the plane and crew back safely on the ground. That was not on its advertised list of capabilities but it was a precision device in the hands of a good radar operator. We had good operators. My destroyer experience with SG radar had educated me on what that equipment and a good operator can mean to survival. It was not long before radomes began appearing on the noses of commercial transport aircraft.

VPB-107 had been re-named VP H/L-7 just before its second deployment to Kodiak in June 1947. The new nomenclature stood for Heavy Land Patrol Squadron Seven. It did not mark any change in mission.

For the next and final deployment with VP H/L 7, the Operations Officer took me aside and spent an hour telling me that our new Commanding Officer deserved an experienced copilot to help him during his first exposure to Aleutian flying, especially for the airbases and terrain surrounding them. Otherwise, he implied, I would have been given my own plane and crew. It took some mental adjustment to swallow that. My logbook shows a formal, seal-embossed entry, dated 8 June, 1948. The entry states that in accordance with a ComAirPac bulletin, I was fully qualified as PPC in June 1948. Retrospectively, it appears that the extra log notations even to the point of embossing a seal were an attempt to reduce the pain in a pilot who did not become PPC for operational flight purposes during the tours of his squadron between June 1946 and June 1948

My flights with the new Commanding Officer, Lieutenant Commander Ed Hogan, rank high on my list for enjoyment and appreciation of his demonstrated expertise in naval flying. He was an excellent instrument pilot. Later in my naval service, I commanded three patrol plane squadrons flying versions of the P2V *Neptune* aircraft and flew as PPC more than a thousand hours with my own crew. It just came kind of late.

In our flights together, Hogan put greater trust in my flying ability, particularly on instruments, than Burris had done in our squadron's first deployment. That was understandable. While I was with Hugh Burris, I was a real novice. By the time I flew with Hogan I had some pretty good instrument credentials, all accrued in the Aleutians.

Our third Kodiak-based tour took me into more airfields on more varied assignments than the earlier tours. In those days, some naval air bases had utility squadrons flying a variety of aircraft for a variety of flight assignments. We did not have that luxury in Alaska. The duty patrol squadron often performed utility duties.

We departed Whidbey March 7, 1948 for this final deployment. The relatively new crew was airborne in our PB4Y-2 aircraft with Ed Hogan who was both our PPC and our squadron Commanding

Officer. Again, Kodiak closed in while we were en route and we went to Anchorage. On the 9th, we got into Kodiak after two GCA approaches, the first one aborted with wheels and flaps down on final approach due to GCA ground equipment troubles.

The next month saw this crew airborne on the Alaskan-Aleutian tour that was scheduled for all newly deployed pilots, with Ed Hogan being the newly deployed pilot. First stop was Anchorage again, on April 9, 1948, although as had been the case with Burris on the first deployment, Hogan and I had already been there once. We went on to Ladd Field at Fairbanks on that same day. This was a tight one. Blowing snow, visibility less than a half-mile. I made the GCA approach. There was a ridge that crossed at right angles to the approach path about a half-mile short of the runway. There were red lights spaced along the peak of the ridge. I seem to recall that the one directly on the flight path to the GCA runway flashed while the others did not. Ed Hogan said he caught a glimpse of the flashing red light and put his hand on the yoke while I flew her on. Then he barked, "I see the runway, I'll make the landing, you stay on the gauges." Well, he was the PPC and the Commanding Officer. So, what's a man to do? I relinquished the approach duty and we landed very smoothly. He also congratulated me on the GCA approach. I began to feel better about this deployment.

Then we went back to Kodiak, then off to Fort Randall, then to Adak and then on to a flyover of Attu and a landing at Shemya. Eastbound, we had the option of taking the return trip to our base at Kodiak in two jumps, landing at Adak for a RON-Remain Over Night, then on to Kodiak. When needing to get back to Kodiak for another operation, we could make the Aleutian return trip as a single segment and give up the training benefit of the extra landing en route.

Next it was back to Fairbanks, for a briefing. The Navy was sending its photo squadron, VPP-1, to map Alaska. Nine PB4Y-2 aircraft configured for photography, along with their photo-mission trained crews, needed a dedicated airbase from which to make their flights and on which to do the first stage reduction of their photography to ground coordinates. The U.S. Army Air Corps agreed to help us put Big Delta field, a satellite field to Ladd Field at Fairbanks, back into operation. But the Navy was to do the grunt work. Commander Hogan and our crew would be the lead plane in to help get the field going again. After our briefing at Ladd Field, we took off for Big Delta, just a puddle jump away. We made the first landing there that had been made since the end of hostilities in World War II.

The Alaskan summer was upon us along with hordes of huge bugs. After surveying what would have to be done first, and making a first report by radio, we returned to Kodiak. Later, while airborne on our missions, we came upon pairs of VPP-1 aircraft flying their "flight lines." They flew most of their tracks above ten thousand feet. If one tiny cloud showed up in the photo-negative between them and the earth below, that entire flight mission had to be repeated.

For all Aleutian chain flights, we now operated our ECM equipment continuously, logging new radar transmissions in Siberia, their frequency, their location and any other electronic information we could deduce with our equipment. Although this was our primary mission, and we worked at it studiously, it was still pretty much ad hoc. There was no prescribed routine. We never had any briefings based on other patrols with requests to look in again on installations already logged to see if there were changes or new conditions. We worked off our own squadron's previous logs and attempted to assemble a composite. But, by this time we had a better understanding of what the equipment could do and increasingly took more interest in the ECM subject.

Perhaps our Navy should be given the benefit of the doubt. Just possibly, a situation room somewhere was recording carefully everything we turned in and were assembling the first composite information. If they treated each of our patrol reports as new information, and used it to check against all prior information, they could then intelligently correct data against equipment or operator inconsistencies. One could reason that if they gave us specific

256

assignments, perhaps, in executing those assignments we might "try too hard to please." All of this is conjecture. I did not feel then that what we were doing was part of a scientific method. And, just maybe, the whole state of our ECM art in 1946 and 1947 had not approached a coherent body of knowledge. It was possible that the very first databases were still being constructed.

Squadron aircraft found a welcome at every Aleutian landing field except one. For reasons never determined, NAS Attu seemed inhospitable even though the Japanese were gone and the personnel there "were all on our side." The main objective in landing at as many bases as possible was to "learn the territory" for a time when a squadron plane might have to land there under less than ideal conditions. Possibly Attu station personnel felt "put upon" when itinerants would come in to stay overnight and ask for tours of the battlefields and caves where so much blood was shed less than three years before. One story went that in each short summer the caves containing undiscovered bodies still had the stench of death.

On one trip to Attu, our aircraft took a pass over the abandoned U.S. airfield on Amchitka Island. We discovered that it would not be an optimum choice for an emergency landing due to the enormous amount of debris that had collected on the runway in just the two years that had elapsed since U.S. forces had ceased operations there.

The first visit to Attu was especially important for all squadron flight crews because it provided a good look at Shemya on the way. This was an atoll to the east of Attu on which there had been constructed a 10,000 foot runway with full landing lights, a good, unobstructed low frequency radio range approach. And most important, Shemya had a GCA unit. Shemya had very low minimums (Cloud ceiling limits were set low and visibility limits were set low for qualified pilots. 300-foot ceiling and 1/4-mile visibility would be an example.) Very little of this small atoll was much above sea level.

Fort Randall and Fort Glenn also had good low frequency radio range instrument approaches but mountainous terrain nearby required higher landing minimums. Adak, with its jagged mountains demanding precision approaches and an early pull-up similar to Kodiak, had a GCA unit and it was just as busy as the one at Kodiak.

Fifty-five years have now passed since the men of the first "tours of duty" following the end of World War II patrolled the air over northern ocean waters in their attempt to obtain early knowledge of activities that might someday lead to a direct threat to the United States.

Allowing two years for a Whidbey Island serviceman's tour of duty, more than 25 sequential "tours," with complete changeovers of personnel have occurred. This spans a period begun by the last man in my squadron to go home in 1948 to the first man or woman to join a new millennium squadron at NAS Whidbey in a deployment rotation. With two or three squadrons at a time in that rotation, and nine planes per squadron, each squadron with 250 men and women, the rough calculation suggests that 20,000 of our military personnel have kept "watch" in the north Pacific on just this one mission. Countless, boring flight hours have gone into thousands of logbooks. Death and tragedy have struck at takeoff, at landing, and during those long patrol flights.

Consider the family involvement. Almost three generations of U.S. service families have been represented. Only the quiet sense of accomplishment shared by those who served and those who remember those who served, constitute the reward. Navy patrol squadrons at NAS Brunswick, Maine with forward bases in Iceland, have matched that achievement over the North Atlantic. And Connies (Lockheed *Constellation* aircraft) patrolling the DewLine along with U.S. Air Force interceptors in revetments along northern coasts, always ready to scramble, have been another major part of what might collectively be called, "watch dog" missions. These efforts have been undertaken for just one reason, to keep from getting surprised.

Chapter 12- Experience Counts

B y the onset of World War II, civil airline pilots in the United States had amassed thousands of hours of instrument flying in support of their airline schedules. Those schedules left little choice. Except for hurricanes and violent summer thunderstorms at destinations, schedules were not lightly tinkered with. The schedule was king.

Army Air Corps bomber pilots' transiting to and from targets in World War II received little recognition for the tedious hours they flew and their return-to-base instrument approach challenges. From these combat missions many flight crews never made it back. Sometimes, their aircraft, though flyable, had taken enemy anti-aircraft fire damage and crew casualties. Crews recorded long hours, and the hours conducted under instrument conditions were, if noted at all, regarded as simply collateral to the primary mission.

U.S. Army, Navy and Coastguard airmen and their British and Canadian counterparts from Coastal Command made impressive contributions to the Anti-Submarine Warfare effort against the U-boats. Many paid with their lives. When Admiral Doenitz ordered his submarine commanders to stay surfaced in groups for passage across the Bay of Biscay, he equipped his U-boats with extra AA guns and ordered anti-aircraft gunnery resistance to ASW aircraft. The heavily armed *Liberators* would go in guns blazing during a depth charge run. Some times, both aircraft and submarine combatants met their end in the same action.

Adding to the complication for many of those missions was a home base in England or other Atlantic rim base, under solid cloud cover often extending right to the ground. The return often required an add-on trip to an "alternate" landing field, often a strange landing field. Military flying in Alaska, though the patrol missions were never as numerically high as bombing raids over Germany, or ASW missions in the Atlantic, or transits across the north Atlantic to the British Isles, was just as full of weather challenges.

Schedule accomplishment and mission accomplishment, unthinkable just a decade earlier, was partly the result of the airframe and engine development that met and surmounted the challenges of intensive flight schedules, weather fronts and enemy fire. With their ever improving equipment, United States' pilots proved more than equal to the complex tasks that faced them.

Airline schedules made instrument flying an imperative. The military flight mission in World War II sometimes deferred to a weather impediment. There were good reasons. Destination weather was often less certain; reporting facilities and meteorology data were scarce. Success in achieving combat objectives could be compromised. The base airport chosen for return often made all options for an alternate landing airport doubtful.

For mass formation bombing missions, instrument flying en route was usually not an option. In addition, in the earliest days, it was understood that the military pilot did not have the depth of instrument flight experience as his airline counterpart. That distinction has gradually disappeared over the years. But, the airline pilots accumulated the instrument experience first.

With the war over, the sheer number of pilots that the military aviation training systems had produced, helped propel U.S. commercial transport aviation into a 50-year period of unprecedented growth covering the last half of the twentieth century.

One revealing progress point for aviation, especially for pilots, occurred when pilots could obtain life insurance without aviation accident exclusions. David Hinson, who served as a Northwest Airlines pilot, became Administrator of the Federal Aviation Administration in 1993. On the 70th Anniversary of the Airline Pilots Association (ALPA) in August 2001, Mr. Hinson spoke on the subject of milestones. Mr. Hinson reminded his audience, preponderantly pilots, that not until 1940 could airline pilots get life insurance. Up to that time, all of their insurance policies had an exclusion that meant that the insurance policy did not apply when the pilot was flying. This author can personally attest that it was 1950 before New York Life Insurance would be the first to write a Naval Aviator life insurance policy without a flight exclusion clause in it. The premium was a little more but the event eased a burden for military pilots who had become dependent on "flight pay." The Navy Mutual Aid Association revised aviator premiums in 2003 to be the same as the standard premium paid by all others of comparable age. Airlines and pilots adapted readily to instrument flying after 1935 but it took decades for insurance companies to accept the favorable mortality data.

Experience counts in the cockpit. That experience counts even more in flights where an aircraft encounters instrument weather.

An experienced pilot can be surprised. Even with my Aleutian flight experience, and pilot hours in large aircraft, my toughest wrestling match with an aircraft occurred in a twin-Beech on an instrument clearance out of NAS Brunswick, Georgia August 3,

1956. My copilot on that flight was Ed Hogan, my second skipper during my Aleutian deployments. After Kodiak, he had commanded a hurricane squadron out of NAS Boca Chica (Key West), Florida.

We both agreed later that a Georgia storm cell, completely overlooked by meteorology during our briefing, that caught us in its grip just moments after takeoff, had been our closest to "losing it" in the air during our aviation careers up to then. I fought the controls, just to keep the wings level. Forget the altitude, as we did not control that, the storm did. We were like a leaf in the wind. He nursed the two engines, whose cylinder head temperatures dove toward zero. He managed to keep power on one while the updrafts kept us aloft until we emerged behind the front over North Carolina. Whatever our required checkpoints, we were not able to make them. We were never even questioned about them!

We were soaked, not from sweat, but from the green water which dominated our cockpit during the worst of the battle. The aviation machinist mate who examined our plane at NAS Anacostia (in a suburb of Washington, D.C.) after we landed there told us that one engine would have to be replaced.

Muscle challenges have receded into history as aircraft requiring direct pilot strength on the controls have aged out of the active inventory. With jet propulsion, aircraft have been equipped with hydraulic systems to provide the muscle needed to move control surfaces. The twin Beeches, Douglas C-47 and C-54 transport planes, *Liberators* and *Fortresses* came earlier in the aircraft design cycle and required human strength to move the surface controls.

An occasional scan of aviation magazines reveals beautiful new single engine planes with excellent instrument panels and equipment. Many single engine pilots have flown many instrument hours in modern aircraft. I have the utmost regard for them. I became accustomed to two (or more) engines.

There remain many arguments for having two pilots. Two pilots, with two sets of flight controls and two sets of instruments, have been provided so that one pilot can check on and back up the other and both can check on the instrument panel. Even with the advent of "boosted" controls, the redundancy that two pilots can provide is valuable, and essential if other lives are at stake. And not just strength, but the ability to get at least one set of hands and feet on all controls, is another two-pilot factor.

Let me offer an example of a situation that was saved because there was a second pilot. In August of 1948, while flying a JRF-5 (the two-engine Grumman *Goose,* an amphibian aircraft) with Lieutenant Commander Gerry Peddicord USN in the right hand seat, the need to have strong hands reach essential controls was driven home. We were both attending the U.S. Naval Postgraduate School then located on the U.S. Naval Academy grounds in Annapolis. To get flight time, we were flying out of the Naval Air Facility across the Severn River from the Naval Academy. It was strictly a seaplane base so we would taxi on wheels and then waddle the plane down a ramp and then raise the landing gear when safely afloat. This day was just a couple of months after we both had first qualified in an amphibian aircraft. Each of us had made only a limited number of water landings.

The wind was brisk but the Severn River is usually fairly placid and takeoff was smooth and uneventful. We had decided to make water landings to add to our experience, but the Severn was crowded with Midshipmen sailors so we went down the Chesapeake Bay a few miles. I noticed that an old two-masted Chesapeake sailing schooner was heeled over quite a bit. That observation did not hit home as it should have. The water was pretty rough. I came in for the first landing try. The aircraft hull skipped on a crest and started to settle into a big trough. It was all I could do to hold the yoke back in my lap with two hands. Gerry sensed the danger immediately and hit full throttle on both of the Grumman's engines. She lifted straight up, we flew off, and abandoned any thought of adding to our small store of water landings. Thank God for a copilot or we'd surely have drowned in water I had no business trying to land in.

On another JRF flight out of the Naval Air Facility at Annapolis, Gerry Peddicord was the pilot and I was the copilot. We went up to Rochester, N.Y., landed, chatted briefly with my mother and father who had come to the airport to see us, and took off for

Annapolis. Afternoon thunderstorms dotted the Maryland and Chesapeake Bay area. The *Goose* got pretty hard to control. Gerry and I were both wrestling with the controls. It was suddenly very dark. We saw the old Baltimore River Airport on the peninsula next to Sparrows Point, Maryland. We called for a landing. The tower operator quickly grasped the situation and gave us a landing priority on the first runway we could make. Gerry put the *Goose* down smoothly, we waited out the storm, then went over to Annapolis and called it a day. The JRF was a challenge to land in any kind of wind, especially crosswind, with her close-coupled wheel-set. I was never keen to test the instrument flight capability of the *Goose*.

Just three years after the two JRF events, I was making a night flight to qualify another pilot in a P2V-2 (Lockheed *Neptune*, early version) at NAS Chincoteague, Virginia. The left-seat pilot at the flight controls was an aging Lieutenant Commander. We were using the North runway and the approach to it was over the water and over a seawall, where the runway abruptly began. It was a relatively short runway, perhaps 5,000 feet. Our P2V-2 with its two R-3350 Wright engines was a project plane, not encumbered with turrets or nose guns, so it was relatively nimble and the 5,000-foot runway was ample even in a light wind. It was very dark but the visibility was good and the runway lights were plainly visible. For whatever reason, the man being checked out made a long final approach and kept getting lower and lower over the water. At the last moment, I could see that the seawall was above us, and the approach had deteriorated to one that a young fighter pilot might experience coming in for a carrier landing below the flight deck. I shoved the throttles forward with my left hand. The plane went up like an elevator and plopped down on the end of the runway. The man in the left seat was startled and upset. He finally cooled off and thanked me.

My thoughts after that first landing included the question as to whether the pilot had been worried about the length of the runway. Could he have been worried that it was too short, since he was accustomed to landing transport-type aircraft on Chincoteague's main instrument runway, with its length of over 9,000 feet? Or had he just plain lost some of his night vision capability?

Darkness has its challenges. Seawalls have their challenges. As the nation's air traffic control system improved, many continental U.S. airports added an important feature. Their instrument runway approaches became equipped with a series of approach lights that began well before the touchdown end of the runway. One feature of the lights was a set of strobe lights that repetitively pulsed like Roman Candles and moved down the centerline of the approach path to the landing end of the runway. Even airports where the instrument approach was over water added these very helpful approach lights. San Francisco was one I admired.

Pilots who take off on an instrument flight and are almost immediately in the clouds, climb according to their clearance instructions to assigned altitude. If the assigned altitude is higher than the cloud tops, it gets brighter and brighter and finally the aircraft breaks out on top of the cloud cover into full daylight. Having that experience, a pilot approaching a landing with the strobe lights first has the confidence that they head to the runway and help keep him on the centerline. As the water vapor layer (fog) that separates the plane from visual contact with the ground gets thinner and thinner, those approach lights get brighter and brighter, just like that sun in the climb-out example.

For the Navy airfields that made up most of my instrument approach experience, the strobe approach lights were not available. Their use on approaches to runways that end in seawalls would have been welcomed. There is a spot short of any seawall that gets darker and darker as the plane gets low and the distance to the end of the runway gets shorter. The mind can play tricks, and some reliance on instruments, and particularly a correct altimeter, is recommended until the aircraft is definitely *over* the end of the runway.

Each pilot will have his or her own set of experiences. These are like a reserve, to be called upon when the next few minutes of a flight depart from a norm. These may not be strictly instrument flight experiences but they share one aspect of instrument flying, the first time these are encountered, one is delving into the unknown.

Max Mahaffey served in the South Pacific in World War II on the aircraft carrier, USS Steamer Bay. He was a radarman in the Combat Information Center (CIC) and the ship was a CVE, a class that became known as "jeep" carriers. When he returned to his Texas home after the war, he enrolled in college and joined the ROTC. He was called back to service once again and served in personnel assignments. When he was really back from war the second time, he entered the automobile business, and for much of his adult civilian life owned a Ford dealership.

The flying bug was strong in Max. He learned to fly in Dallas. He bought an Aeronca *Chief* "side by side" for $500 and with it came flying instructions from the seller, an instructor-pilot. That deal resulted in forty hours of flying and a private pilot's license. When Max sold the Aeronca for $485, counting the gas and oil and other expenses, and the $15 discount to the next owner, he had spent a net of $85 for the flight time, instructions and pilot's license. It is not hard to see how Max could become a successful Ford dealer.

Max later bought a twin-engine Beech *Queen-Air.* A retired Conoco aircraft mechanic with an A&P license overhauled the Beech's two engines. While waiting for his Beech to be readied for flight operations, Max took instrument instruction from an airline Captain. Max rented time in a Cessna 172 and the flights were conducted out of Hooks Airport in Tomball, Texas. He successfully passed his instrument check-ride in 1977 and became single engine, instrument qualified. Within a month the Beech was ready and he passed his multi-engine check ride and became multi-engine, instrument qualified. He flew the Beech for 22 years.

Mahaffey recallrd his first flight on a filed IFR flight plan. It was the very day he completed all the qualifications. He loaded his family for a trip to the shore, flying to Rockport, Texas. The weather was intermittent instruments, and while directed to lose altitude on the approach at a sink rate that was pretty fast for the Beech, he recalls passing over the Non-Directional Beacon (NDB) higher than specified. Assisted by breaks in the clouds he completed the approach without a go-round.

Another aircraft Max owned was a pressurized Cessna 421. He found it to be fast, and expensive.

Max Mahaffey's years of instrument flying involved the higher frequency Omni-Range stations known as VOR. His instrument training got right down to fundamentals. The airline pilot instructor would put covers over appropriate instruments to simulate loss of electrical power, and Max then had to maintain flight using needle-ball, airspeed and barometric altimeter. In 2003, Max owned an A-36 Bonanza and was still flying.

Almost every rank, privilege or recognition in flying is built on how many flight hours you have. If the reader recalls pilot MacSpadden getting command of his own B-17 plane and crew after he had accumulated "34 hours" of copilot time, be assured that that decision stemmed from his demonstrated fast acquisition of skill along with what superiors might have called, the "exigencies of war." In early flight training, some distinction is given to "solo" time as opposed to "dual" time. Later on, hours, just plain hours, become the passion. Stearman instructor Verschoyle was memorable for his 10,000 hours. Though seeming an elderly man to the students, in his early thirties in a group where many students looked ahead to their 20th birthdays, what interested the students even more was his flight proficiency and his ability to pass it on.

Most copilots in multi-engine aircraft are willing to "put in time" as their contribution to the opportunity to learn from experienced pilots. Most also want to avoid the commentary, "willing to be a copilot" that marks a person content to stay in the right hand seat. Actual instrument time is needed but pilots also need to become detail-oriented, skilful, plane handlers, especially around airfields near man-made or topographical challenges..

There was a role-model pilot, especially when it came to instrument flying, in our Alaska-deployed squadron. He was Lieutenant Commander Leonard H. Snuffy Wagoner. He was Operations Officer of our Aleutian patrol squadron for three advance-base tours. I occasionally flew as his copilot. He was great at decision making. Snuffy had 12,000 flight hours in 1946 when most of us had less than one thousand.

Snuffy Wagoner put every bit of his experience to work for other pilots during the two years we served in an Alaska-deployed squadron. More than any Operations Officer I encountered in naval aviation, Lieutenant Commander Wagoner studied his pilots. He knew what experience they had and what they needed to acquire. He set about to address their lack of experience in this or that aspect of flying while keeping an even handed approach to their operational flight assignments.

Wagoner never sent a boy on a man's mission. He built strength and then used it judiciously. Though he never bragged, it is fair to tell readers that he was an outstanding fly-fisherman. Alaska was a dream come true for fly-fishermen.

There is at least one offsetting story to the high flight-time pilot as the infinitely wise pilot. While our squadron was on its first deployment to NAS Kodiak, a major U.S. airline had a crash near Annette Island, Alaska. This was a passenger flight in progress between Seattle and Anchorage. In the accident investigation that followed, the pilot was deemed to have made a key mistake. The plane went down and all aboard were lost. That airline Captain had 15,000 hours of flight time. I thought a lot about that incident and that pilot. It was very hard to reconcile then though it would not be so hard now.

Our 1946 ECM flights were a far cry from the quality of the missions of the Lockheed EP-3 aircraft that made an emergency landing on Hainan Island on April 1, 2001. In 1946, we had no intelligence officer in the squadron, and I do not recall that there was even one attached to Fleet Air Wing Four. Certainly, there was no one trained in electronic surveillance intelligence. We learned by doing. We read the equipment handbooks, listened to our CO, the XO and the Operations Officer, took off and did our best. A lot depended on the native intelligence of the radiomen and radarmen in our flight crews.

Many young World War II military pilots were thankful that at least over the early legs of their deployment to their advance operating bases, a domestic airways system was in place. Those military pilots in turn helped establish airway and traffic control systems extending over the northern rims of the Atlantic and Pacific Oceans. Success in flying the north Atlantic was vital to victory in Europe in World War II. Success, though greatly compromised, in flying the north Pacific helped blunt any intention that Japan might have had in expanding their early Aleutian success. After World War II, both the North Atlantic and the North Pacific became areas in which tests of our resolve in the Cold War were met. And for the airline transport business, these northern routes proved to be essential.

In 1946 a severe ear infection could keep a pilot on the ground. (My own piloting experience never included a pressurized military plane.) A substitute pilot could be assigned. In my deployment in Alaska as copilot for my Commanding Officer, Ed Hogan, then a Navy Lieutenant Commander, I could see that he filled half the dresser top in his room in the Bachelor Officer Quarters with ear medicines. His ears were always in pain in flight, but he never missed a flight during my duty period with him.

Commercial airlines' "backup" in terms of pilots, crews and equipment set a mission execution standard that military aviation can only applaud. Both the U.S. Navy and the U.S. Army Air Corps operated air transport counterparts to civil aviation. These were, respectively, the Naval Air Transport Service (NATS) and the Military Air Transport Service (MATS), the latter an outgrowth of the Air Transport Command. Those organizations maintained schedules comparable to their commercial aviation counterparts, with the added challenge of destinations where airfields were located more sparsely than U.S. airline destinations.

Military flying for patrol or reconnaissance has not attempted to match the schedule discipline maintained in commercial transport aviation. Operational military flying done for patrol or reconnaissance involves weapons systems and electronic surveillance responsibilities that civil aviation does not face. Added to these requirements in military aviation is "mission creep" which often becomes "mission leap." The next mission you might have to undertake would have no counterpart in aviation history. In Alaska, my squadron was sent north in 1947 to escort the ships of PET Four to Point Barrow on Alaska's north coast during its brief summer of long days. "PET Four" stood for Petroleum District Four, in the U.S. federal government inventory of its precious oil reserves. Keeping ships and their drilling platform equipment clear of ice fields meant long hours for our PB4Y-2 *Privateer* aircraft. The landing field at Point Barrow, Alaska, was too small for our aircraft to land on; a temporary home base was at best hours of flying time away.

Orders to perform this air escort duty came to our Kodiak based squadron with no prior warning. The PET Four ships were on their way. Do your duty. It was not heroic in any way but it is an example of how flight requirements of Navy over water patrol aviation differs from civil aviation. The pilot of a commercial transport aircraft in passenger service always has a place he or she is supposed to go. He or she has little flexibility on where to go and not a lot of flexibility on when to go. "Stretch" is a word that fits military flying.

Joseph D. Waldroff, Major USAFR, who retired in 1972, had one instrument flying challenge for which no instrument flight school could have specifically prepared him. Here, first, is how he became a pilot.

"While I was going through recruit training (sometimes called boot camp) at Lackland AFB, Texas, the TI (Tactical Instructor, the guy who gives you an especially hard time and teaches the recruit the basics of military discipline) came around one day and asked for volunteers for the aviation cadet program. My opportunity literally fell in my lap. I volunteered, among others, and much to my surprise and relief, I passed all the entrance tests. I was selected for entry into the Aviation Cadet program and began the program in January, 1953."

In Primary Training, Waldroff flew a souped up Piper *Cub*, then the T-6 *Texan*, and went on to Basic Training in a T-28, and finally the T-33, the Lockheed *Shooting Star*, his first jet. The Armistice in the Korean War diverted him from his anticipated F-86 program, to multi-engine training in the B-29 in Operation Blow Torch.

Waldroff was then assigned to MacDill AFB in Tampa, Florida and spent the next 11 years flying the B-47, which he described as "probably the slickest and the most dangerous and unforgiving plane" in his flight career.

With Viet Nam ramping up, Waldroff found himself flying the B-52D out of Anderson AFB on Guam. On the 9th of July in 1968, on his first mission in full command, his aircraft was assigned to refuel from a KC-135 over the Philippine Sea on his way to Viet Nam with a 50,000-pound bomb load. The ejection seat on the D model would go down only, with no tilt and no fore and aft movement. The sky was all lightning and thunderheads, and the aircraft was in and out of the cloud tops. It was turbulent. Waldroff was #3 in a 3-ship cell. Waldroff, in his words:

"I didn't think we would be able to find the tanker, the weather was so bad. We rendezvoused with our tankers using their radar beacons and eventually, visually, when we were getting uncomfortably close before spotting them. We closed in and began the grueling task of attempting to fly formation while flying in and out of clouds, lightning all around, and heavy turbulence. It was an environment just built for introducing extreme vertigo. I don't know how many times I made contact with the tanker and broke contact. By the time we reached the end of the refueling track, I hadn't taken on even half of my fuel. I was pretty hyped up and I realized I would have a heart attack if I didn't settle down and try a little calmer approach toward getting that fuel. It would be embarrassing since the others in the flight were apparently succeeding at getting their fuel. The tanker lead called on the radio announcing the end of the track, effectively ending my chances of getting anymore fuel. I had just broken contact for the umpteenth time when all this happened and I fully expected to see the tanker start turning right. Instead, the boomer (refueling boom operator on the tanker aircraft) gave me the signal to come on back in. I was clear to make contact again. Relieved that I had one more chance to get my fuel, I did move back in, made contact and stayed in contact until I had my fuel. That tanker crew came out of Kadena in Okinawa. I regret to this day not looking that crew up when I finally got to Okinawa to offer at the very least, a beer to the crew for sticking with me until I got my gas (JP-4)."

More and more flight situations are now simulated in advanced training devices that can anticipate and mimic actual experience. There will never be a substitute for actual experience. While actual experience adds to experience, there are some actual experiences that pilots would not care to repeat.

Chapter 13- Aids & Manuals: Information Systems

E
arlier chapters have introduced aircraft systems that are relevant to instrument flying. Basics, like fuel management and flight control anti-icing systems have been touched on. An aircraft must stay in the air to make instrument flying relevant

There are also some aids that have helped make the pilot's job a little easier. These deserve some mention.

WW II Navy officer Bill Rowan served aboard the attack transport, USS Doyen, in the Pacific war zone. He went to work for Sperry (gyroscope design and development) right after the war. In shifting to peacetime, Sperry found little interest from a vanishing shipbuilding market and much interest from aircraft manufacturers.

Rowan's penchant for memorabilia gives us a glimpse of the Sanderson Flight Computer, SC-3.

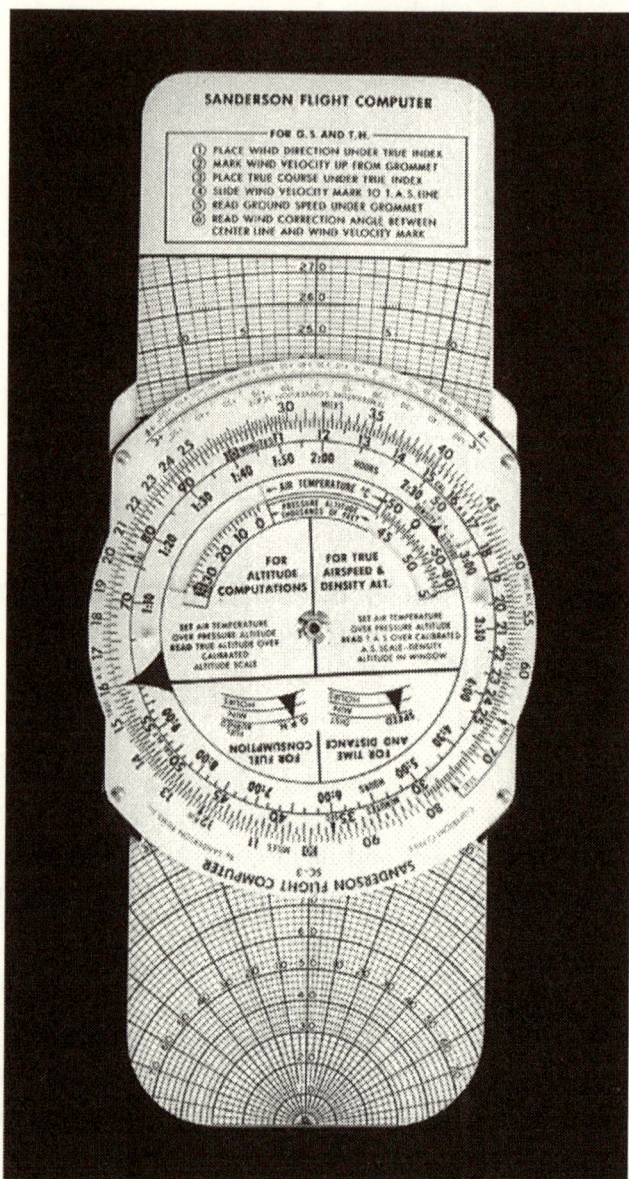

Illustration 24 - Sanderson Flight Computer

A subtitle on the computer is labeled, For G.S. and T.H. Those initials stand for Ground Speed and True Heading.

Discovery of the Sanderson took me back to an orange flight suit, hanging untouched in a basement closet for over 25 years. The pockets were quickly emptied of their contents. Sure enough, there was a Mark 8B computer, in aluminum just like the Sanderson, manufactured by Virginia Plak Company for BuAer (The Navy's Bureau of Aeronautics).The 8B is exactly the same as the circular center core of the Sanderson. It lacks the long rectangular base plate of the Sanderson. The Mark 8B was more of a pilot's aid and the Sanderson would have been a navigator's assistant, with its oblong template for solving wind speed and drift angle.

"Computer" is stretching it a bit if one is fussy about words. These devices fit more realistically into the "slide rule" category. The 8B is a circular slide rule. The Sanderson does not physically fit in any pocket of a flight suit so that reinforces a recollection that it was more often brought aboard by a navigator in a carry-on case.

The Sanderson computers came with a warning. "Do not leave plastic computers and plotters exposed to excessive heat or direct rays of the sun." The early models were plastic but all the later issue came in aluminum.

The Sanderson package also contains a checklist for Sanderson models SC-1 through SC-4 inclusive, plus a "Student Pilot Guide" dated 1946, issued by the Department of Commerce, Henry A. Wallace Secretary, and the Civil Aeronautics Administration, T. P. Wright, Administrator. In the four Roosevelt Presidential terms, Henry Wallace served at different times as Secretary of Commerce, Secretary of Agriculture and Vice President.

In a "Prefatory Note" in the Student Pilot Guide, F.M. Lanter, Assistant Administrator of the Civil Aeronautics Administration, informed student pilots that the guide contains a summary of rules on which the student will be examined on Civil Air Regulations before a cross country solo flight is permitted. It covers Part 43 of the Civil Air Regulations (those existing then, of course) dealing with

General Operation Rules and Part 60 on the subject of "contact flight rules."

In Part 60, it was noted there that "25 questions would be found on the examination and a passing grade of 80 percent was the minimum requirement."

Examples of regulations: "You are not permitted to pilot an aircraft carrying a person except a private, commercial or airline transport pilot."... "The minimum proximity of aircraft in flight is 500 feet (except by pre-arrangement of the pilots)..."
"Experienced pilots consider it unsafe to indulge in aerobatics at altitudes less than 1500 feet." Those Civil Air Regulations are part of history and some are quite different today.

The lines above do explain the interest that so many solo pilots had in obtaining a private pilot's license. That license permitted them to take passengers aloft.

The term "license" brings the following out of my personal archives:

ACA-170 certificate No. ITL 1352261, dated 09/25/56. It was issued by The Department of Commerce, Civil Aeronautics Administration, signed by the Director Office of Aviation Safety, and it indicates that I have been found to be properly qualified to exercise the privileges of COMMERCIAL PILOT with Ratings and Limitations of "AIRPLANE MULTIENGINE LAND INSTRUMENT."

Reading the back of the certificate, I learn that I am in violation of the provision that I notify CAA of a change of address within 30 days. Just now, as I examine that rule, I realize that I have changed addresses more than 20 times since the address I submitted when the application was approved was an actual address. That address was a fine home out on beautiful East Avenue in Rochesterg276
, New York in the Brighton section. My mother had a small apartment at that address. I frequently used that address, because as a Navy itinerant, I lacked a permanent address. That Rochester address has been bulldozed into what Rochestarians call, "The Can of Worms," a highway-interchange gone wrong.

In an earlier chapter, there was a description of Boston & Maine Airways' pilot Hazen Bean and his Stinson Trimotor flight out of Boston into clouds. He used his turn indicator to keep the wings level while he climbed slowly and finally got on top of the cloud bank. For perspective, Hazen Bean undoubtedly had many counterparts who had encountered comparable situations, and found a way as Bean did to surmount the challenge. The difference for my benefit and for aviation's benefit is that Captain Mudge of Northeast Airlines chose to relate Bean's story.

The expression, "needle-ball and airspeed" best characterized an era of defensive instrument flying that a skilled pilot might use at that time in aviation history. Using needle-ball and airspeed for instrument flight was used primarily when one got caught in instrument conditions that had not been anticipated. If anticipated, instrument-flight, totally blind and without a visual horizon, was to be avoided.

A Navy instrument flight manual of the 1940s era (specifically, NAVAER 00-80W-1, dated 1944) contrasted an early method, "needle-ball and airspeed," known also as the "1-2-3 system," with a later method known as the "attitude system."

For the 1-2-3 system, the manual told the reader, "The rudder governs the turn needle, the ailerons govern the ball bank indicator and the elevators govern the air-speed indicator needle." That was how the NAVAER manual expressed the 1-2-3 system, otherwise known to those who did not read manuals as "needle-ball and airspeed." It is a good thing that Hazen Bean had not read that manual. He kept his plane on a steady course using his ailerons to keep the wings level. The ball helped the pilot to avoid putting his aircraft into a skid, provided he kept the ball centered with rudder. Without a visual horizon and with no gyro horizon, a skid would put G-forces on the plane and its pilot and lead to disorientation for the pilot. Page 7 of a later 1945 Navy publication, NAVAER 00-80W-7, is more helpful.

"The (turn) instrument is activated by a gyroscope which is rotated by air entering the case through a jet. Although a suction of 4 inches Hg. (Hg is the abbreviation for the element, Mercury) is supplied by a mechanical pump, the pressure differential between the inside of the case and the surrounding atmosphere is kept constant at 2 inches Hg by means of a restrictor valve. The gyro rotor is so mounted that it precesses whenever the airplane turns, causing the indicator needle to move off-center."

And so we are reminded that Hazen Bean's turn needle involved our friend, the gyro.

An interesting piece of collateral information is that the turn indicator was noted as the only flight indicator that continued to provide valid information if the aircraft went into a spin. The 1944 Navy manual also added the following statement:

"In the attitude system, he (the pilot) thinks and acts in exactly the same manner as he would in contact flight."

It's as though wishing would make it so. That 1944 manual reads now, nearly 60 years after it was published, as quite likely the transcription of a classroom instructor's spoken words. It appears to be an effort to persuade pilots who had atempted some instrument flying by needle-ball and airspeed to convert to the new attitude system as a better system. Since student pilots in our World War II military classes had not been flying by the 1-2-3 system, and most in fact had not been flying at all, the ground instructor's effort to convert students was at best, academic, and at worst, confusing. In fact, neither of those alternatives was going to be successful. Even more puzzling, the gyro horizon was already in use.

The emphasis that seems to have been almost totally overlooked in language intended to persuade one to leave one practice for another, is the huge change brought about by the introduction of the gyro horizon to the instrument panel in the cockpit. That gave a pilot a horizon. It was a sea change in instrument flight. The earlier instruments had powerful virtues and would help one be a better pilot and would remain relevant, but the real message was that cockpits could now have a horizon at all times. It was the gyro horizon. There was no "attitude system" without it. It changed flying.

The experience of pilot Hazen Bean in his "conversion" to the use of the turn needle stands out in one more respect. It was vital for Bean, with the instrumentation he had then, *not to turn* the airplane. The later addition of the ball in the bottom of the turn indicator helped a pilot who could not always "feel" his aircraft, to make a coordinated turn, avoiding slipping and skidding. Even later, training exercises emphasized patterns one could fly to "calibrate" the turn needle, and deduce how many degrees per second one would be turning in a specific airplane with a "one needle-width turn." With the needle and the ball, the rudder and the aileron, in reasonable control, one still needed to know what was happening due to the action of the plane's elevator. The altimeter would indicate if the plane was going up or down, but only yielded a result, a new altitude that aircraft had arrived at. The rate of climb indicator would tell the pilot whether his aircraft's nose was up or down, but it is a "jumpy" instrument-it does not integrate at all. Oversimplifying a bit, the altimeter needle is too slow for "blind flying," and the rate of climb indicator is too fast. This set of instruments was never going to be adequate for planned instrument flying and could only buy limited time for the best pilots when they ran into unpredicted weather conditions.

The earlier Stearman trainer pilot had the very basic instruments, airpseed, altimeter, turn needle with ball, and rate of climb or descent indicator. Provided that he or she stuck to contact (visual) flight rules, there was a visual horizon. With that combination, a Stearman pilot could learn smooth, coordinated flight under visual flight rules sufficient to satisfy the fussiest check pilot.

For instrument flying, the gyro horizon needed to be added to that earlier basic flight instrument set. This proved to be the instrument that the pilot, with some training, would need to achieve smooth, coordinated flight in the thickest of clouds. It was a substitute for the visual horizon and provided an indication of nose up or down or level and wings level or dipped left or dipped right. In the case of smog over a city or a region with some lights, the gyro horizon is friendlier than any hazy visual horizon.

Illustration 12, the Lockheed *10 Electra* panel, told the story. Complete "dual" instrumentation was not yet achieved in that aircraft but the "makings" were there. The vital flight attitude control indicators were placed in the center of the panel where both pilots could see them. The altimeter location favored the pilot and is just behind the right rim of his control wheel. The gyro horizon is top left center. Airspeed is just below. Just to its right is the turn needle with its ball in the same enclosure below. To its right is the "rate of climb or glide." Its needle is at nine o'clock, the "zero" for this indicator, appropriate for a plane on the ground.

Early instruments were introduced into aviation use, one at a time. Today, when introduced, many would be denoted a "system," but in early aviation that term was little used. There certainly are systems in aircraft today, worthy of the term, but there is an element of salesmanship involved when the term is overused.

It took the military and its big contractors, sometimes now referred to as the military-industrial complex, to bring the term "systems" into aviation. Many of the systems can be called "information systems." "Avionics" was another term that came along in the last half of the 20th century. That term introduced electronics into aviation systems.

The APS-15 radar on the PB4Y-2 or the APS-20 in the later P2V aircraft were conceived and installed as systems. Antennae, receivers and transmitters including magnetrons or klystrons, and visual displays, have all been defined as subsystems. When these are put together to provide a user-function, the whole came to be called a system. The same was true for the Electronic Countermeasures (ECM) system. The navigation system, LORAN, came to aviation as a system. Later, flight control systems more and more leaned to electronic sensors and transmitters that could act or react at electronic speeds.

Long before use, and overuse, of the word system, the introduction of redundancy was a design objective in aviation. The Stearman biplane was the first hands-on experience for many fledgling pilots in the early days of World War II. The Stearman engine was started with an assist from a ground mechanic who got hold of the prop and gave it a pull, and got out of the way. In cold weather, a bungee cord was attached to the tip of the prop, and perhaps a gas truck would perform the extra duty of pulling on that cord. Later, compressed air in a cartridge became available on some aircraft and finally electric starting came to aviation. Those were improvements.

During those engine starts, the Stearman pilot had his magneto lever on "both." Later, with the engine warmed up and before takeoff, the pilot would rev up the engine and look for any change in revolutions per minute (rpm) as he tested his magnetos, first on "right" then on "left," to see if there was any appreciable drop in rpm from that indicator when the switch was on "both." That was basic redundancy. It is the in-flight redundant systems that are of greatest interest, particularly if instrument flying is in the plan.

Any example of a navigation system for our new century would include the Global Positioning System (GPS) with its indicator (display) in cars or ships or aircraft representing one essential part of such a system, with satellites and data links contributing the other essential elements.

The magnetic compass has been important to mariners and to aviation. It needs constant attention for a correct reading. There is "variation" in the earth's magnetic field, a correction for which needs be introduced to determine true heading. Each magnetic compass has its own "deviation" signature, another correction that needs to be entered.

An important system that came to aviation use in World War II was the IFF system. IFF stands for Identification, Friend or Foe. With the system turned "on" in an aircraft, a transponder reacts automatically to an interrogation signal from a ground station or "dew line" aircraft keeping watch along the northern parallels. The object is to make sure that all aircraft entering a defined airspace are identified as friendly. In war, "friendly" is the opposite of "foe," or at least unfriendly. In peacetime, friendly means that "you, and we now know who you are," are specifically located in an air traffic control geographic location grid. Pilots who have failed to energize the IFF in their aircraft have risked their lives. First, they are not being deleted from the potential "foe" status. They have risked the lives of other "friendlies" by being an unknown and perhaps uncontrolled target or even a wholly undetected target in increasingly crowded air traffic control airspace. In the heightened alertness after September 11, 2001, the IFF system's importance can hardly be exaggerated.

The extremely rapid progress in aviation between 1949 and 1959 reached a milestone in 1952 with jet-powered commercial flight. The jet airliners gradually took over from the Douglas DC-7s and Lockheed *Constellations*. Jets and prop-jets have now provided a half-century of airline passenger safety and comfort. Since everything happened a little faster with jet propulsion, the air navigation systems and the air traffic control systems all had to perform with greater solution accuracy and faster responses. By this time the concept of redundant systems had fully taken hold. The dual magnetos of the early reciprocating engines led to at least one backup in an aircraft for every vital flight control system, including instruments.

Intelligent data collection has been essential to safety of flight. Delivering good information to the pilot is a first step. As aircraft increased in size, power and capability, the instrument panel grew in number of indicators until space to put them became a designer's (human factors engineer's) challenge. The first of two main messages that instructors delivered very early in flight training was that those were *indicators*, devices that communicated something about the basic performance of something else. The second message was, "Do not let your eyes become locked on any one indicator. Scan a selection of basic indicators on a regular routine."

The terms, indicator, gauge, and instrument are being used interchangeably, to mean devices that communicated to a pilot the amount of, or rate of, something. Strictly speaking, the instrument itself contains a sensor and a processor. It is most often not on the "panel" and is located in the information chain before its indicator. Pilots tended to refer to the "panel" as the structure on which the indicators were mounted and then to refer to it as "the instrument panel." In early aircraft, with gravity fed fuel systems, the gasoline gauge was the instrument and the indicator bundled into one.

The U.S. was constantly upgrading aviation systems all during World War II. Changes were evaluated rapidly. High volume flight operations records were sought to provide good statistical bases for change. Since combat pilots and flight crews were already at risk, the improvement looked for by military aircraft designers may have occasionally been weighted higher than the negative of premature introduction.

Aircraft accident reports often revealed that more testing would have been in order. The accident turned out to be, in effect, a missing part of a test program that failed to achieve one key objective, safety. In military aviation in the war days, a new design aircraft could become operational too soon, and the early experience would tell if this were the case. Changing designs always came a little more readily in military aviation than in passenger aviation.

The commercial transport skies today grind out more "mean time to failure" data than any other enterprise that I can think of. The jet engine has leveled the playing field between civil and military aviation, insofar as accumulation of valid power plant data is concerned.

Aviation owes much to the field of "information science." That was true even before such a field became recognized as such. The flight data recorder and the voice recorder required in today's transport aircraft come at the end of the chain. These help drain that last bit of information that might prove to be actionable data from an aviation accident.

The objective to lower the ennui and fatigue and tension of pilots and ground air controllers has moved forward but high subsonic speeds and crowded skies means that the margins are tighter today. Air Traffic Control meets this crowded sky and is just able to hold its own. The same is true on the ground where the oversight function is identified as Ground Control. It is crowded there too.

The Triumph of Instrument Flight

The day in which the Corps of Engineers or the Navy Seabees could go in and hack out an aircraft runway in record time has passed. In populated areas, it takes ten years to construct new runways and approaches and it requires the introduction of many, many ground systems. In my home state of Massachusetts, the aviation authorities are trying to add one new runway at Logan Airport. It could be a long time before a new runway is approved for Logan Airport in Boston.

During the last half of the 20th century, aviation invested heavily in development and refinement of aircraft and ground systems with hands-off instrument landings an important objective. With such aircraft as the Boeing 757/767/777 series, and the later Airbus 300 series aircraft, the hands off instrument approach landing is now an approved procedure in the commercial air transport business.

Instrument flying, around the clock and around the world, has provided an opportunity for direct human contact so enormous as to defy any method of measurement. Leaders rely on face-to-face contact. World history is made from human contact. World histories have yet to be written that would include the monumental impact of dependable human flight anywhere, anytime.

The events of September 11, 2001 found the airplane in use as a weapon on a clear day in the northeastern part of the United States. Instrument flying that day was not required. The deed was accomplished by 19 men who could not have pulled it off that day had the weather in the northeast been anything other than cavu, ceiling and visibility unlimited.

The next chapter is a fast forward to the present day in instrument flying.

Chapter 14- Hands-off Landings

Faith made this story possible. The early inventors and pioneers of flight had faith. The engineers, builders, investors, pilots, air controllers, airport operators, flight and ground support personnel and passengers kept the faith. I am grateful that their dedication made possible my years in flying. As an aviator, I had a safe, undistinguished career, and there is merit in that.

There are about fifty years to cover here, from the 1950s to the fourth year in the new millennium. It took almost all of those years for pilot proficiency and technology, and the confidence that these had effectively matured together, to move commercial aviation to accept landings under full instrument control with passengers aboard. Hands Off! Fifty years for that last fifty feet may sound like overstatement, but the triumph of a fully blind landing can hardly be overstated. A number of elements had to fall in place first.

The Triumph of Instrument Flight

In the late 1950s, Bell Aircraft Corporation pilots at the Niagara Falls, New York Airport, sat in their cockpits, hands-following but not hands-controlling their aircraft while the aircraft made landings and takeoffs under full automatic control. In these flights, the objective of the Bell Aircraft engineers was to configure Navy planes for blind landings aboard aircraft carriers. The military can do these things experimentally and operationally. Those efforts succeeded and the blind landing capability exists in the Navy carrier fleet. Some pilots are still not keen about the full automated approach and landing. The Navy in the 21st century has an additional aid. With global positioning system (GPS) navigation, the pilot can always locate the carrier. Just as helpful, the carrier itself can often find clear space with some horizontal visibility above the water to conduct aircraft recovery operations.

By 1940, regular instrument flight had become routine along with pilot-controlled letdowns and landings using radio range approaches. Within a few years, at some airfields, the final approach could be assisted by a Ground Controlled Approach (GCA) controller. A technology known as Instrument Landing System (ILS) came soon after. Hands-off landings were still a few decades in the future. Commercial aviation was not ready in 1929 with Sperry's gyro stabilizer, or in 1959, to turn over its flight controls to electronic systems and gyroscopic stabilizers for takeoff, flight, and landing.

Military and civil aviation experiences are entwined in many aspects of U.S. aviation. Some differences between civil and military practice have occurred. Not sharp distinctions, but understandable differences in their emphasis on the subject of preservation of life. Risks that are acceptable in the military are not acceptable in commercial flying, certainly not when passengers are involved. And when a military flight is dedicated to the transport of passengers, the differences disappear.

In 1950, the end of the reign of the piston engine could be foreseen.

Early transport aircraft were not pressurized or were pressurized to fly only at relatively low altitudes. Fuel efficient jet engines and pressurization technology were partners in higher altitude flight profiles. Pressurization freed the crew and passengers from the need to don oxygen masks.

The altitude requirement escalated rapidly as the number of flights in the airspace increased. In addition there was a weather advantage. Cumulus cloud buildups (thunderheads) can rise above 50,000 feet. Detouring around the upper reaches of those buildups permitted a safer, less turbulent flight for the later jet-powered, pressurized, commercial aircraft. For one period of years when the Boeing 707 and the Douglas DC-8 ruled the transport skies, the windows told the story. "Tested to 39,000 feet" was the marking on passenger cabin windows. By then a passenger, I hoped the pilots had read the window markings.

Earlier aircraft flights had no choice. If they were to proceed, they had to penetrate weather, and the choice of altitude to penetrate was often the critical decision. In air traffic control's first years, controllers did not have the option with available technology to send aircraft off the airways system defined by low frequency radio range stations to make detours around weather. The introduction of ground-based microwave radar with a plan position indicator (PPI) scope centered on an air traffic control (ATC) location permitted that station to identify (with the help of IFF-identification friend or foe) and track each aircraft in that ATC airspace. This was more positive than an aircraft reporting its own position. When the two were redundant, that is, the pilot's low frequency radio range position report and the ATC radar gave the same position for the aircraft, the system was working with a much higher degree of certainty. With these tools in place, even lower altitude aircraft could be vectored around storms and could even be vectored into positions and talked down to lower altitudes where visual approaches to landing at an airfield could be undertaken.

Microwave radar was a great forward leap for technology in World War II. It was quickly put to civilian use after the war. We have seen how pilots in the fog-bound Aleutians put the APS-15 radar to work. One advantage of x-band radar at the shorter wavelength end of the microwave spectrum was its small form factor. Early radars like CXAM on Navy ships required huge "bed spring" antennas that stood out even in the complex of spars and other equipment on busy masts. Raytheon-manufactured SG radar on later Navy ships used the x-band spectrum and came with an antenna that fit into a very small profile.

So it was on the *Privateers.* In our Navy's patrol squadrons, the x-band antenna was housed in a small protrusion below the aircraft, called a radome, quite aerodynamically clean. Longer range radar known as S-band, was the type found, for example on dew-line Lockheed *Constellation* aircraft. The antennae were so large that in their flyable configuration, that they dominated the aircraft profile.

Precision approach radar (PAR) systems, a combination usually of S-band for longer range and x-band for close-in accuracy, were rapidly adapted for expanded use in air traffic control centers in the United States following World War II. All major aircraft control centers gained the ability to give aircraft "vector" directions to letdown positions, and then give directions to the pilot to line the aircraft up for landing. In many instances this removed the necessity for lengthy radio range letdowns to approach and land at the airfields served.

An onboard radar system for transport aircraft was not overlooked. U.S. military air transport services had the first opportunity with x-band radar which had been launched into war service with a lot of secrecy. 1946 was the first postwar year. General Electric had developed the APS-10 radar, a lightweight x-band radar system. It was adopted by the USAAF Air Transport Command in 1946 and fitted to one of its C-54 (civilian DC-4 and Navy R5D) transport aircraft. Aerodynamically, its antenna was placed in a small faired housing under the plane's belly. First Lieutenant Milton Rhodes, along with George E. Ballweg and Joseph H. Andre, Jr., who had both previously been in the armed forces, have been publicly recognized for their contribution to the demonstration of onboard radar applicability to transport aircraft. The subsequent interest of the U.S. Navy and American Airlines led to the placement of the antenna in a radome right up in the transport aircraft's nose, where its descendants ride today. Dr. Milton Rhodes gives Peruvian International Airways credit as the first commercial airline to adopt the APS-10 technology with its antenna still configured under the fuselage.

The airborne radar system, once it had been packaged effectively on transport aircraft, gave the pilot an ability to "see into the clouds ahead." When the pilot can perceive severe turbulence on the radarscope, on or near the aircraft's planned flight track, he or she can seek diversion from the flight track for the safety and comfort benefit of the plane and its occupants.

The effectiveness of any radar used for ground search is enhanced by the height of its antenna above the earth. Antennae at 35,000 feet can see more than antennae on the ground. The jet engine, the pressurization of the cabin, and radar joined together to improve the safety and the quality of flying. The aircraft and its pilot simply had more options.

Before the defeat of Germany in World War II, the Luftwaffe had introduced both jet fighters and rocket plane interceptors into combat. Too late to change the outcome of the war in Europe, Germany nevertheless pioneered the operational jet age. England was not far behind with the U.S. a close third. Both the United States and Great Britain had test versions of jet aircraft well along in development programs by V-E day.

My first experience with jets in the U.S. was the Lockheed *Shooting Star*, a single-seat jet fighter plane. The squadron I reported to in 1951 received a two-seat trainer version (TV-2) of this aircraft to begin checking out middle-aged (anyone over 30) pilots. At this time, the Navy fighter jocks, with their new steam catapults and canted flight decks (both of which were British ideas) became operational on carriers then supporting both propeller and jet aircraft.

For multi-engine flying, I can recall United States Air Force pilots at Long Beach Airport making touch-and-go landings about 1950 in a twin jet bomber about the size of the World War II B-25

Mitchell. Those early twin-jets took a lot of runway for takeoff and had to stay pretty close to an airport. Fuel consumption rates were high and fuel capacities were low to keep weight down so that these planes of limited takeoff thrust could get off the ground.

JATO, for Jet Assisted Take Off, was an early thrust-enhancer in a support role. Afterburners were then added to jet engines to provide more takeoff thrust in the launch of military jet aircraft. I can recall hearing successive afterburner booms emanating from Westover Field, Massachusetts, near my home, when a squadron of F-102 or F-106 aircraft would be scrambled. Those reminders of the Cold War took place before Westover's fighters and its B-52 bombers were transferred and Westover became a reserve base with C-5 transport aircraft.

In the early days of operational jet squadrons in the military, tail pipe temperature was a required part of the jet powered aircraft check off list. If the tail pipe temperature was too high, engine thrust would be down, takeoff distance lengthened and serious heat damage to metal could work its way back from tail pipe toward the heart of the power plant. Often, flights would be rescheduled for hours when the tail pipe temperature readings would be lower.

One of my memories of commercial jet flight was a United Airlines Boeing 707, a short version, making its maiden flight about 1959 from San Francisco to San Diego. This plane landed into a beautiful Lindbergh Field sunset, letting down very carefully over the El Cortez Hotel.

In the 1950s, the Air Force introduced the B-47, a range-starved nuclear delivery platform. It was complemented, then superseded, with the approval of many an Air Force pilot, by the B-52 of enduring operational life.

British transport aviation gave us the first commercial transport jet turbine aircraft, the four-jet DeHaviland *Comet.* After a number of incidents and accidents, this aircraft was retired from service. Travelers connecting through O'Hare Airport in Chicago, Illinois, recall one parked there for years, abandoned, too costly to fix or too chancy to fly to a decent burial in England. Her four jets were faired into the wings, as were those of the Navy's P-6M, an ill-fated four jet seaplane built by Martin in Baltimore. Both of the XP-6Ms crashed and the United States' effort to create a military seaplane with jet power ended, at least for my lifetime.

The Navy tried twin-jet carrier aircraft to deliver fat nuclear warheads. The AJ was a fat aircraft of short operational life and quickly forgettable capabilities. Douglas got the Navy successfully into multi-engine jets, with its A3-D for carrier-based nuclear delivery. The Navy added two jets to the two Wright 3350 propeller engines on the Lockheed P2V to create the P2V-5F series that extended the useful life of that successful patrol aircraft. In my own flights as pilot of that aircraft, we used the two jets to shorten our takeoff runs. Jet-prop aircraft also came into the inventory. For civil aviation and for short haul airlines these have maintained some performance advantages. But, by and large, the pure-jet has won the day. It took a little time.

Power plant development for aircraft propulsion is a dramatic story. The essential point here is that power plant progress has made its mark in its contribution to instrument flight.

The jet engine has proved the most reliable of all aircraft propulsion choices. It has had an impact well beyond its reliability. When first used in military fighter aircraft, it forced the domestic air traffic control system to incorporate important improvements in instrument flight procedures. The early jets were fuel-limited. The military developed TACAN, a passive air navigation system in the UHF range, to support reduced time penetration profiles for jet powered aircraft at weathered-in destination airports. The lengthy high cone, outbound leg, low cone procedures took much too much time. Early jets, particularly, required new, faster, penetration procedures at weathered in airports. All aviation benefited.

The fuel per mile efficiencies eventually became very good. That was not enough. The U.S. Air Force made in flight refueling a standard practice to support longer flights, and the Navy followed suit. All-weather performance for jet fighters became part of the design, development and manufacturing plan. With the new performance capabilities, the fatigue challenge shifted to the pilot from the aircraft system. In larger transport aircraft like the Boeing 747, having two pilot crews aboard became the standard procedure for long flights.

With airspeed, altimeter, rate of climb, the turn indicator and the magnetic compass as "givens" in 1930, and with some trepidation, let me offer my summary of progress:

Essential to instrument flight, 1930s: The gyro-horizon flight instrument; the radio navigation systems including low frequency radio range stations, non-directional beacons, airborne radio direction finder for these low frequencies and then its automation, airways network and control; crystal controlled megacycle band, "always on" voice radio

Supporting instrument flight, 1930s: Carburetor heat; the anti-icing systems for flight surfaces, propellers and airspeed; the directional gyro and the autopilot

Advances, 1940s: GCA and ILS precision approach systems; better anti-icing systems; x-band radar on the ground; x-band radar in the aircraft; higher frequency (hundred megacycle) air navigation and voice radio systems; IFF

Advances, 1950s: Higher altitude pressurization of aircraft; the jet turbine engine for its reliability and altitude performance; inertial navigation systems

Advances, 1990s: Hands-off landings

We need also to acknowledge the pilots who adapted so successfully. Few have even noticed the accomplishment. The pilots that matriculated with new technology into the era of all-weather jet aircraft marked the leading edge of a new breed of military pilots and a new breed of transport pilots. These men and women made contributions not only to execute missions requiring penetration into instrument weather, but their new destination-airport weather penetration techniques, with time-abbreviated approach and letdown procedures, have benefited all aviation.

Hands-off Landings

I have endeavored to tread lightly on the technology subject, sticking to what the technology accomplished and leaving out the design details.

The instructor personnel involved at hundreds of civilian airfields, and the training they have given and promoted, the young pilots they have graduated, along with the Aircraft and Power plant (A&P) licenses that have been earned, have made a variety of aviation careers attractive and challenging. The flight simulators that took the place of the Link Trainers are making an enormous contribution to pilot training. (These simulators were also involved in the training programs elected by some of the hijacker pilots who flew the death planes on September 11, 2001.)

I salute the Fixed Base Operators (FBOs), many of whom struggle to make ends meet and keep a facility going. They deserve recognition. They persevere, often at a sacrifice in pay and emoluments, for the love of aviation.

I recognize and salute commercial airlines. I am now in a modest way, a member of an airline family. One of my sons has made American Airlines his career, not as a pilot, but as reservations agent, ticket counter agent, ramp agent, and baggage agent. His wife has been an American Airlines overseas boarding agent. With her gift of the Spanish language, she was chosen to help open several South American terminals for her airline. Another son has a wife who is a flight attendant on American Airlines' South American runs. Another son's wife has just retired from more than 30 years of flying as a stewardess for Delta Air Lines and earlier as a flight attendant for Northeast Airlines. Her recognition of the value of Robert Mudge's story of the Yellowbird got me launched on this book.

My own hands-on activity in the pilot's seat of Navy aircraft came to an end in the early 1960s. From then on, my understanding of both commercial and military aviation has come from reading, from flying as a passenger, and from contact with those who have been direct participants in aviation progress in the United States in that period. I have learned from my considerable experience as a passenger, and from all of these next-generation family alliances, that the success of an airline in 2003 is built on employee tension, from the cockpit to the tarmac. The stewardess of 1935 and her passenger shared the excitement of aviation. The flight attendant of 2003 often has a grim, tense, look.

Airlines work hard to get flights out on time, as carefully loaded as possible and as full as allowed with law-abiding, paying, passengers that can be attracted to its services. I am almost a little too able to see what is happening in the scenes and behind the scenes when I have been an airline passenger, at times a frequent passenger. Every employee of a scheduled airline in this new millennium is a Lifeguard at Shark Beach. In today's competitive, terror-threatened, global environment, it would not work any other way. I am hopeful we can return to times in which airline flying can be a more pleasurable experience.

I have reflected on this and worry about it and do not have any idea how we might relieve that tension and still achieve the results we demand.

When I was a child growing up near the New York Central railroad tracks in western New York State, I could hear the big freight going through every night about 2 a.m. Its steam whistle was a thrill. When the snow got too high even for an emergency steam engine's plow during harsh winters, I would wake up because I did *not* hear a whistle that night. For the past twenty years, a small twin engine plane has come over my home every morning in the 4 a.m. darkness. Those are surely two radial engines, like the twin Beech of yore, and I can hear the pilot synch-ing his engines some mornings. In occasional bad weather, I have missed him or her though that plane's on-schedule reliability has been so good that I am sure it made it to Bradley Airport at Hartford later in the morning. Where did it originate? I had pretty good binaural hearing up to five years ago, so I tracked that plane from Portland, Maine. Even on clear nights, it was obviously on the Bradley Field (Hartford, Connecticut) approach that takes most instrument flights over my house.

Why is that little plane making the trip so regularly, weekdays and weekends? Well, I can speculate that it has been bringing fresh lobster to Hartford. This has been my last active connection with aviation. Just as with the steam engine pulling that midnight freight, a radial engine throb awakens wonderful memories.

Today, young ladies are fully involved in all aspects of U.S. aviation. Many have already become high-time airline command pilots and some have become fighter pilots in the military.

Content from three pilot sources are now going to be quoted here. The three are Chad Mingo, Robert Mitchell and Frank Davis. Their thoughts arrived just before the original draft of this story was completed in 2001.

The first is an e-mail from Navy pilot Chad Mingo. I have never met Chad. His e-mail arrived in my in-box because it was forwarded by a family to a list of military e-mail addresses compiled by WW II Ranger, Carl Lehmann. My e-mail address was on one of those lists. The F-14 *Tomcat* is a durable single seat carrier aircraft made by Grumman. The F-18 *Hornet* is a newer two-seat Navy carrier aircraft. Mingo is flying a *Tomcat*. I have edited out aboard-ship paragraphs to stick to the flying episodes.

"28 October 2001

Hi Folks,

Had a mission tonight that went really well. Sweaty (our girl pilot) was on my wing and she hung in there really well. We went out to the tanker (the first of three times) and it went ok, but three and a half hours later, after the moon had set, it was so friggin' dark. We all have our lights off so the bad guys can't see us. To tank we have to take our night vision goggles off, and it takes 20 minutes for your eyes to get used to the dark again. So I came off the goggles and tanked immediately. All I could see was the dark mass of an L-1011(a tanker aircraft converted by the military from the Lockheed L-1011passenger aircraft) and the basket of the drogue (a flared-end open tube that passes the fuel from the tanker aircraft to the plane being refueled-the drogue streams down from, and behind, the tanker aircraft ahead) we plug into. The air was a little bumpy and there was no horizon. I tried to stare at the basket and fly formation off of that, but I started to get vertigo. I was in a turn with the tanker but I did not perceive it. I was bouncing around and getting dizzy. It is the hardest thing I have done in a while.

The combat stuff is going well. Our four ship(a flight of four aircraft), of two *Tomcats* and two *hornets* (I will never capitalize the plastic plane!) was going after stuff...and coming off target we started getting anti aircraft artillery coming up at us. They could hear our jets and were shooting at me. It looked like Roman candle balls coming up in streams. I saw on the mountain where it was coming from and rolled in on the site. We got a designation, and I came off and felt a thump under my bird. Now I was pissed. We had good engine readings and the hydraulic system was good, so I was not too worried about the jet. We watched that spot on the ground with our system and when they shot again, we were able to pinpoint where it came from. Next pass they got a thousand pounds of love riding a laser beam shining on their heads. It is strange to say that killing people could be satisfying, but I wanted to cheer. 'Oh, so you want to shoot at ME?' The jet was fine for the trip home, and we landed uneventfully, if a night carrier landing with no moon at all can be called uneventful.

I took some pictures the other day, and some from a night strike through my goggles...they are awesome, I just wish they did not limit the field of view so severely. It is like looking through two toilet paper tubes. The countryside is so barren. Nothing but rocks and dirt, and more sand than you can imagine. Who would live there? The river valleys have some agricultural development, but as you go further North, it is Grand Canyon like. I would love to go raging around in all the terrain, but it is too dangerous below a certain altitude. We don't go below it.

I don't have much to tell you about except work. Have not been working out so much, and movies are right out. We have our first 'Beer Day' coming in about a week. If we are at sea for more than 45 days straight, they give everybody two beers. Somehow, people manage to get more. I might be doing some scrounging.

There really is nothing like being in a tightly knit organization. Even more so when you are living day to day, trying to make the most of a bad situation.

Hope you are taking care. I am looking forward to getting home and saying hello in person. Chad"

The American Heritage Dictionary's second meaning for "vertigo" is the one most applicable to a word that two pilots quoted in these pages have now used. Both of them used it in conjunction with air-to-air refueling. For "vertigo," American Heritage states, "confused; disoriented state of mind." Let me risk a little extension of the dictionary phrase in connection with flying. In clear visibility, with a good grasp of an earth horizon, a pilot does not normally get vertigo. If he engages in acrobatics and lets go of reality, he can become disoriented, confused or dizzy. The pilot who gets inadvertently into instrument conditions where he has no earth horizon and has not prepared a substitute, can get vertigo. The pilot who is successfully flying on instruments is proceeding according to an artificial construct of the earth world that replaces the real world. Irrespective of good grasp of the earth world, or good grasp of an artificial world that successfully replaces it, a pilot can become transfixed in a highly focused task. In-flight refueling is such a task. The pilot being buffeted by turbulence, for example, and attempting to chase the refueling attachment could experience vertigo and would have to force himself or herself back to an effective flight orientation whether flying VFR or on instruments. As that early instructor told me, do not focus on a single instrument. Constantly scan all the relevant instruments.

I have endeavored in the early chapters of this story to make the important point that military aviation and civilian aviation have been very important to each other. They were almost co-dependent during the formative days of U.S. aviation in the early part of the 20th century. Gradually, during the last 50 years of the 20th century, the bond has loosened. Each of these components of aviation is now quite self-sufficient.

Yes, the commercial airlines are still happy to see a cadre of trained, young, military pilots knocking at their doors for openings in pilot ranks. But we are not likely to again see contract civilian pilots manning operational military aircraft to establish new air routes needed for ferry requirements. We will still see and are seeing civil aviation pilots flying troops in charter transport aircraft. And Reserve and National Guard aviators who fly for airlines for a living are being called to active duty for aviation duties that cover the gamut of the military aircraft inventory.

Some chapters have centered on events in which I have in some way participated. The contributions to our country of civil airline pilots, general aviation pilots, Navy pilots, Army pilots, and pilots in the Air Force, defy measure. It was never a challenge in the writing of this story to make a special effort to look for examples to relate. In telling the story that I wanted to tell, I came upon example after example of the valor, the ingenuity, and the pioneering that both civil aviation and the military air services have meant to the United States. Watch a Coast Guard helicopter crew on TV as it makes a rescue in a storm at sea. That takes proficiency of a high order.

I'll go back once more to the Aleutian flying I did in 1946-48 to illustrate the value of GCA to military pilots at airfields before ILS existed. The two principal airfields for Navy pilots were at Kodiak, Alaska and at Adak, Alaska. Each had a low frequency radio range letdown and approach from the sea toward an instrument runway that had mountainous terrain directly past its far end. When making low frequency radio range approaches at either field, mandatory pull-ups were required well short of the instrument runway at a non-directional beacon if the pilot had not gained visual contact by that point in the approach. Both fields had GCA units and thank God for that. On a GCA approach, the pilot turns control of his aircraft heading and altitude over to the short interval vocal commands given by a ground operator (the GCA controller) who can see the plane on special radarscopes. The polished vocal practice, a result of much training, of the ground controller included a requirement that he or she never be silent for any sustained period. The pilot followed the directions of the controller in flying his plane right down to touchdown. The skill of both pilot and GCA controller was directed to keeping the aircraft very close to the desired position so that corrections were always small. A safe touchdown resulted from a collaborative effort.

Let me add here a fragment from an e-mail received from an FAA official who was in the GCA "shack" at Shemya some years after my time there. A Navy A-6 (now EA-6) had been aloft on a long flight and had to come back into Shemya when the Aleutian weather went "zero-zero." At the very end of the approach, as the aircraft was at its flare-out phase, the GCA controller told the pilot to pull up and go around for another approach. There was an awkward silence and the pilot then came on and said he was unable to follow the instruction. Reason: He was taxiing on the duty runway and wanted a ground vehicle to come out and direct him to the flight line. The folks in the GCA shack had not even heard the plane as it passed them and obviously had not seen it. In my own direct experience in the 1940s, I have seen aircraft at NAS Whidbey Island make successful GCA-controlled landings in fog with no ceiling and little horizontal visibility. It was attempted and for the most part successfully completed when alternate landing fields "shut down."

About the middle of my Aleutian tour, in May of 1947, our Privateer aircraft were outfitted with new electronic equipment bearing the designation, SCS-51. Many of the airfields we used were just being equipped with the ground electronics installation necessary for the SCS-51 equipment to work. Known in the commercial airline world as ILS, for Instrument Landing System, the SCS-51 system provided the pilot with constant glide path and azimuth information in graphic presentations in an instrument display right on the instrument panel. The pilot actually "sees" whether he is high or low from the correct glidepath and right or left of the correct glidepath. It is a very good system and in more advanced forms it is used today.

The pilot's gyro horizon and gyro compass indicators were vital to the "small correction" concept of a GCA approach and were just as vital to the "small correction" practice in the ILS approach.

The Triumph of Instrument Flight

First use of ILS in commercial aviation is credited to Braniff Airways in 1947. Commercial airline, air freight, and corporate aircraft pilots would almost always choose to use the ILS system over GCA, when both were available, because the pilot stays in complete control. When the pilot reaches landing minimums and cannot see the runway, he or she can execute a "missed approach procedure" and take the plane back to altitude. Commercial pilots believe in their abilities and wanted intellectual as well as hands-on control of their aircraft during takeoffs and landings. Commercial pilots, many of whom are ex-military or military reserve pilots and have used both, did not minimize the value of GCA. Most would certainly have used GCA without question when it was the only option, but their choice was ILS.

World War II military pilots welcomed GCA because it gave them a chance to get back on the ground safely when a low frequency radio range approach or an Automatic Direction Finder (ADF) approach would still leave them up in the clouds. GCA was a life-saving solution that came during the war to some military bases. There was no SCS-51 in those war years. A GCA endearment that I recall was the intimacy of the attention given by a ground controller during the critical period of a pilot's descent to the ground under instrument conditions.

ILS in its modern embodiments takes most of the load for instrument weather situations involving low ceiling and low visibility approaches and landings in the United States. ILS is passive, and not only in the sense that the pilot keeps control of the aircraft. With ILS, there is no personnel crew on the ground to be paid and trained and on watch 24 hours a day. For the most part, ILS and its system descendants have become the standard.

For those readers interested in pursuing more viewpoints on how low ceiling, low visibility instrument approaches and landings are handled, a little web searching is a good first step. First, the acronym "GCA" will now fetch such groups as the Green Communities Alliance, Gun Control Alliance and Global Coalition for Africa. Not too helpful. One must insert the complete terminology, "Ground Control Approach," to discover that two full GCA systems are archived at the Wright Patterson Air Force Base (WPAFB) Museum.

At the website, www.wpafb.mil/museum, one discovers that the final resting place of two complete GCA systems, one originally in use at Keesler AFB, in Mississippi, and the other that had been in service at Wright Patterson Field, are in the U.S. Air Force Museum at Wright Patterson Field. The Keesler unit remained in service until 1980 and the WPAFB unit until 1978. As improved after World War II, these units consisted of a search radar system with a 45-mile search radius, a two-way voice radio system, and a precision radar system for use during the 11-mile final approach to the runway. Those web pages include a brief statement on how this equipment was used. For example, "It (the precision radar) alternately scans in both the vertical and horizontal planes to track the approaching aircraft's line of descent and course. The controller advises the pilot by radio of any changes in glide-path or course needed to accomplish a safe landing." For glide-path control, the oral instruction would be in the form of "increase your rate of descent" or "decrease your rate of descent."

One historically important paragraph on the WPAFB museum website cites the Berlin Airlift in 1948-49 as an example of GCA's critical performance. All ground routes to the city had been sealed off by the Soviets and the western powers undertook to supply the citizens by airlift. Hundreds of lives of flight and airport service people were at risk everyday when the Berlin airport was under instrument conditions. GCA was the way that millions of Berliners received essential supplies during the Soviet blockade. Young Berliners recalled the candy that the pilots brought them. Older ones would more likely remember that the cargo on many flights was coal to heat them.

The insertion of "ILS" into a web search engine leads to discovery that the acronym is in use by many organizations that are not remotely connected with instrument flight. One helpful result turned up by a search engine in 2001 resulted from "Instrument

Landing System" and one very helpful listing from that insertion, was,

home.sprynet/~jayschnell/Ils1.htm.

(The website is no longer current. Readers who know how to use the web's archiving tools can find it. The next paragraph contains webmaster/pilot Jay Gerald Schnedorf's phrases, in quotation marks, that attracted me to his description of altitude changes involved in an instrument approach.)

In a page headed, "Instrument Landing System," Mr. Schnedorf visualizes a precision instrument approach as "a child's slide at the park." He likens the non-precision approach to "a series of steps on a staircase." For the non-precision approach, Schnedorf cited two examples that might be available to a pilot. One is a directional system such as a passive Localizer. Another is an active system involving an Airport Surveillance Radar. Using that radar, an air traffic controller can vector a pilot on a series of headings and tell him or her at what point to descend and how much altitude to lose. Active or passive systems can aid a pilot in bringing his aircraft toward the instrument runway on a series of headings, the last heading being the correct landing runway heading. The precision approach systems that Mr. Schnedorf cites are the Instrument Landing System (ILS), the Precision Approach Radar (PAR) and the Microwave Landing System (MLS).

As a direct consequence of placing a draft version of this story on our publisher's website (www.daileyint.com) in November 2001, I was privileged to enter into dialogues with two recently retired airline pilots in early 2002. Relevant portions of these dialogues follow.

With his words, "We've come a long way; baby," Delta Air Lines Captain Robert E. Mitchell, who retired in 1999, brought retired Navy Captain Franklyn E. Dailey, Jr. up to date on "hands-off landings" under Instrument Flight Rules (IFR) conditions. In an early chapter, I had written (and have now removed for reasons that will become obvious), "Commercial aviation is not ready in 2002 for this mode (hands-off landings) of operation." The lines that follow contain the response of Captain Mitchell on 02/12/2002 to my out-of-date sentence.

"In fact, the present generation aircraft (typified by B-757/767/777) are equipped for just that, and the crews so trained. It is common practice and approved procedure to engage the autopilot/flight director and RNAV (horizontal) and VNAV (vertical) at 1,000 feet agl (1,000 feet above ground level) after takeoff and not touch anything (including the brakes) until you reverse the engines on roll-out. Normal minimums for these aircraft going into a large airport that is Category III equipped, is just 600 feet runway visual range (no ceiling requirement at all). In essence, you don't see anything except the green centerline lights as you roll out!"

On 02/13/02, Captain Mitchell added a follow-up:

"Well, that is pretty much what computers have done for instrument flight and approaches in the last 20 years or so. I found as an instructor that getting a student (maybe with as much as 15 - 20 thousand flight hours and no previous experience in the 'glass cockpit airliners') to grasp the concept was no small challenge. You must realize that a lot has probably changed in the years since my retirement."

"The auto-flight system and controls in the B-757/767/777 aircraft are almost identical. In fact, the FAA issues an ATR rating (Airline Transport Rating) that is common to all three aircraft. My ticket shows 'Airline Transport Pilot: DC-9, B-757, B-767 (the 777 came just after I retired).' The system is comprised of the autopilot, autothrottles, autobrakes, flight director, RNAV and VNAV. All of these components are part of a larger bundle of 'magic' called the Flight Management System."

"The autopilot is pretty much the same as it has always been, just refined and refined. However, there are three separate autopilot systems that automatically engage in the approach mode to give redundancy. The autopilot may be used without any of the other autoflight components (and are the same as in a DC-6 or DC-9 plus or minus some details). The only restriction is that it cannot be used by itself without these other components below 1,000 feet agl."

"The auto throttle system is used most all of the time and is turned on/off by a switch on the glareshield. It sets the power for takeoff, will maintain a selected airspeed or mach number and is somehow (magic again) connected to the Flight Management System so that it will maintain a cruise airspeed/mach number that is the most efficient for that flight segment. The autobrakes must be used for takeoff (procedure) and are selected by a switch. They will apply maximum braking to all wheels if the throttles are manually retarded to idle for a rejected or aborted takeoff. They may be used for any landing, visual or instrument, but must be used for a Category III approach/landing. The flight director (two separate units, one for the captain and one for the first officer) is a standard dual-cue system (orange bars superimposed on the attitude gyro called the ADI or Attitude Directional Indicator) which may be used alone (hand flying) or coupled with the autopilot. It can be controlled manually by entering the desired heading and vertical command (altitude hold, selected vertical speed or go-around mode). It can be used in conjunction with the autopilot and/or the RNAVand VNAV."

"RNAV is the horizontal navigation system which is based on position information automatically gained from the DME (Distance Measuring Equipment), from two separate VORs (omnirange), and is backed up by three INS units (which become primary when out of range of VOR i.e., ocean crossing). This information is displayed in the cockpit on the HSI (Horizontal Situation Indicator)." (Author's Note. I am inferring that INS stands for Inertial Navigation System.)

"Flight plan information for RNAV and VNAV (and the Flight Management System) is entered by the crew into the CDU (cockpit display system) which is a very small computer screen and keyboard located on the center console between the pilots. There are two of these units; one for the captain and one for the first officer. If memory serves me correctly, this system even has the capability to download all this flight plan data via an inter-link with the company's flight control (dispatchers), thus not requiring a manual entry by the crew." (This paragraph was condensed from a clarification of 02/18/2002 received from Captain Mitchell.)

"The Flight Management System recognizes airways, ATC charted fixes, airports, etc. When engaged, it will provide heading information to the autopilot and flight directors, and fly the entire flight from the departure point (including any published instrument departure) to the initial approach fix at your destination. You can program it to fly direct from fix to fix or fly an entire airway route, ie: J22 to DCA, J14 JFK direct BOS. (Author's Note: From memory, DCA is Washington National, now Reagan, JFK is Kennedy, formerly Idlewild, and BOS is Boston, for Logan Airport.) You can change anything en route at any time if you so desire. RNAV does not know anything about altitude. If you only engage RNAV, then altitude management is strictly the pilots' responsibility."

"VNAV (vertical navigation) is the altitude portion of the system. You must enter the desired cruise altitude and the altitude at which you want to be at the initial approach fix (it even has the capability to put you over the runway threshold at 50 feet...but that isn't used). When programmed, VNAV is usually engaged at 1,000 feet agl. Along with the autoflight system, it will climb the aircraft to the selected cruise altitude, level off, and retard the throttles to the selected cruise power setting. At the descent point (computed from the altitude at which you wish to cross a specified point) it will again retard the throttles and begin the descent, keeping you informed all along as to how the descent profile is coming along. There are, however, safeguards to ensure that you do not climb or descend without proper clearance."

"In the approach mode, the autoflight system uses ground based ILS systems just as it has for years. In very bad weather conditions however things change a lot. All major airports now have instrument runways which have been designated as Category III runways. These ILS units and runways must meet a much higher standard and must have a lot of additional components."

"Category III is further broken down into Cat IIIa and IIIb and the above rules likewise apply. In both Cat IIIa and b, ceiling is of no concern, only runway visual range RVR (as measured along side the runway) is controlling and in the case of IIIb it can be as low as 300 feet! The crew and aircraft must be qualified for Cat III and the aircraft must be coupled to the autopilot, flight directors, autothrottle and autobrakes. It is a completely hands-off approach and landing. The only physical movements the pilot must make is to properly program the approach, lower the gear and flaps, arm the auto spoilers and reverse the engines after touch down. There is no requirement to see anything! You just hope and pray that all those little electrodes are getting the right signals and when you stop you're on the runway and not off in the grass somewhere. The aircraft will flare, touchdown, throttles retard to idle, the nose wheel settles on the runway, the brakes apply and centerline guidance rolls the aircraft to a stop! As I mentioned, the pilot may see a few of the green centerline light as the aircraft rolls out, but that is not a requirement. The hard part now is taxiing to the terminal. I must admit that it took quite awhile to completely trust the system and even then it was not a very comfortable situation. One other requirement: max crosswind component to initiate a Cat III approach is 10 knots."

"I realize that this is a quick, down and dirty description and I hope it helps. You would not believe the problems we had in training with 50+ year old 727 captains who had not been trained on a new aircraft in 10 - 15 years and the word computer scared them to death! It was a giant step! The young guys who had seen all this magic in the military in some form or another had no problem at all. Would you believe that the Navy now has full autoland to come aboard the (aircraft) carriers!"

"As for me, I entered pre-flight in the fall of 1958 and spent 8 years in the Navy flying S-2s and A4s. In my last year, I was an instructor in an instrument flight training unit. I went with Delta in August 1966 and retired in 1997. I flew the DC-6/7, Convair 880, DC-9, DC-8, B-727, B-757 and 767 and the 767ER. I spent 5 years (1986-1991) as an instructor in the Flight Training Department on the 757/767 which was treated as one aircraft. My last year there I was a senior instructor charged with training new instructors. The last six years were on the ER flying to Europe. I was based in Atlanta all 31years."

Captain Mitchell's words inform the reader that the military pilot/commercial pilot dialogue of 1949 on the merits of GCA versus ILS would find no parallel in 1999. The passive electronic ground systems of 1999 owe their heritage to ILS. The military pilot of 1999 and the commercial pilot of 1999 would be talking about variants in packaging the electronic components but would have no issue about what the components accomplished and what the pilot relationship to them was.

The remarks quoted next are based on several telephone conversations with Frank Davis, a recently retired United Airlines pilot. The key phrase is "one green light" and its context is the line of green lights down the centerline of an instrument-equipped runway first introduced to this story by Captain Mitchell. These two veteran pilots do not know each other. Neither saw, at least before publication, what the other had said or written.

United Airlines Captain Frank Davis retired from that airline in September of 2001. His final years with United were spent flying overseas in the Boeing 777. He served at various periods as a flight instructor in Boeing 727, 757 and 767-type aircraft and during other periods as a ground instructor in United's extensive family of aircraft simulation devices. In one conversation with him, Davis commented on the close family ties of the Boeing 757,767 and 777 aircraft, while also noting that the 777 actually incorporates systems to make automatic in-flight broadcasts of aircraft performance data back to United Airline's ground maintenance facilities.

In an overnight stop at Denver with a Boeing 777, Captain Davis came back out to fly the same aircraft the next morning. He discovered that one engine had been replaced while he slept. He was concerned enough to call his San Francisco maintenance base before taking the plane out again, questioning them on how the decision to change an engine had come up when the flight crew of the evening before had found no fault with the power plant. He was assured that there was no outstanding problem with that engine but that data transmitted to the ground station informed them that the engine was nearing its limit for hours of operation before maintenance. The ground supervisor explained that United had the skills and the spare engine available at Denver and wanted to anticipate the engine replacement routine while the opportunity presented itself.

Contrast this with the military procedure in the 1940s. After an engine change, an aircraft would receive a test flight of some duration before resuming operational schedules. And the aircraft would be in the hangar for up to several days for maintenance on engine and airframe on 30, 60, 90 and 120 hour checks.

Boeing has scored with the pilots who fly the 757/767/777 series of aircraft. Even though competition with Airbus Industries has been fierce, and every fraction of a gallon of fuel was counted in range and efficiency calculations, the electronic package in the 'seven-five, seven-six, seven-seven' aircraft counted heavily in their acceptance. The procurement decision came down not just with airline management concurrence but with the crucial acceptance by the airline pilots who would fly the Boeings. The instrument flight package was a factor in acceptance.

A Texas A&M graduate, Frank Davis began his flight career with the Air Force at primary flight school in Lubbock, Texas. He flew and appreciated the value of GCA instrument approaches in 1964. He made ILS part of his capability in 1967. While admiring fully the merits of these two methods of getting a plane safely back on the ground in instrument flight conditions, when there was a choice pilot Davis ultimately preferred ILS.

An airline pilot repeats flight profiles, from a take off at one regularly visited airport, then along a familiar route path to a landing at another regularly visited airport. This repetition of a given point-to-point experience occurs many more times than with the military pilot. Does the airline pilot become bored? Definitely not! Experience tells him or her that each flight segment, repeated in identical symbols many times on the traveler's departure and arrival screens, is always different, notwithstanding the repetition on the flight display boards.

Let me use a personal, non-flight, analogy. My family lived in the Mission Hills section of San Diego, California, for three years and I had the rare-in-life opportunity to walk to my technology job down the hill to a business area called Five Points. It was just a two-mile walk. San Diego is called the city of the short thermometer. As a born easterner, I had always heard the criticism of California that there were no "seasons." Despite the compelling seascape of Coronado Bay in my broad view each morning, I became enthralled with the daily changes in the beautiful foliage in my short gaze. An airline pilot flying the exact same point-to-point segments sees comparable subtle changes every time he or she flies. That not only takes boredom out of the job, it regenerates diligence in the application of the human senses to the job at hand, safe flight.

Frank Davis makes clear his love of flying. When conditions were VFR, he would often hand fly his aircraft to an assigned cruise altitude of say 39,000 feet, and then shift to autopilot. For descent, again providing conditions were right, he would switch out of autopilot and enter the let down phase. When the flight plan is a short segment, most often congested with aircraft, with conditions mostly IFR and therefore even more congested at destination, Frank Davis notes that the autopilot is hooked up at 1,000 feet above ground level after takeoff. This is not the lazy way. The pilots have learned that it is the best way. It reduces pilot workload and lets the flight crew focus on seeing or hearing the seemingly minor detail that makes this flight just slightly different from the last time over this route.

Each airline has its own standard procedures. Davis calls this "the company way" to perform to plan. But, Davis emphasizes that the Captain of the aircraft is in ultimate command and when there is a situation not foreseen specifically in the flight plan and in the airline's page-heavy procedure manuals, the Captain takes charge and does it "his way." In our last exchange of thoughts prior to publishing this story, Frank Davis filled out the Category III airport gradations. Category IIIa requires runway visual range of 600 feet, Category IIIb requires 300 feet, and Category IIIc requires no runway visual range, "zero," as his note to me indicated.

When a destination airport is Category IIIb, meaning equipped for landings when there is no measurable ceiling and just 300 feet of Runway Visibility Range ahead, the airline Captain is in a role defined for the command pilot of an aircraft, a decision role. With many repetitions of "almost the same" prior situations to guide him or her, the human pilot elects to use the autopilot to effect the approach and landing. The Captain has been intellectually persuaded, with experiences repeated enough times to become "reliable data," that the autopilot provides a better way to execute descent, flare-out, and touchdown than the flesh and blood pilot could consistently manage. In this sequence, the cockpit crew can monitor the descent and landing profile and more alertly detect exceptions that might require intervention, such as loss of thrust from an engine.

There are other exceptions. There are always exceptions. For example, if a frontal passage and a possible wind shift might find the landing aircraft exposed to a severe crosswind, the Captain would elect to land the plane himself. This might involve not just the physical intervention but might bring up a second consideration. For such a landing, the pilot might insist on better field ceiling and visibility conditions than Category III allows and if those conditions did not exist at the destination airport, could elect to take the plane to an alternate airport.

After a long airborne segment with a full load of Boeing 777 passengers to Frankfurt, Germany, Captain Davis put the full repertoire of his modern instrumented aircraft to work. It was a Category III landing. On the rollout, the flight deck crew could see just one of those green runway lights in the row of centerline lights. A "follow-me" vehicle was sent out to help direct the aircraft to the terminal.

Ask for a show of hands at an annual convention of the Airline Pilot's Association from those who have flown in military service. Or put the question to a meeting of air controllers. Both queries would result in a strong showing of hands from those with military backgrounds. Those who made it with military training would applaud those who made it entirely with civil training. The feeling would be mutual. That connection has made for strength.

The record of safety in flying is unmatched in any other form of human transport. It is not even close. The global performance of aviation is testimony to its pilots, its ground crews, the FBOs, flight attendants, designers, engineers, businessmen, regulators and controllers, and embracing all of these, its discipline.

I hope by now to have made it clear that a collateral theme of this story is that the United States has set a notable mark in civil aviation.

A citizen of the United States can be proud of the role the country has played in establishing the record of instrument flight.

Aviation Humor

In an address to Airline Pilot's Association (ALPA) members on the occasion of the group's 70th anniversary in August 2001, former FAA Administrator David Hinson told of a flying event in which he was a relatively junior copilot on the Boeing *Stratocruiser*. Those were the days when the command pilot, like his Northwest Airlines Captain that day, talked 'only to God,' and the copilot mostly kept quiet and did the paperwork. The *Stratocruiser* was a 4-engine B-29 *Stratofortress* reworked for airline use. Its cabin had two decks.

Hinson was doing his copilot paperwork on a flight in the *Stratocruiser* from Buffalo to Detroit, a short up-and-down 15-minute flight across Lake Erie. As the plane steadied out on heading for landing at Detroit, Hinson finally got up the courage to ask the Captain if he, Hinson, should put the wheels down.

The Captain's answer: "Put them down? Who told you to put them up?"

Index

Index

Index

Index

Index

Index

Index

Index

Appendix - Source Citations

Books, Publications and Spoken Word

Robert W. Mudge – Command Pilot (Northeast Airlines) and Author, Adventures of a Yellowbird: The Biography of an Airline; Copyright 1969 Branden Press, Boston; Copyright has reverted to the author.

Brian Garfield - Author, The Thousand-Mile War: *World War II in Alaska and the Aleutians*; Copyright 1969 by Brian Garfield; Bantam edition, 1982.

Walter J. Boyne – Author, *The Smithsonian Book of Flight*; Copyright 1987 Smithsonian Institution

Anne Morrow Lindbergh – Author, *North to the Orient*; Copyrights 1935 and 1963 Anne Morrow Lindbergh; published by Harcourt Brace & Company, First Harvest edition 1967. Chapter Twelve, Fog-and the Chishima, pages 85-88. The author was the radio operator in the crew of the *Sirius..*

Edward Pearson Warner – Lecturer and Author; delivered the first of a series of lectures at Norwich University on November 21, 1937 on the subject, *Early History of Air Transportation.* Copyrighted by the University in 1937. This material was later published in book form by Maple Press of York, Pennsylvania, copyright 1938.

Samuel Eliot Morison, Author, History of United States Naval Operations in World War II; Volume VII, *Aleutians, Gilberts and Marshalls*; Copyright 1951.

Samuel Eliot Morison, Author, The Oxford History of the American People: Aviation, 1903-1960 pages 893-897; Copyright 1965.

Don Fortune, Author, personal correspondence, excerpts from the voyage of SS Taku to Cold Bay in Chapter 8. Originally published in Amateur Writer's Journal Jan./Feb./March 1993.

James Forrestal, with Editor Walter Millis and in collaboration with E.S. Duffield, *The Forrestal Diaries*, pages 144-145, The Viking Press. Copyright page torn, but about 1950.

Booklet *Glenn H. Curtiss Architect of American Aviation* Lord & Field Publisher, Copyright 1998.

Ben Yagoda, Author, as quoted in *Booknotes*, Brian Lamb, first paperback edition copyright 1997 National Cable Satellite Corporation; pages 49-50; interview September 25, 1994 on Yagoda's book, *Will Rogers: A Biography*.

Standard Quarterly Review, quarterly issues from April 1929 to and including January 1932, published by the Standard Education Society, Chicago, Illinois, Carl R. Fisk Managing Director.

Quarterly, *The Lamp*, a shareholder publication of ExxonMobil. Spring 2001 issue, article pages 5-9 entitled, "Flying with ExxonMobil: From Air Force One to vintage planes, we fuel a fifth of the world's aircraft."

The Holley Standard of July 21, 1927 and the Brockport *Republic-Democrat* July 21, 1927. Microfilm records at Drake Memorial Library, SUNY Brockport, search directed by Mary Jo Gigliotti.

Reference Manual for Instrument Flight, Academic Phase, copyrighted by Northeast Airlines, Inc. revised July 1943. 263 pages.

Aerospace Historian; winter, December 1991 pages 231-240; "Radar: Wartime Development-Postwar Application AN/APS-10," by Milton Rhodes.

Instrument Flight Check for F.E. Dailey, Jr., written test 30 Sept. 62, air test 09 June 62, report CNATRA-Gen 3720, conducted by N.E. Marston, all signers and subject holding standard ratings.

Navaer-4111, Logbooks (3), pilot Franklyn E. Dailey Jr., October 1944-June 1962.

Navaer-80R-19, Introduction to Naval Aviation, January 1946.

Navaer 00-80V-66, The Pilot's Guide for the PB4Y-2 Privateer, 1945.

David Hinson, Address to ALPA member banquet, August 2001, on the occasion of their 70th anniversary. As seen and heard on public TV broadcast.

Correspondence- (some points clarified by telephone)

J. Frank Durham - Private Pilot; mail and e-mail.

Major Joseph Waldroff USAF Ret.- B-52 Command Pilot; refueling in tops of thunderheads; e-mail correspondence.

Captain Harry Carter USN Ret.- PB4Y-1 Pilot and Navigator; mail and e-mail correspondence.

Allene Rollier Niehaus – Correction to Lt. Apollo Soucek's second high altitude record from 'nearly 43,000' feet in earlier text to 43,166 feet. E-mail correspondence. She is a cousin of Navy Lieutenant Apollo Soucek, later, Admiral Apollo Soucek.

Ann Richards – relaying communication from F.E. MacSpadden, B-17 Command Pilot; he became command pilot of a B-17 after 34 hours as copilot. E-mail correspondence.

Hugh Burris Commander USN Ret.-Command Pilot PB4Y-1 and PB4Y-2, R5D and Lockheed *Constellation*; personal recollections of Aleutian flying; mail correspondence.

Leonard B. DiNapoli Commander USN Ret. - radioman in P2-Y2 and PBY-3; recollections of early Alaska flying; mail correspondence and photo of squadron of P2-Y2 aircraft in flight.

Stanley Hogshead - Captain USN Ret.; as plotting officer of U.S. detroyer Bailey in WW II at Battle of the Komandorskis; e-mail correspondence with excerpts from speech given in San Diego, CA.

Chad Mingo, Lieutenant USN - pilot F-14 *Tomcat*; Afghanistan missions 2001; refueling and carrier recovery; e-mail correspondence.

Robert E. Mitchell - Delta Air Lines Captain; blind landings in Boeing 757/767; e-mail correspondence.

Frank Davis - United Airlines Captain; blind landings in Boeing 757/767/777; telephone discussions.

Max Mahaffey - Private Pilot, with added qualifications for single and multiengine instrument flight; e-mail correspondence.

Steve Sisk – e-mails, 02/08, 02/09/04, more on Privateer formation flying accident in Chapter 9, Wartime Pilot Training.

Dr. Milton Rhodes – e-mail 12/28/03 and letter 01/09/04 on APS-10 radar and radomes..

Correspondence – Historical Societies

Ferguson Historical Society, Ferguson Missouri; Corresponding Secretary Ruth Brown e-mails; Ferguson Notes January, February 2003; color copy original parchment scroll July 13-30 endurance flight Dale Jackson and Forest O'Brine.

Beverly Historical Society & Museum, Walker Transportation Collection, Paul Larcom, Aviation Curator; meeting in Framingham, MA, telephone conversations, paper on *Operation Bolero*. Also, Richard W. Symmes, Curator, Beverly Historical Society and Museum, Walker Transportation Collection; telephone conversation.

Jell-O Museum, Leroy, New York; news clips from *Leroy Gazette*, *Leroy Pennysaver*, and *Journal-American*, of events commemorating Donald Woodward Airport, covering year of airport founding, 1928 and the decade following; Ruth Harvie, staff researcher at Jell-O Museum used Museum index to find and then make copies of articles for author.

Illustrations

Illustration 1 Curtiss *Jenny*; Glenn H. Curtiss Museum; digital photo by author.

Illustration 2 Stinson *Detroiter* in near background; photograph in the Walker Transportation Collection, Beverly (MA) Historical Society.

Illustration 3 Curtiss *June Bug* of 1908; Glenn H. Curtiss Museum; digital photo by author.

Illustration 4 Newton F. Foner's Airplane Engine patent; reproduction of cover of U.S. Patent 1626457.

Illustration 5 Lindy and his autograph; reproduction of snapshot photo in Dailey family collection.

Illustrations 6, 7, 8; Turn and bank indicator, direction gyro indicator, gyro horizon indicator, Navaer 00-80W-7, 1945

Illustration 9 A drone with two chase planes; reproduction of a photo in the Dailey family collection.

Illustration 10 Link Trainer in use; Boston-Maine Airways photo, courtesy Robert Mudge. Inset, Link Trainer; Binghamton (New York) Regional Airport public lobby; digital photograph.

Illustration 11 Stinson *Trimoator*; photo courtesy of Robert Mudge.

Illustration 12 Lockheed 10A *Electra* panel; reproduction of photo in Walker Transportation Collection, Beverly Historical Society.

Illustration 13 Ladies fly, including Amelia; reproduction of photo by Robert Stanley; Walker Transportation Collection, Beverly (MA) Historical Society.

Illustration 14 Low Frequency Radio Range; pilot Franklyn E. Dailey Jr. sketch from author's memory, smooth illustration by Claire Keefe, Wilbraham MA.

Illustration 15 Northeast Airlines DC-3 taxiing from ramp of Boston Airport; photo courtesy of Robert Mudge.

Illustration 16 North Atlantic by air-1941; reproduction of drawing for author Paul Larcom's article on Operation Bolero; The Yankee Flyer, Journal of the Massachusetts Aviation Historical Society.

Illustration 17 The North Pacific; reproduced from outlines of Naval Air Transport Service (NATS) Squadron VR-5 chart, smooth illustration by Claire Keefe, Wilbraham, MA.

Illustration 18 A Formation of Navy P2Y-2s; reproduction of a photo in the Leonard DiNapoli family collection.

Illustration 19 Navy pilot with wings; reproduction of snapshot photo in Dailey family collection.

Illustration 20, Aleutian Chain via Airways, VR-5 chart

Illustration 21 Radio Range Letdown Chart; pilot Franklyn E. Dailey Jr. sketch from memory, smooth illustration by Claire Keefe, Wilbraham, MA.

Illustration 22 Navy PB4Y-2 *Privateer*; reproduction of photo in Dailey family collection.

Illustration 23 Coming Home; two views; reproduction of photo slides in Dailey family collection.

Illustration 24 Sanderson Flight Computer; digital scan of photo of computer, in the collection of pilot Franklyn E. Dailey Jr.

Web Sources

(Caution! Assume the life cycle of website and e-mail addresses to be short)

www.arinc.com ARINC.

Jayschne@sprynet.com The e-mail address of Midwest Airlines pilot Jerome Gerald Schnedorf III. The phrases he used (Copyright 1997) to describe altitude changes in instrument flight approaches can be found in Chapter 14 of this book. The quoted phrases were found to be effective when Schnedorf was instructing at Louisiana State University. As a working pilot, changes addresses frequently. His cell phone number is 414-698-6577. The author reached him by phone at 877-632-2572 on 08/26/2003 to confirm the insertion in Chapter 14 and the contact information.

www.wpafb.af.mil GCA, Wright Patterson Air Force Base.

www.wpafb.af.mil/museum/early_years/ey19a.htm Link Trainer at WPAFB.

www.navfltsm.addr.com/howitbegan.htm Air Mail service in early years. Copyright Charles Wood.

www.navfltsm.addr.com/ndb-nav-history.htm Low frequency radio range and other low frequency air navigation aids. Copyright Charles Wood.

www.navfltsm.addr.com/howitbegan.htm Light beacons. Copyright Charles Wood.

www.geocities.com/CapeCanaveral/Lab/4515/doolittle.htm James Doolittle details.

www.geocities.com/CapeCanaveral/Hangar/7107/html/engine.html OX-5 Aviation Pioneers; history of the Curtiss OX-5 Engine.

www.centennialofflight.gov/wbh/index.htm Wright brothers history.

www.nasm.si.edu/research/aero/aircraft/curtiss_j1.htm Curtiss J-1 *Robin* details.

www.eaa231.org/Museum/Robin/Robin.htm   More on Curtiss Robin aircraft and Curtiss Museum, Hammondsport, NY.

http://avstop.com/Stories/2.html General Aviation. Stories of Interest.

www.mapsirmuseum.org/linktrainer.htm Link C-3 Trainer, Air Museum at Akron-Canton Airport, North Canton, OH. Portions Copyrighted 1998 Aerospace Education Center. Site: Copyright 2003 James Kohan and MAPS Air Museum.

www.hangarline.com/trainer.htm From organs to aircraft; more on the Link Trainer.

www.crh.noaa.gov/lmk/history 1.htm National Weather Service history, 1644-1970.

.